# EDUCATION IN THE VEDAS

# EDUCATION IN THE VEDAS

R.P. Singh

KALPAZ

ISBN: 978-93-5128-170-2

Price : ₹ 890

First Published, 2016

*Published by*

Kalpaz Publications
C-30, Satyawati Nagar,
Delhi – 110052
E-mail: kalpaz@hotmail.com
Ph.: 9212142040

*Printed at:* G Print Process, Delhi

**Cataloging in Publication Data—DK**
Courtesy: D.K. Agencies (P) Ltd. <docinfo@dkagencies.com>

**Singh, Rajendra Pal,** 1932-2015, **author.**
Education in the Vedas / R.P. Singh.
pages cm
ISBN 9789351281702

1. Education—India—History—To 1500. 2. Education in literature. 3. Vedas—Criticism, interpretation, etc. I. Title.

LA1151.S56 2016 DDC 370.954 23

Cover Page:
Mr Kalyan Banerjee

***Dedication***

My Dear Wife Vimla Singh

# Contents

# Preface

"The person who is only able to recite the Veda, but does not understand its meaning, is like a post (sthanu) or a mere load-bearer (bharahara); but he who understands the meaning will attain to all good here and hereafter, being purged of sins by knowledge.

Words simply learnt by rote, but not understood, will not enlighten when uttered, just as fuel, be it ever so dry, will not blaze if it is put into that which is not fire." Yaska, Nirukta

The present book is an individual's bumbling effort in the twilight of his life. With numerous scholarly works on the Vedas already available in libraries across the world, the motives of a novice attempting to bargain a place in a densely populated terrain can easily be suspect. Also, while numerous Sanskritists appear to be busy offering exposition of each and every aspect of the sacred ancient lore, one could always ask the question: where is the need for anyone like me, who has had no curiosity about it until recently should have suddenly felt so enamored as to break into a branch of study reserved for those who have for long taken it upon themselves as a calling. I think my answer lies in the query itself. For me it is a labor of love.

I wish to find answers to several questions. May be there are answers already available: Surely, I am not aware of them. Better still, I am interested in trying to find my own answers, which to say the least is not tantamount to reinventing the wheel. Perhaps it is like getting on top of the Mt. Everest. True, hundreds of adventurers have been on its top but for anyone undertaking the arduous task for the first time, to experience the pleasure of a difficult undertaking is by itself absolutely exhilarating. It would appear as though the mountain peak keeps calling for more and more climbers to achieve what their predecessors legitimately claim they have accomplished already. The same is true for the Vedas. To he able to read them and even to partly understand them is an experience by itself.

This work is addressed to those who like me know very little the Vedas but they are curious to know a lot more about them. Those that agree to explore new grounds traveling across turbulent seas and possess the where withal of patience to get rationally persuaded by the arguments (which is a treat) the Vedic text itself offers, for them this book will offer a welcome edification.

In reality, the book attempts to answer following questions.

Who wrote the Vedas? Did the Vedic Seers come from outside the present-day geographical territories of north India?

Can we get a glimpse of the real Vedic society through Vedic text? To what extent were those people different from us; and, were their life and society as complex as we find living it today? What is common between the Vedic people and their modern day counterparts/ descendents? Are the Vedas really relevant for us? Do they contain any history?

Unfortunately. everyone is not agreed on the answers to these queries. For starters the scholars are almost equally divided on the answer to the first question: Did the Seers and their folks belong to the soil of India? Yes and no. Majority of scholars hold the view that they came from outside the Indian sub-continent A few equally competent people who should know better than the most say. *No, they were natives of the soil.*

I find no reason to be very different from my predecessors. Why must these doubts lead us astray from our original intention of knowing more about the Vedas and not bother to find the answers its text offers? While I shall pursue the path of reason and limit my quest to the Vedic text, I am notable to restrain myself from citing what Max Muller wrote around 1879 or so. Though the citation is little large than necessary but I still prefer to transgress the limits because everyone may not have access to this book published originally in 1882.

But before one reads what I cite below, one must realise for once that this time around Europe got interested in our past. Europeans were on the ascendance and Indians were on the decline. For lack of patronage during the Muslim rule in India, Hindu learning was limited to the few struggling courts of the Hindu rulers or to the confines of solitary hutments where the lamps of ancient wisdom still bumtunaided but without attracting public notice. The fact that Hindu learning survived in obscurity and neglect, thanks are due entirely to the innumerable Brahman families who put their ancestral devotion and reverence to this lore higher than their personal security and affluence. If Muslims had their Akbar and Dara Shikoh- patrons of the ancient Indian lore, the British too were not found wanting both in curiosity and patronage. To name a few they had their Sir William Jones, Thomas Colebroo, H.H. Wilson and many more of similar taste and proclivity. I am citing Max Muller because his motives were clearly unacceptable. If a person of that type and proclivity could write what I am about to cite then it is possible to say that there ought to be some truth in what he said. (India: What can it teach us?)

"The Veda may be called primitive, because there is no other literary document more primitive than it; but the language, the mythology, the religion and philosophy that meet us in the Vedas open vistas of the past, which no one would venture to measure in years. Nay, they contain, by the side of simple, natural, childish thoughts, many ideas which to us sound modem, or secondary and tertiary, as I called them, but which nevertheless are older than any other literary document, and *give us trustworthy information* of a period in the history of human thought of which we knew absolutely nothing before the discovery of the Vedas." The word ' discovery' needs to be noted.

He goes on to meet an objection that the Vedas do not represent the people but only a fraction of the priestly class. He says, "So far from denying that the Vedic hymns represent only a small and, it may be, a priestly minority of the ancient population of India, the true historian would probably feel inclined to urge the same caution against the Old Testament and the Homeric verses also."

Max Muller compares the wisdom of the Greeks with that of the Indians. "The knowledge of the Self is really the Vedanta, that is, the end of the Vedas. The highest wisdom of the Greeks was 'to know ourselves' and the highest wisdom of India is 'to know our Self'. "It is in this way that he equates the best of Europe with the best of India and finds that the latter despite all the handicaps and deficiencies like 'lack of practical and fighting virtues of the West', still made the greatest conqueror of antiquity (Alexander the Great) stand" in wonderment before the Indian Gymnosophists that he could not communicate with them in their own language, and that their *wisdom could not reach him except through the contaminating channels of-sundry interpreters.*

It is very interesting the way Max Muller looks at the world religions and then tries to assess the Indian way of life and offers an opinion.

"Now we may seem to know a great many religions-I speak here, of course, of ancient religions only, of what are sometimes called national or autochthonous religions-not of those founded in later times by individual prophets or reformers.

Yet, among the ancient religions we are seldom certain, what after all is to be regarded as the most important point-their origins or their gradual growth. The Jewish religion is represented to us as perfect and complete from the very first, and it is with great difficulty that we can discover its real beginnings and its historical growth. And take Greek and Roman religions, take religions of the Teutonic, Slavonic or Celtic tribes, and you will find that their period of growth has already passed, long before we know them, and that from the time we know them, all their changes are purely metamorphic - changes in form of substances ready at hand.

Now let us look to the ancient inhabitants of India. With them, first of all, religion was not only one interest by the side of the many. It was the all-absorbing interest; it embraced not only worship and prayer, but what we call philosophy, morality, law, and government-all was pervaded by the religion. Their whole life was to them a religion everything else was, as it were, a mere concession made to the ephemeral requirements of this life."

What then can we learn from the ancient religious literature of' India-e-or from the Vedas?

"It requires no very profound knowledge of Greek religion and Greek language to discover in the Greek deities the original outlines of certain physical phenomena. Every schoolboy knows that in Zeus there is something of the sky, in Poseidon of the sea, in Hades of the lower world, in Apollo of the sun, in Artemis of the moon, in Hephoestos of the fire. But for all that, there is, from a Greek point of view a very considerable difference between Zeus and the sky, between Poseidon and the sea, between Apollo and the sun, between Artemis and the moon.

Now what do I fmd in the Vedas? No doubt here and there a few philosophical hymns, which have been quoted so often that people, have begun to imagine that the Vedas are a collection of Orphichymns. We also find some purely mythological hymns, in which the Devas or gods have assumed nearly as much dramatic personality as in the Homeric hymns.

But the great majority of the Vedic hymns consists in simple invocation of the fire, the water, the sky, the sun, and the storms, often under the same names, which afterwards became the proper names of Hindu deities, but as yet nearly free from all that can be called irrational or mythological. There is nothing irrational, nothing I mean we cannot enter into or sympathise with, in people imploring the storms to cease, or the sky to rain, or the sun to shine." (This stage Max Muller calls is the *childish* stage of human mind).

"Now, it is exactly this period in the growth of ancient religion, which was always pre-supposed, or postulated, but was almost everywhere else, that is clearly put before us in the hymns of the Rgveda. It is this ancient chapter in the history of human mind, which has been preserved to us in Indian literature, while we look for it in vain in Greece or Rome or elsewhere.

*"Supposing that the Vedic hymns were composed between 1500 & 1000 B.C. we can hardly understand how, at so early a dale, the Indians had developed ideas, which to us sound decidedly so modern!* ..The answer to this query he sums up by saying," we must some what modify our conception of the *primitive savage*, and remember that things hid from wise and prudent have *sometimes been revealed to babes."*

One would not like to improve upon his judgment, except that it had better be taken with a tablespoon full of salt. In any case this would not be the general view and decidedly not of all scholarly Indians.

This is one reason why we must endeavor to find out the Truth, as we understand it. One question that bothers everyone is: How are we sure that the seers of the Vedas were not human? Three difficulties have been pointed out: (1) The proper nouns found in the body of the text of the Vedas are in fact common nouns i.e. a proper noun like Vashishth or Vishwamitra in reality is a common noun for *prana* and *ear* respectively. (2) There are mantras that are supposedly composed by multiple rishis. (3) For instance, in Rigveda 66.19 and Samveda 627, 1464 a well-known mantra has supposedly been written by 100 rishis. The quey is logical. Is it reasonable to argue that a mantra of 24 syllables was composed by an army of one hundred rishis? And, lastly, several rishis get addressed in superlatives. Surely, it is difficult to defend such a usage even in extraordinary circumstances. A related matter also needs to be addressed. Each mantra is supposed to be addressed to a devata. Who is that deity? According to *Yaskacharya* in his Nirukta "when God, desires to impart instruction about a particular object the term devata stands for the properties of the mantra. (Ya tain uchhyate saa devata)." Still, there is no agreement about any of these explanations. While the Western scholars insist on the commonly explained reasons for the usages, Indian scholars continue to advance their arguments refuting the same.

I have tried to keep myself away from these hair splitting arguments. We all know that scholarship is all about one-upmanship. Since I have no claims to Vedic scholarship I can afford to keep myself away from this genre of logic.

My presentation is based on the citations of the Vedic text and my arguments flow from the Vedas themselves. Beyond that I have nothing more to add. I want to thank Dr Lata Chandola for help in proof reading.

**R. P. Singh**

711, Express Apartment

Plot No. 17, Sector 4, Vaishali,

Ghaziabad - 201010 (UP)

Tel: 0120-4132229
Mob: 9582401042

# Chapter - 1

# The Vedas and their Message

### Introduction

"O! Omnipresent Lord, the giver of happiness, may we subjugate the wicked folk on this earth where the sages perform the Yagnas. May we associate the ignorant moving in the dark with the learned and thus spread freely the system of education as propounded in the Vedic hymns. Thus, as my light of knowledge is valued by all; so should yours. The ignorant moving in the dark are opposed to the learned disapprove for their antagonism to knowledge; should be brought round to the path of virtue by hundreds of means available and let the restriction on them be not removed till their enlightenment. May the wicked be not blessed with prosperity, and the pleasures of knowledge. O Ye dutiful may yet persistently follow the path. Yajurveda Ch.1/26.

The Vedas can be read for different purposes, as they are capable of giving more messages than one can imagine. In fact, it is impossible to understand everything they say and why do they say what they actually say. Majority of the Indians regard them as revealed books because no human being could have been so wise as to cover all themes and subjects, besides all aspects of human life as they do."

Probably for this reason alone that F, Max Muller wrote the following:

"What can be more tedious than the Veda, and yet, what can be more interesting, if once we know that it is the first word spoken by the Aryan man?

The Veda has a two-fold interest: it belongs to the history of world and to the history of India. As long as man continues to take interest in the history of his race, and as long as we collect in libraries and museums the relics of the former ages, the first place in that long row of books which contain the records of the Aryan branch of mankind, will belong forever to the Rigveda."

So much for the glory of the Vedas! This praise comes from a man who learned Sanskrit and the Vedas only to make Hindus Christians.

I have read and interpreted the Vedic hymns only *to discover and present the type of society it was that helped produce such a marvelous compendium of eternal truths.* I have no intentions to fix either their historical date or discuss the authenticity or otherwise of each hymn. *For me the Vedas are the oldest and the most venerated documents of the ancient Indians.* Therefore, for me they mean only two things. One, they can help us reconstruct the ancient Indian society which gave them to us. Two, besides being esoteric they also speak of the conduct of ordinary human beings. On both of these counts they can be immeasurably helpful in achieving my purpose.

The Nairukta: This method is pre-eminently philological Devi Chand in his translation of Yajurveda has enumerated several ways in which the Vedas can be interpreted. They are:

(1) The Nairukta is the first method in which there is an insistence on going to the birth and development of Vedic speech. This is the most fastidious, thorough going and perfectly critical method and is hard to apply by an ordinary scholar.

(2) The second method is historical or Aitihasik and was evolved by Yaska it consisted in elucidating a Vedic passage by referring to particular events in history. The names of kings and great men in India have conformed to Vedic words and it was never difficult to find a name which conformed to the Vedas. With the passage in time both these methods were abandoned because they led astray a scholar who used either of the two methods. Sayancharya however used these methods and misled vast number of scholars. The fact is that names that occur in the Vedas are not of any historical person. Instead they symbolise some power and not any individual.

(3) The mythological method was to collect tales prevalent in the society and were utilised to explain Vedic realities. Like the historical this method was found very attractive and highly appealing and hence its acceptance.

(4) The scientific: After the Nairukta method this is the most difficult among all methods. It consists in identifying Vedic truths and with natural phenomena and presenting them as physical-scientific truths. This method though difficult is mostly adopted because it alone yields the right meaning.

(5) The intuitional or the most esoteric: This is an extremely difficult and abstruse method because it is both hard to learn and even harder to apply. In terms of explanations there is hardly any way to explain any meaning or phenomenon. It deals with God, the soul, and the human body taking account of he external world as an 'outside' phenomenon.

(6) The ritualistic Perhaps this is the easiest and least bothersome method. The example given in this connection is that at the time of child's tonsure it is used with reference to the barber. There are several passages that can be explained only through this method and the example given is that of the mantras of Rgveda 20 to 119.

It is incidental that out of curiosity I have attempted to place (in temporal terms) the Vedas in the light of archaeological evidence of the Indus Valley Civilisation available till date. There are several theories about the Aryan invasion in India in general and on the Harrapan sites and the latter's total destruction in particular. There are scholars who have accepted more or less uncritically the theory that Indra, the Aryan warlord, succeeded in Aryan occupation of the destroyed territories. I find it hard to accept any such theory for the simple reason that such an extensive habitation as the Harrapan (in advanced stage of material prosperity) could have been destroyed by essentially pastoral/nomadic Aryan tribes. In fact, the evidence cited to support this particular theory is not even persuasive. There are scholars like Romila Thapar who have even advanced a chronology of the ancient India's civilisational march in her book *From Lineage to State.* But then she is a class apart.

There are, however, others who are more circumspect than her. For instance, (Dilip K. Chakrabarti, *The archeology of ancient Indian cities, our*, 1995, p. 124) records the view, "in its Phase III, the last period of Harrapan occupation, one of the two entrances of its western gate system was blocked completely and the other was partially closed by a screen wall. In the same phase an additional salient was added to its northwestern corner tower. These archaeological indications were interpreted as signs of the Harrapans being on the defensive and thus on the decline. The Rigveda provided the literary data with its wealth of references to the fortified strongholds of non-Aryans and the tale of their destruction by the warlord Indra." One is advised to go through Chakrabarit's book and read the conclusion where he clearly mentions in the chapter Problems and Perspectives p. 276 the first issue is the problem of 'state formation' in early historic India and the other is the historic urban growth. He goes on to suggest, that "there was not a homogeneous Harrapan empire. On the contrary, if we look at the latest political history of the entire region, we are likely to argue in favour of the idea of a number of separate kingdoms throughout the distribution of Harrapan zone." No one is likely to agree with the thesis that the presence of a few skeletons, bones and artifacts are proof enough of some major invasion or destruction of a culture as extensive and as advanced as the Harrapan's.

Incidentally yet another observation that needs be paid attention to is from (The cultural heritage of India, Vol.1, edited by S. Radhakrishnan, p.128, Ramakrishna Mission, reprint 1993), which says, "It is notorious that the cow, which was prized as wealth and considered aghnya by the Rg-Vedic Aryans, and the horse, which played an important part in their life, do not find a place among animals depicted in the Indus valley sites, the place of the cow being taken by the bull. while of the horse no trace is found." I have no intentions of trying to pretend being more knowledgeable than the author of this essay but one thing that appears to be missing is the possible cause of the absence of cow on the seals. The cause could be very simple. Being Shiva worshippers the bull received prominence over the cow and hence its absence. There is reference in the Rigveda that Aryans disapproved of phallus worship. The phallus-worshippers are taken to be unchaste, lustful, and non-bramhcharis. Reference to phallus worship are to be found in Rg. X.99.3; 1.105.8; X.27.19; 33.3 It goes to prove that Lord Shiva is the original deity of the Indus valley people. If this suggests the antiquity of Shiva worship, one should accept the other implications as well.

At the same time I am no one either to endorse the truthfulness or contradict the veracity of any statement that scholars keep on making about the ancient Indians. It is as yet not established beyond any reasonable doubt that Aryans were not the natives of this country itself and that they did not come from any foreign land. (See, The Cultural Heritage of India, op.cit. p.139) where the author raises the point that it is probable that the native inhabitants of the valley could have been non-Aryans.) I have my own doubts about the whole matter. We also have scholars like R.C. Dhanda (The Harrappan Origin of Hinduism, p.120; Book links Corporation, Hyderabad, 2001) who claim that Sankhya-yoga philosophy is "rooted in the non-Aryan and non-Vedic world - view whose origin goes back to Harappa civilisation and beyond." Similarly, it is possible to point out that Lord Shiva combined with Vedic god Rudra becomes the First Cause. He becomes the Great Lord Maheshwara- the Supreme Purusha among several other purushas. (See, *Svetasvatara* Upanishad)

I shall show from the Vedic verses when I cite in the appropriate context evidence that the Rgvedic people were not averse to constructing large buildings, using baked bricks, exhibiting detailing knowledge of vastu shashtra, imparting instruction in geometry and mathematics, devising various methods of teaching, learning to write etc. It is these people who constructed vedis for their yagnas and used a variety of ishtikas (baked bricks) for the purpose. The textual evidence however refuses to uphold the oft-cited thesis that the Vedic people destroyed an urban culture only to revert to their pastoral ways. In fact, my readings of the Vedas suggest that the Aryan achievements intenus of civilisation were more than modest and that there was no need to have destroyed any particular civilisation although it is true that they had enemies whose destruction they did desire. But their constant references to the presence of enemies and their desire to see their eventual destruction might not necessarily be related to the Indus valley civilisation. I am conscious of the fact that the Vedas are also the finest form of poetry. Poetry perse is open to multiple interpretations. In my opinion a poem is as good as its reader. Interpretations are subject to the sensitivity and the level of the understanding of the reader neither more nor less. Only a poet tends to use words that can logically carry multiple meanings.

I am interested in finding out what kind of society did the Vedas consider was ideal for the humans. I am also interested to know what kind of knowledge did they possess or message did they propose to give us. Why were they so anxious to preserve what they had spoken or talked about? Was it that they thought the society should remain forever "static and not change with time? Like these there are a million questions the answers of which I propose to find out. Clearly, I am no preacher and what I write is not meant to propagate any Vedic religion anywhere in the world; therefore, my work should be accepted on its face value. My write-up is only an individual's voyage of discovery" the results of which are as uncertain as my hope of being able to complete this task with any measure of success.

For my purpose I have accepted mainly the translations produced by Veda Pratishthan, New Delhi. Svami Satya Prakash Sarasvati and Satyakam Vidyalankar did the English translation for that Trust. The other set of translation I have with me is of 'Sarvadeshik Arya Pratinidhi Sabha, Maharshi Dayanand Bhavan, Ramlila Ground, New Delhi.' Occasionally, I have also consulted Satvalekar's translation. Several other respectable volumes too have been occasionally consulted. I have had neither the time, nor the ability or age in my favor to have read the Vedas in original Sanskrit. For my purpose translations and a few historical-sociological references have sufficed. I also do not make any claims about possessing any particular scholarship. With the kind of limited knowledge and purpose I have in my mind I do not think I need to offer any excuses or seek anyone's forgiveness.

It is not easy either to date the origin of the Vedas or to support its eotemporary culture through archaeological evidence. Talking of the Indus Valley Civilisation and its relationship with the Rgvedic Aryans R.C. Majumdar talks of "a peculiar problem". He says, "The Indus Valley Civilisation is known only from archaeological finds and there is no literary evidence throwing light upon it, while the Rgvedic culture is known only from literary evidence and no actual remains of it have yet come to light. The result has been unfortunate. The archaeological remains are visible and make an easy impression upon the mind, whereas literary evidence couched in a dead language and contained in a book which few care to read, suffers by comparison." (See, Studies in Cultural History of India, pp. 5-6, editors Guy S. Metrauk & Francois Crouzet, UNESCO,1965).

The other difficulty is the language of the Vedas. Of course there are ways to read it and understand it but then not the way Sayana has understood it or the Western scholars attempt to do so. Gurudatta cites Patanjali's Mahabhashya Ch.-III, Sec-III, Aph.1 to record, "ancient authors and commentators without any exception, regard all Vedic terms to be yaugika, whereas some lokika terms are regarded by some as rudhi also." He goes on to say, "This principle, the European scholars have entirely ignored; and hence have flooded their interpretations of the Vedas with forged or borrowed tales of mythology, with stories and anecedotes of historic or pre-historic personages." In his scholarly work (The Wisdom of the Rishis, edited by Vedanta Tirtha, Arya Pustakalaya, Lahore, 1896) Guru Datta offers various examples about the place where scholars who ignored the principle of regarding all Vedic terms as yaugika have erred in the understanding of the Vedas. For example, according to Muir, certain historic and pre-historic personages are mentioned in the Vedas, viz. the rishi Kanvas, Gotamasin Rg. 1.42.2; and 71.16 etc. The truth is that if only they had consulted Nighantu of Yaska they would have known that learned men were commonly given these names and those they were never taken to be proper nouns. Similarly, he refutes the Yam-Yami dialogue as a discussion between twins about sex but according to Nirukta 7-26; 12-10; and 12-11 Vaivasvata is sun and in the allegory of Yam-Yami they are merely shown to be conversing about the control of one's passion. Just as with the appearance of the Sun the darkness is gone similarly as one controls one's passions the darkness of the desire evaporates. This is one reason why I have tried to adhere strictly to the translations of Indian scholars devoted to the study of the Vedas.

What is most intriguing about the Vedas is that they come all of a sudden not unlike a bolt from the blue without any precedence/ continuity or knowledge of the state of society that produced them. We know practically nothing about the pre-Vedic people, the state of their material/literary development, their social organisations/ customs or preferences etc. The usual support for any historical statement that one derives from subject are as such as archeology, written word etc. provide no help to an individual trying to piece together a picture of the time that preceded the Vedic age. In fact, a Marxist like S.A. Dange for instance has with the help of Engles tried to superimpose our contemporary logical analytical system on the times to which he doesn't appear to have had any clue.

People believe the Vedas to be revealed or Sruti i.e. heard and not written down by any human being. A clear distinction must be made between a Sastra and Sruti. A sastra is systemised presentation of a subject. The same cannot be said of a Sruti. Instead of regarding them to be socio-historical documents the Vedas are Holy Books or sacred literature. Numerous scholars do not subscribe to this view point. I include myself in that class of individuals.

For the uninitiated a few elementary facts need to be recounted. According to Vishnu Purana, the original Veda was first revealed to the rsis consisted of one lakh verses. These verses were divided into four parts. With the passage of time a mix up occurred and several portions of the Vedas became obscur. In the beginning of the Dvapar age, Krishna Dvaipayana resuscitated the Vedic study and classified the work according to the four ancient divisions of Rk, Yaj us, Saman and Atharvan. As is universally known the Vedas are four in number. The Rgveda-revealed to Paila consists of 10,552 mantras (in 1028 Suktas), the Samaveda r. vealed to Jaimini consists of 1875 mantras, the Yajurveda, revealed to Vaishampayan consists of (the Vajasaneyi Samhita text) of 2,086/1984 mantras of which a few are in prose, and the Atharvavedas revealed to Sumanta consisted of 5987/5977 Suktas (a few of which too are in prose). Because of the oral tradition the Vedas were called shruti because they were unwritten. They survived for a longtime through their purohits like hota, udgata, adhavaryu and Brahma. Later on they were collected in four samhitas. If one liked one could easily accept Tilak's dating of the Vedas, which according to him were composed in four stages starting with 6,000 BC until 500 BC. Since we are told that Vedavyas prepared the final edition of the Vedas during the reign of Yuddhishthira, there is no difficulty in accepting this proposition. But then it does not mean that everyone is likely to agree with this assertion. The fact is that the purists do not accept this proposition.

It may interest some to know that Sukta means what is pleasant to hear or something nice that has been said. In all, the Vedic Sarnhitas (as distinguished from the literature based on the Vedas such as the Brahmanas, Upanishads, and Aranakyas etc.) consist of 20,500 mantras. The other thing worth noting is that a number of Rgvedic verses appear in the other Vedas too. The Vedic prose is rhythmic. The Vedas contain the earliest recorded poetry and prose literature of the human race. The Vedas are not systematised knowledge with a set of any scientific terminology.

Sarnhitas means compilations. The Suktas and the mantras that are compiled under Rik are called Rik Sarnhita or the Rgved. Similarly, the mantras compiled under Sam or Yaj us are called Samveda or Yajurveda. The Atharvaveda is so called because Rishi Atharvan wrote a substantial part of it. For a longtime the Atharvaveda was not regarded as part of the trayi tradition. Generally, it is believed to be the last Veda because its content reflects a society very different from the society in the earlier Vedas. It seems by then the Aryans had come in contact with the local tribes and aborigines who believed in sorcery, magic and other satanic powers and all these impacts got reflected in the mantras of this particular Veda. In her book A Short History of the Vedic Literature, Eastern Book Linkers, 1994, Delhi, (p. 9, Hindi) Dr Pushpa Gupta advances reasons for accepting the Atharvaveda as the last Veda. According to her: (a) religion had peaked by then, (b) it deals essentially with the material world that deal with mundane occurrences of human existence, and (c) there after no new prayers were written. I am unable to resist the temptation from citing the mistake Hiuen-Tsang, an ancient Chinese traveler, committed by mentioning Ayurveda in place of Atharvaveda. R. K. Mookerji in his scholarly book Ancient Indian Education, (Asia, p. 505) attempts to explain away this mistake by citing from Watter's note thus: "(the traveler) had in view those Vedic works were then in writing and known to the brethren in north India. Some of these Buddhists were converted Brahmans as it was perhaps by some of these as has been suggested that the Vedas were reduced to writing." But he fails to explain how by reducing anything to writing a name would get so drastically transformed. The reality may be that Ayurveda was very popular then, hence the mistake.

It may be noted that a Sukta may contain one or many mantras. The absence of any uniformity in the Suktas is remarkable. While a mantra may have been written by just one Rishi/Seer-is-one who can see much beyond the physical eye, a Sukta may contain several mantras written by a whole family or even a group of families. At times it is possible to attribute or identify the writer of a mantra but there are a few mantras that defy this kind of deciphering.

I should like to explain the meaning of a few terms generally used while talking about the Vedic literature. For instance. the Sukta means good poetry, or Mantra means speculation or summary of thought presented in quintessential form. The term Samhita means compilation. On the basis of the meaning and the nature of the content the Vedas are called veda-tray. This use does not denote that the reference here is restricted to three Vedas only and the fourth Veda i.e. the Atharvaveda has been excluded. At the same time it is generally taken to mean that only the first three Vedas count and the fourth does not get similar weightage.

However, on the strength of the Veda and Vedanta sutra it is possible to say that all the Vedas were given to us by God himself. "From that Great Yagna or Supreme Lord, the rcas (the Rgveda), and Sarna (Samveda) hymns were born. Therefrom the chhandas (the Atharvaveda) were produced. The Yajus (the Yajurveda) had its birth from it." (Rgveda. X. 90. 9; Av, XIX. 6.13). The Vedas were given to mankind at the earliest stage in human development but they carry message for all times to come. This is one reason why they command so much reverence from all Aryas.

Though technically the word Veda means knowledge/gyan, the Indian tradition holds that the Vedas contain both the contents and purpose of the karmakaand i.e. the sacrificial rituals as well as the jnankaand i.e. the spiritual knowledge. On the basis of these twin purposes of the Vedas the sacrificial aspect of them is contained in the Brahmanas and the gyan/or the spiritual aspect of the knowledge is dealt with in the Upanishads. In fact, Apastamba titles both the mantras and the Brahmanas as the Vedas.

On the basis of internal evidence it has now been possible to see a kind of development in the Vedic society. It is illogical to imagine that this vast literature could have been produced at one time. This is one reason why numerous scholars have devoted their life time to trace a gradual development in the ancient society from a simple, nomadic people to a highly advanced, complex society with vast empires and elected Parliaments/Assemblies. If a Marxist scholar S.A. Dange has seen traces of primitive communism in that society and analysed it on the lines suggested by Engles, there are others for whom the ancient society being idyllic was perfect in every sense of the term.

It is however commonly agreed that the Vedas existed in the oral form long before they started being regarded as a body of Divine revelation. It may not be possible to pin point the exact date of their birth but it is definitely possible to say that the final and the fourth version of the Vedas got recorded during the Mahabharata time. This means the duration of their writing stretches to more than a thousand years or so. What is most surprising about the Vedas is their survival for such a long period of time in their oral form. An elaborate system was designed to commit them to memory in a flawless manner, which by itself is a marvel of human skills and achievement. If the ancients lacked talent in certain aspects of human knowledge/skill they more than made up by preserving so marvelously well such a voluminous literature for posterity.

We stand at a point in history when we believe all mysteries attached to human existence like survival perse and its future are about to be unraveled. The developments in science and technology have brought us to the present stage when we are unwilling to accept that humans could be forced to accept any limits. It therefore becomes necessary to evolve a perspective for understanding the nature and content of a society that is no longer around. What we find today is only a faint resemblance with the original. There is no need either to defend or ridicule the past.

It is believed that internal evidence available in the sruti / or what was revealed or heard is indicative of the gradual complexity of language development that took place then. The ancients preserved the Vedas through oral tradition. It is common knowledge that to keep any language unchanged fora longtime issimply impossible. A living language will invariably change both because of its natural tendency to absorb new words and idioms in its repertoire and to keep modifying pronunciations with each successive generation. This linguistic reason forced the ancients to devise a system that prevented such a change to occur. They therefore evolved a regular disciplinary system known as the vedangas i.e. the limbs of the Vedas. It was felt necessary to lay down general rules for pronunciation of words properly. Change in pronunciation leads to change in the interpretation and meaning of the words. This necessitated the formulation of shiksha and chhandas. The vedangas are six in number. They are: (1) Shiksha (orthography), (2) Chhanda (prosody), (3) Nighantu (lexicon), (4) Jyotis (astronomy), (5) Vyakarana (grammar) and (6) The Kalpa (rituals). The ancients also divided knowledge into several areas of specialisations. These knowledge areas are called the up (mini)-Vedas or the minor Vedas. These are: (1) the Ayurveda (the science of medicine and cure), (2) the Gandharva-veda (the system of aesthetics) and (3) the Dhanurveda stands for the system of defense sciences, and (4) the Arthaveda means economics or the science of wealth i.e. the production, distribution and utilisation of wealth. For the development and growth of this kind of knowledge it is more than obvious that the ancients must have taken a very longtime. In fact, the form in which the Vedas themselves have been made available to us makes an interesting reading. On the basis of some internal evidences, which are corroborated by tradition and literary testimony, it has been observed that the Vedas were compiled four times in all. The present day shape of the Samhitas represents the fourth and the final compilation. The first compilation took place in the realm of king Sruta of Ayodhya; the second compilation was undertaken at the instance King Srutayu of Videha; third time it was done during the reign of King Brahmadatta of Dakshin Panchala while it was the war-crippled regime of Yudhishthira that saw the final version prepared by Veda Vyasa.

The fact that the Vedas underwent four times editing means that a few mantras were either added or deleted. It is possible that this explains some kind of design behind the repetition of the mantras in the Vedas and the sequencing of the various Suktas. In fact, one of the reasons why Atharvaveda has been declared to be later day writing and compilation is because it contains material, which the earlier Vedas do not even refer to. On the basis of its content it has been declared that the Atharvaveda is not only a much later composition but its content also suggests a distinct flavor and depth. At an appropriate time and place we shall go into this issue at length.

The three types of contents of the Vedas as referred to earlier by the term trayi have been simplified here for the lay reader. They are knowledge (gyana), the code of action (karma), and the upasana (worship).

The word rk stands for knowledge, yajuh for karma, and the sama for love of God or devotion, and dedication. No rigid boundaries are observed in any of the Vedas (Samhitas). The Vedas do not accept the demarcation between the empirical, ephemeral, and the world of absolute reality. They hold out that whatever is born, movable and the immovable, changeless or changing everything in the cosmos is pervaded by that Supreme Being alone, the one who is the Creator of all and the One who knows all. In fact, the entire universe exists within Him and there is nothing beyond Him. There are numerous Hymns on the pre-Cosmic form of the Creator and also on the Creation itself. The Atharvaveda is called by various names. Its most popular address however remains Atharvaveda.

The Vedas are principally about the Creation and the Creator, but this aspect of the Vedas does not have any bearing on the subject that I have in mind. Therefore, with good deal of hesitation and considerable regret I have ignored this aspect totally. I have made only a few passing references about a couple of concepts and practices in which modem day Hindus also have considerable faith. But that does not mean that I believe the Hindus alone are inheritors of this ancient treasure. On all hands, the Vedas are acknowledged to be the heritage of the entire human race. Everyone is invited to share this common treasure. For instance. Indians by and large believe in almost the zero spatial dimension of the soul and in its transmigration. Indians also believe that the Soul is indestructible and is an infinitesimal part of the Divine Being. That is what the Gita lays stress upon and that is what we in India largely believe in. There is a very large number of people among the Hindus too who do not subscribe to all this but that somehow does not make them non-Hindus. That is the large-heartedness of the Indian culture and society. One's personal opinion in this regard seldom creates dissensions in an ordinary Hindu family.

In a Vidya Bhavan Publication one A.C. Bose has discussed the issue whether the Vedic poetry is 'primitive' in nature. Bose says if by primitive is meant primitive poetry or it means some kind of a tribal song or a ballad than nothing could be farther from the truth in the case of the Vedic poetry. He cites an example to make his point. He says no primitive poem would possibly sing the following:

Thought was the pillow of her couch,

Sight was the unguent of her eyes. (R. X. 85.7)

Before I start discussing Man and Society and their mutual relations in ancient India let me mention in passing the classification of knowledge and literature that Indians have had since time immemorial. Thereafter. I should also like to touch upon the social meaning two major classifications of ancient knowledge are the Srutis or the Vedas and the Smritis i.e. what was remembered and written down and the laws of memorisation. Whereas we have already mentioned a thing or two about the Vedas but I have not of the yagnas. Read for instance Yajurveda XXX 5. and subsequent mantras and learn first hand about the society the Veda itself describes. "O God! Create a Brahman, who knows the Veda and God, for propagating the knowledge of God, and the Veda; a Kshatriya prince for the safety of the kingdom; a vaishya for rearing the cattle; a shudra for hard labor and service. Cast aside the thief, who steals in darkness; the destroyer of heroes; who passes his days in jail, the eunuch mentally disposed to licentiousness, the dacoit bent looting and harming people; the harlot full of lust; and the bard disposed to abuse!"

Each Veda consists of an organisation, which enabled ordinary persons to understand that each Veda is also called the Samhita or the collection of the hymns, which may be prayers or the mantras that deal with either cosmic or mundane matters. The interpretations of each Veda are compiled and presented in the Brahmanas. Each Veda therefore has to have its own *Brahmanals.* Four of these Brahmanas are supposedly more important than others. They are Aittaraiya (Rigveda), Satapatha (Yajurveda), Sama (Samaveda), and Gopath (Atharvaveda). The Brahmanas explain difficult terms and concepts used in the Vedas. There are several other Brahmanas too but all of them have not survived. The Shatapath, which forms part of the

Yajurveda, is written in prose-the first ever prose written in Sanskrit language. It is better known or most discussed because it records the attitudes and longings of the ancient society. What is most surprising is that very little has changed in Indian society in the past more than 3500 years or so. In number of ways we are surprised to find the same maladies that we are afflicted with today bothered the ancients as well. For instance, povert, gambling, beggary, dishonesty, jealousies, adultery and rivalries etc. that we find so common these days were not unknown then as well. Since they suffered from ailments like impotency cancer, anxiety, covetousness etc. one is led to conclude that there is very little in terms of misery whose absence we could gloat about this day.

Towards the end of each Veda there are certain chapters or parts, which deal with the mysteries of life and creation. These parts that contain esoteric messages are called the Upanishads. Although the number of these Upanishads is not commonly agreed upon the important ones are eleven in number. They are: Isha, Ken, Katha, Prashna, Mundaka, Mandukya, Taittaraiya, Aittaraiya, Chhandogy , Brihad-Aranyak, and Shwetashwara.

One must also mention here that for the first time in this country we have a varna-vyavastha or an arrangement and organisation of people's lives according to their functions in life. Broadly speaking, all the basic functions of a society are performed by its own people through commonly understood designations such as, the priests, warriors, businessmen, agriculturists and by those that undertake residual jobs for which the most impoverished are generally found fit. The term Varna has been used in the same sense as class in the West. It is the nature of work that defined one's class. It is a historical reality that over a period of time the class got transformed into caste in India. We continue to remain caste-bound inviting in vectives from all and sundry. In the Vedas themselves there are hymns that contradict each other in regard to castes. Interestingly, the castes signify profession and they were changeable according of the profession one engaged in. It would appear that the rigidity that came to characterise caste later on did not exist then. I am repeating here what I have already stated earlier only to remind us that caste and class are historical realities and need not be misinterpreted. There are numerous references in the ancient literature that the change of caste was fairly common and the two primary castes/classes continually changed their caste groups to undertake each other's social obligations. If Vishvamitra was permitted to do so, so were others to join the caste they elected for. There is a reference in which King Bharata (son of Shankuntala) asked Bharadvaj II - a Brahmin by birth to take over the reins of his empire which he accepted gladly on the condition that his progeny will be entitled to retain their original as well as the assumed caste. This gave rise to the birth a caste category called *kshatropeti* Brahmins. It has been pointed out that inter dependence of the priest and the ruler was a necessity. But once either of the two wished to show total independence of each other-defying the norm, it created tensions. This explains to some extent why open hostility and dissensions between the Kshatriyas and the Brahmins, which would come to the fore at the slightest pretext.

The Vedas use the term Varna instead of Jati or caste. The Atharvaveda (3.XXIY.3) talks offive varnas and not off our castes. This is endorsed by other Vedas too. Therefore, there is need to revise our opinion about the origin of the castes and the association of rigidity with it. I should like that some authentic research were to clear the doubt about the Vedic sanction of the caste as a social division and not as part of economic activity. In fact, the Vedas talk of panch janaya as well, which means that people belonged to five types.

This caste rivalry later on came to dominate the social discourse largely due to the question of fixing primacy in society, which eventually led to the birth of organised religions like Buddhism and Jainism. These religions accorded no special place to the Brahmins. Indeed they ignored them entirely banishing them from their fold Even so for a very long time caste mobility remained a recognised fact of ancient life. This explains why and how Satyakam Jabal was declared a Brahmin. He showed the characteristic of Brahmins i.e. truthfulness; and not the manner of his birth.

I personally believe that conflict always leads to progress whether it relates to ideas or functions. There is need to mention the meaning of the term Shudra. They were perhaps the original inhabitants of this land but being aborigines they were accorded the lowest rank order. In the Atharvaveda there is a specific mention that God makes no distinction between either castes or gender but the Indian society has doggedly refused to obey the command of the Lord God.

"The teachings of the Vedas are universal. Yajurveda 26-2 clearly enjoins all learned persons to preach Vedic truths to all, the Brahmanas, the Kshatriyas, the Vaishyas, the Shudras, the Chandals, the degraded and the for lorn. Dwijas, the twice-born alone are not entitied to study the Vedas. The Shudras and even women are equally entitled to read the Vedas. Persons like Kavish Aylush (the seer of R.Y.X. 30) a shudra by birth, vide Aitraiya Brahrnana 11-19' and women like Lopmudra were the seers of the meanings of Vedic texts and their names are from times immemorial attached to the Vedic verses. God is not partial to anyone caste... or a section of people." Introduction to Yajurveda, p.6, Devi Chand. M.A.

I think the ancients believed in organising themselves into a well-oiled society. Therefore, it should come as no surprise that they should also have divided the life span not unlike society according to human abilities and functions. Each stage is called an Ashrama. While the first stage is that of the student i.e. Brahmacharya, the second is that of the householder, the third is of gradual withdrawal from worldly affairs and the last one is of total renunciation i.e. Sanyaas.

As a few of the Upanishads or their parts required complete concentration they were also called the Aranyakas i.e. those sections that were to be read in complete isolation in the jungles/forests. Besides the up-Vedas and the six vedangas, which I have already mentioned, there were six other branches of knowledge that constituted memorised literature or the smritis. These six branches were: (1) The Dhannasastras are the laws of human conduct-personal as well as social as enunciated by Vidur, Shukracharya or Chanukah; 18 Srnritis-variously written by Manu, Parashar, Yagya valkya, and Vashishth; (2) Kautalya shastra (Economics, Politics, and Law or the art of the runninga state/state craft), (3)The Puranas (18 out of 108) are normally regarded important. The Puranas are a record of the past but because their authors employed certain metaphors, allegories and codes that it has not been possible to compare them with books of modem day historians. Scholars like Pargiter and several others including one Kennedy have retrieved them from complete oblivion, obscurantism and disrepute into which they had unfortunately got trapped. Of these the Bhagvat Gita is accepted as the most important, (4) Itihaas i.e. history (or literally it means *that is how it happened)* can be discovered in both the Epics and the Puranas. The two great Indian epics are – the Ramayana and the Mahabharata, (5) Agam i.e. sects such as Vaishnava, Shaiva, and Shaakta; and (6) Philosophical systems, which are, divided into two main branches: the atheists viz. the Charvakas; and the theists and they are; Vaisheshik (Kanad), Nyaya (Gautam), Sankhya (Kapil), the Yoga (Patanjali), Purva Mimansa (Jaimini), and Uttara Mimansa. These are also called the Vedanta i.e. the end of the Vedas (Vyas). The names given in the brackets are of those who were founders of these schools of philosophy or thought. This then has been the range of knowledge made available to us by our ancient counterparts.

I have mentioned all this to avoid confusion later on because other than the Vedas no other branch or part of the ancient knowledge has been cited. I have therefore scrupulously avoided getting bogged down by some later day discussion on the same subject or section of the ancient lore. My interest is restricted to the text of the Vedas.

The Vedas are believed to be the source of all knowledge. The Vedas themselves acknowledge that God alone is the source of divine knowledge or for that matter of all 'forms of knowledge'. My interest is only in the forms of knowledge that the Vedas contain. But before I do that I should like to deal with the fact how and why exactly they took so long to be written down and why an elaborate system was created to memorise them in a perfect form.

To the question whether the Vedas were written or revealed the answer is unequivocally No. *There is every reason to believe that they existed orally as part of the cultural heritage of a group of people.* They got written or were given script much later. Therefore, the next question is HOW did they come to us and do they mean really the same as we understand after reading them? Perhaps, yes, because we do have a long list of interpreters. Let me briefly touch upon the stock of knowledge that we have today. Its definitive version is unlikely to come anytime too soon.. According to H.R. Divekar (Rgveda Sukta Vikas, Motilal Banarasidas, 1970) the Western scholars did the initial work. It is they who are primarily responsible for the discovery arrangement and interpretation of the ancient Indian sacred and secular Sanskrit literature. We must value their opinions as well. While Indians themselves were later day entrants in the area, they had the intentions of trying largely to claim proprietary rights over this vast sacred literature. They advanced their so-called religious/spiritual versions. It should surprise no one that this area now constitutes a contested terrain. There are today (logically enough) several interpretations of each hymn and similarly, we have several opinions and suggestions about the origin of these literatures. Even the dates and authenticity of each and every version available today continues to be hotly debated. To avoid confusion and help the reader to take his/her individual decisions in this regard I offer choices for them to select. H. H. Wilson, a known name in the field has given his opinion on the various books/ mandalas of the Vedas containing the material essentially differing in cultural levels and their multiple authors.

He says "The absence of any obvious dependency of the suktas upon one another is sufficiently indicative of their separate and unsystematic origin. That they are compositions of the patriarchal sages to whom they are ascribed, is sometimes, apparent from allusions which they make to the name of the author or of his family; but these indications are of unfrequent recurrence, and we must trust in general to tradition, as preserved by the Anukramanikas for the accuracy of the appropriation. Their being addressed to the same divinity is a less equivocal test of community and they probably were composed in many instances by the heads of the families, or of schools following a similar form of worship, and adoring in preference particular deifications. Besides the internal evidence afforded by difference of date; and we find some ascribe it to the ancient rsis, while others admit to their being of new or newest compositions. The great variety of metres employed shows also a progressive development of the language, which could have been the effect of long and diligent cultivation."

To the Indians this view point is by and large unacceptable. They hold that the Vedas originated in their perfect form and there is nothing evolutionary about them. On this controversy, the Prathisthan's scholars offer an alternative opinion. I cite the same for consideration.

"It is to the credit of Dayanand and later on also of Aurobindo to have declared in unequivocal terms that the Rgveda is one in all its parts. To Dayanand, not only the Rgveda, but all the four Vedas go to constitute the Single Veda, even as Aurobindo says," whichever of its ten Mandalas we choose, we find the same substance, the same ideas, the same images, the same phrases. The Rishis are the seers of a single truth and use in its expression a common language. They differ in temperament and personality; some are Inclined to a more rich, subtle and profound use of Yedic symbols; others give voice to their experience in a barer and simpler diction, with less fertility of thought, richness of poetical image or depth and fullness of suggestion. Often the songs of one seer vary in their manner, range from the utmost simplicity to the most curious richness. Or; there are risings and fallings in the same hymn; it proceeds from the most ordinary conventions of the general symbol of sacrifice to a movement of packed and complex thought. Some of the suktas are plain and almost modern in their language; others baffie us at first by their semblance of antique obscurity. But these differences of manner take nothing from the unity of spiritual experience, nor are they complicated by any variation of the fixed terms or formulae. In the deep and mystic style of Dirghatarnas Aucathya as in the melodious lucidity of Medhatithi Kanwa, in the puissant and energetic hymns of Vishwamitra as in Vasishtha's even harmonies we have the same firm foundation of knowledge and the same scrupulous adherence to the sacred conventions of the Initiates."

In a way both Dayanand and Sri Aurobindo are one in accepting a kind of uniformity and congruency in the entire Vedic fabric texture. Still there appear to be fundamental differences between these two great scholars. Aurobindo believes that the names preserved in the Sarvanu kraman is acted as the media for the spiritual knowledge found in the Vedas. But following Yaska, "Swami Dayanand Saraswati holds the view that these revealed hymns existed much prior to the names that appear in the **Sarvanukramanis.** Therefore, these Rishis whose names we are referring to here are only interpreters and not the media for the spiritual experience that Aurobindo is talking about. In other words both deny the authorship to the mortals whereas while one regards the Rishi as the medium, the other insists that they (the Rishis) in reality are mere inspired interpreters and no more."

For me this debate is not central to the purpose I have in mind. It is a fact that even for the revelations too there is need for a medium.

All religious books that the mankind claims to possess today needed one or the other to function as a kind of medium – their designations notwithstanding. In the case of the ancient Indians if the Rishis played that role there is no need either to rationalise the event or feel apologetic about it. Indeed, there is every reason why we must feel proud that we were chosen for a gift like the one that we got in the form of the Vedas.

We are lucky that not only we have today the Rg. Samhita and the Pad-Pathas but also the indexes that carry the individual names and the genealogies of all the Seers associated with the Vedas. Katyayana composed **Sarvanukramni** (edited by Macdonell, Oxford, 1886) and as its name indicates, it is a collection of various indices for the Rgveda This work gives, in the form of Sutras, the first word of every hymn, the number of verses in that hymn, the name of the family of the Risi to whom the verse is ascribed, the devata (the deities) or the subject title to which the hymn is devoted, and the meter or the meters in which it is composed.

In the Rgveda 1.164.23-25 we have the following description of the meters we are referring to. It should been ough for an intelligent person to appreciate that these Rishis themselves knew what meters they were using and why. The reader is free to interpret the same the way one likes. The mantras are:

"On the tree, whereon the beautiful birds taste the sweetness, where they all rest and again bring forth their offering,—on its top, they say, the fruits are sweet, but the one who knows not the father (of the Universe) has no privilege to enjoy it.

They, who know, the support of the gayatri (24 syllables) on gayatri, the support of the tristubh (44 syllables) on tristubh, and the support of jagati (48 syllables) on jagati, know the eternal.

He, the Lord, constructs the Rks with gayatri prayers; with the rks he constructs Saman; and with tristubh the Yajuh couplet! triplet, he constructs the Atharvan hymns with verses of two or four distiches and subsequently with the syllable; the poets construct the seven meters.

With the stanzas in the jagati meter (48 syllables. He fixed the Milky Way in the heaven, and surveyed the sun in the interspace (or ratnatara psalm). They have declared three divisions of the gayatri meter whence the creator or Lord surpasses in authority and grandeur."

We have another index also known as the **Arsanukramani** which is ascribed to Saunak and it enumerates the rishis of the Vedic hymns according to the Mandalas. There is yet another book of considerable importance for all of us known as the **Brhd-devata** also ascribed to Saunaka. It constitutes a more or less exhaustive manual dealing with the devatas (gods). These gods stand celebrated in the Vedas. Infact, some of the Indian gods and goddesses have foreign origins. One could study the Vedas with some profit for the sake of tracing their genealogies.

It would be wise to remember that there is no history or historical names (as we understand). It was considered very sacred to find proper nouns out of the common terms that occurred in the Vedic text. The stories currently in vogue about these names are a later day creations. Most of the Puranas have continued to preserve these tales.

The Sarvanu kramani provides a list of 407 rishis for the entire Rigveda. The term Risi itself has been variously interpreted. Its roots are mentioned in the Taittaraiya Aryanaka, which means to go upward. Sayana says its roots suggest the meaning as 'to go'. According to the Nirukta the Seers were supposed to have the 'vision' of the mantras. I personally like the meaning of the word rsi, as some one who has the vision of the mantra i.e. a rsi is a drishta – someone who has developed an insight beyond the phenomenological appearances of things. One must distinguish between those that are merely learned i.e. those who have read widely and may be even deeply and intensely. But wisdom comes only after one has meditated or reflected on one's experiences. It is not very surprising to learn that Indians have talked of the 3 stages in the learning – *chintan* (reflection or thinking), *manan* (meditation) and *nidhiasana* (constant deep meditation while sitting in a given posture). It is only in the last stage of meditation that one acquires the ability to look beyond or develop an insight into the subject understudy. An insight is the last stage of discovery or invention. There is no reason whatsoever to doubt that the mantras of the Vedas are indeed the result of a lifetime effort of a rsi's meditation or sadhana.

What is generally not discussed about the Vedas is the fact that in whatever form we take the text it must have taken a long time being written/ revealed or interpreted. The logic of my argument is simple. The Vedas are not considered to be an individual effort even if the source remains the self same Divine Being. The fact is that each Veda has almost three distinct parts and everything mentioned in them is also not very organised suggests multiple efforts and also a considerable time lag in between. Let me cite just one genealogy to support my thesis. The Sarvanu kramani gives the following family tree of Rishi Angiras:

Anginas———>Rahugana———>Gotama

I

-----------------------------------------------------

I I

Nodhas

Vamadeva

I I

Ekadyu

-----------------------------------------------------

---------I

I I

I

Brhaduktha Murdhanvan

Amhomuk

If each one in the present case contributed to the Vedic revelations then the minimum time consumed can not be less than hundreds of years, if not more. Infact, the Pratishthan scholars have suggested that the time lag between the Vedas and the Brahamnas could be even a thousand years or more. There are cases in which the generations went on to be much more than the mere three-generation of a single rsi. For instance, in the case of Atris 50 names have been given. Although the */irstrsi* is the chief of the Gotra or a school of thought or principal contributor bequeathing to the rest of the family a surname. Even today among the Hindus the gotra is an important consideration. No one can marry within the gotra because they are supposed to belong to the same family tree. In the case of the first such gotra the system was that in a *hotr* ceremony the name of the ancestor was given first by a *hotr* priest and another priest who read out the name of the descendents first and then went on to reach the top or to the first head of the family i.e. in the reverse order, was known as the *adhvarya.* It is all known as *pavarocchar.* This is a very strange way to identify one's lineage. But if one went into the logic of the same; one might get surprised to note that this might as well have been the trick to exclude the interlopers.

There are numerous rsikas or the lady-seers. During the Vedic period the ladies were denied the right to be rsis. Some of the famous names are *Lopamudra, Romasa, Vishwavara, Angirasi Sasvati, Apala, Yami, Sraddha, Vasukra-patni, Ghosa, Surya, Indrani, Urvashi, Sarama, Juhu, Vakambhrani and Paulomi Sachi.* While a few of the ladies are real historical personages there is some reason to believe that it would be true for all.

Scholars have attempted to discuss the meters used in the Vedas. They have even attempted to both count the names of the meters as well as the total numbers of the syllables used in of these meters. Numerous complications are listed in attempting this process. But for our purpose it would suffice to learn a little bit about the meters. For instance, in counting the munber of syllables in a meter, only the number of vowels (svara) is counted, and not the consonants with out the vowels. The svaras normally are a, aa, i, ii, u, uu, etc.

The meters are arranged in an increasing series of 4 starting from 24. Thus, it would go like 24, 28, 32 and so on and so forth.

| *Total No. of Syllables* | *Name of Meter* |
|---|---|
| 24 | Gayatri |
| 28 | Usni |
| 32 | Anustup |
| 36 | Brhatpankti |

But these meters do not exhaust the list. There are some more. However, for our purpose this discussion should suffice. Therefore, I refrain from going into the details of the meters.

To the question how the Vedic hymns have to be read we have the following comments to guide us in our effort. Since the Rk Samhita is arranged both in the patha and pada it is suggested that while reading them, one should remember that the padas are considered superior to any other arrangement. The text in which the words stand as joined by the rules of Sanskrit Sandhi is called the Samhita-patha, In the pada patha all words stand alone or by themselves-as they do in Latin or Greek. "For practical purposes, the pada text is far superior to the Samhita text in which the final and initial letters of words are constantly disguised, and therefore liable to different inter pretations."

All Vedic Suktas begin in the following manner: for instance, the first hymn comprising nine verses in the first book of the Rgveda it is written as Seer: Madhu Chandas; Devata: Agni; Meter: Gayatri; and Tunc: Shadja.

The Veda Pratishthan scholars have given us their opinion, which supports the view Max Muller had taken to read the Vedic text. According to the Pratishthan scholars "It is almost certain that neither the Pada nor the Samhita text, as we know now possess them, represents the original text of the Veda, both show clear traces of Scholiastic influence." This is what Max Muller says regarding reading the Rk text. "It is far easier, as I remarked before, to discover the original and natural rhythm of the Vedic hymns by reading them in the Pada than in the Samhita text, and after some practice our ear becomes sufficiently schooled to tell us at once how each line ought to be pronounced. We find, on the one hand, that the rules of the Sandhi, instead of being generally binding, were treated by the Vedic poets as poetical licences only; and on the other, that a greater freedom of pronunciation was allowed even in the body of words than would be tolerated in the later Sanskrit. If a syllable was wanted to complete the meter, a semi-vowel might be pronounced as a vowel, many a long vowel might be protracted so as to count for two syllables, and short vowels might be inserted between certain consonants, of which no trace exists in the ordinary Sanskrit. If, on the contrary, there were too many syllables, then the rules of Sandhi were observed, or too short syllables contracted by rapid pronunciation into one; nay in a few cases, a final *m*ors, it seems, was omitted."

It must be remembered that the readings of the Vedic texts are of two types; pada patha with each word or the term spoken clearly and distinctly, and when these padas are compounded together according to the rules of euphony or *sandhi,* we get the samhita patha; in fact, sandhi is the euphonic junction of final and initial letters in grammar, every sentence in Sanskrit being regarded as a euphonic chain, a break in which occurs at the end of a sentence.

The identified number of accents in Sanskrit is four. They are *Udatta, Anuddata, Svarita* and *Eksruti.* It is quite important to remember that each Veda has its own style of being read loudly. Therefore, each Vedahas his own class of priests. The following pecking order was followed in each case:–

Suppose a Rgedic Yagna is in progress. A Hota is the chief priest. He is entitled by his position in that yagna to half of what comes as a Vedic offering. The next in that order is Maitravarun who will receive half of the half. Acchavak is on the third rung of the ladder. Therefore, his share is the one third of the half. Gravastuta is on the lowest rung of the ladder and therefore he is entitled to the least or whatever remains from his seniors.

In the same way the hierarchy in the case of Yajurveda is Adhavaryu, the leader supported by Pratistatha, Neshta and Unneta. For the Samveda the priestly order is Brarnha, Prastota, Pratiharta and Subramanya. The yagnas themselves were divided according to moonshine i.e. when there was no moon and when there was full moon.

A discerning scholar can easily see from the above description that such an elaborate system was needed for each Veda because there were differences in their presentation and also perhaps because their period of time when they came into existence also differed considerably. It may be a pure conjecture if! were to suggest that the enunciation in each case varied for this very reason as well. Or, it could be because each family that contributed to its recording or interpretation wished to have its identity known through their bench mark pronunciation.

The Vedic sages are positive in their acceptance of life. They accept death and imperfections of life in the same spirit as they do their opposites. For them Truth, Goodness and Beauty are the ultimte values. They accept the Eternal laws (Rita) and the Ultimate Reality. They may be called as intensely religious too as they have a sense of feeling the living Presence of the Divine in their midst in the form of beauty and glory of the living universe (Vibhuti Yoga). Vedic poetry came out of the joyous and radiant spirit, over flowing with love and energy for action, and looking up with serene faith to the Divinity for support and inspiration.

Like joyous streams bursting from the mountain. Our songs have sounded to Brihaspati. ( Rig Veda. X. 68.1)

Perhaps nowhere in the world have the glory of dawn and sunrise and the silence and sweetness of nature, received such rich and at the same time such pure expression. They also have the confidence in the eternity of their poetry. That is why a sage-poet sang,

> Forget not, Singer! This word of thine,
> which after-ages will resound. (Rg. II 1. 33.8)

We must remember that the language of the Vedas and the terms used in them have been a matter of considerable debate. I am writing this only to give my readers an idea how a Divine Book could also be misinterpreted to make its message a property of a section of society. The biggest problem generations faced until Swami Dayanand Saraswati and Aurobindo gave their explanations of the Vedic text was Sayana's interpretation. For so many centuries and the millennia the Vedic text remained obscure because what were made available until then were 'the notion of the times and the practice of the days' when the interpreters lived. For the Pratishthan's scholars none of the Brahmanas, or Aranyakas or even the nirukta could be accepted as the true interpreters of the Vedic text. The older tradition of reading and interpreting the Vedic text must have been lost long back. The Taittaraiya Samhita itself, which is a book that deserves to be treated as an independent text like any of the Brahmanas or the Aranyakas are commonly believed to be the true interpreters of the text. And when even the venerated Brahmanas do not explain enough how can one accept Sayana's interpretation when we are informed that he was born in the fourteenth century A.D.?

The objective of the Vedic revelation (compilation) was manifold. It was to prescribe a code of conduct to the mankind. It was also to tell them that there exists a live relationship between the Nature and the society. Indeed, they are interdependent. Also, the purpose was to initiate the mankind into the mysteries of the relationship with the Creator and His Creation. The idea was to explain the meaning and purpose of gyan (enlightenment), karma (duty and action), and upasana (devotion and love toward God). Man needs to be instructed in all these three hence the need for a special revelation.

The distortions started appearing in the understanding of the purpose and functions of reciting particular verses on given occasions.

This led to a rigid ritualism of the use of the Vedic verses. The term given to this rigidritualism is viniyoga. The ritualistic application of the Vedic text can be both relevant and irrelevant. For instance, the relevant ones are given the namerupa-samriddhi. The initiatory and offering verses are regarded perfect in the ritualistic context. But the overuse of the viniyoga resulted in the complete distortion of them eaning of the Yajurveda until Dayanand delivered it. It may be remembered that the Vedas are much more than mere ritualistic formats. It is because of this reason that I have dared to present a socio-historical analysis of the Vedic content.

Only to illustrate the point how Aurobindo and Swami Dayanand helped rescuing the Vedic text from the clutches of the viniyoga I cite a quote from the former. While posing a problem he said, "Our first duty, therefore, is to determine whether there is, apart from symbol and figure, in the clear language of the hymns a sufficient kernel of psychological notions to justify us in supposing at all a higher than the barbarous and primitive sense of the Veda?" He formulated his psychological theory and explained the mystic meaning behind the Vedic Text. In addition, he explained the terms like sapta-sindhu, the dawn, cow and angiras and the concepts like the lost sun or the Hounds of Heaven.

Having compared the Dravidian languages with Sanskrit he wrote, it did not take long to see that the Vedic indication of a racial division between Aryans and the dasyus and the identification of the latter with the indigenous Indians were of a far flimsier character than I had supposed. But far more interesting to me was the discovery of a considerable body of profound psychological thought and experience lying neglected in these ancient hymns, and the importance of this element increased in my eyes when I found first, that the mantras of the Veda illuminated with a clear and exact light psychological experiences of my own for which I had found no sufficient explanation, either in European psychology or in the teachings of the yoga or of the Vedanta, so far as I was acquainted with them, and secondly, that they shed light on obscure passages and ideas of the Upanishads to which, previously, I could attach no exact meaning and gave at the same time a new sense to much in the Puranas." A few examples are cited below: -

| **Term** | **Psychological sense** |
|---|---|
| Rtam | Truth |
| Dhi | Thought or understanding |
| Raye | Spiritual felicity |

| | |
|---|---|
| Vaja | Homogenous totality of thought |
| Ashva | vital energy |
| Go-Ashva | Light-energy companionship |
| Immortality | State of infinite being |
| Rodasy (Heaven and Earth) | Mind and Body |
| Yajna | Action |
| Yajamana | Soul or personality of a doer |

The Vedic deities are names, powers, personalities of the Universal Godhood and they represent each some essential puissance of divine being.... The gods call man to a divine companionship and alliance; they attract and uplift him in their luminous fraternity, invite his and offer them against the Sons of Darkness and Divisions.

Aurobindo also says, "The Rgveda itself, asserts (Rg. I.164.46) that the gods are only different names and expressions of One Universal Being, who in His own reality transcends the universe; but from the language of the hymns we are compelled to perceive in the gods not only different names, but also different forms, powers and personalities of the one Deva. The monotheism of the Veda includes in itself also the monistic and even polytheistic views of the Cosmos and is by no means the trenchant and simple creed of modem theism. It is only by a violent struggle with the text that we can force on it a less complex aspect."

The Veda or the eternal Divine Knowledge is one. The revealed word of God has come to us in three forms: (1) The Rk. or the hymns pertaining to knowledge; (2) The Yajuh, outlining the details of yajna or action; and (3) The Saman, or the devotional songs. All the Vedas consist of these three or trayi vidyas.

The Lord bethought of Himself: "Verily, if I shall intend against him, I shall make the less food for myself." With that speech, with that self He brought forth this whole world, whatsoever exists here: the Hymns (rk. i.e. the Rgveda), the formulas (yajus, i.e. the Yajurveda), the chants (saman, i.e. the Samaveda), meters, sacrifices (yajnas), men and cattle".

A few Indian scholars have made one complaint against their Western counterparts that although credit must be given to them for their meticulousness and scientificity in their work their "critical study lacked in the sense of that sympathy which a scripture meant to elevate mankind through all times deserves." This criticism is seemingly out of place. Firstly, the western scholars were forced to undertake a job, which the natives had never done before and certainly not with as much care and scientific editing or objective insight as the Westerners had. Secondly, they were not here to admire the ritualism of the 'barbarians' whom they wanted to give light. Even today in the third millennia Indians have not succeeded in removing the impression that for them religion means anything more than mere a ritual. Thirdly, we have ourselves rarely overcome our narrow-mindedness and produced works of any standard on any other religion or scriptures other than our own. Therefore, honestly speaking but for the labour of the Western scholars we would have remained ignorant of our own ancient knowledge. The peculiar tendency of the Brahman scholarship has been its exclusiveness and the overt desire to remain over bearingly proprietorial in their conduct. It was therefore one of those good things that resulted from the evil of colonialism which freed our ancient literature from a private discourse and the stultifying decadence of caste monopoly and brought it to the full glare of the world to appreciate.

The Vedas are Living Books and are not relics of a dead past. The spiritual nature of their content apart, they are a source of all knowledge personifying morality. The personal ethics is outlined in the five yamas and five niyamas. The relevance of both can be judged by reading the bare outline itself. For instance, the five yamas are: non-violence; truthfulness; abstinence from misappropriation of others' wealth; celibacy and freedom from avarice. The five niyamas are: cleanliness; contentment; austerity; study and self-evaluation; and devotion to the Supreme Being. No one can doubt either their universality or eternity. In which age would a civilised society accept violence or theft as legitimate functions of an individual?

For future translators guidance is also readily available. For instance, before translating a text it is suggested that one should be familiar with both i.e. grammar arid etymology. In Sanskrit a single word has multiple meanings. It depends for a meaning on the context in which a word has been used. For instance, the term gauh is a synonym for earth when it is seen to have been derived from the root gam or when it is accepted to have been derived ga with a suffix au. Even a novice would know that gau stands for earth, which is in constant motion. The verb is gaman. The term gau also stands for indriyas, which are seldom under control. Therefore, in the Yogic language they are supposed to be kept under control. It is in that context a rsi says let them (the indriyas/ gau) be eaten up or kept under control. It is this interpretation that has been thoroughly misconstrued. This is what is regarded as an invitation to eat a cow when in reality it means keep the senses under control, and those too in the yogic terminology. The cow is also a synonym for an ammal from the same root. During the BJP-led NDA rule at the center a twist to the meaning of the term was given to this term gau with highly prejudicial interpretations. The so-called secular scholars, though very knowledgeable, did not hesitate to mislead the common man.

Let me state here that while I have no intentions of either picking bones or joining Issues with them, but I find it difficult to confirm their contention. It would be edifying to have here a relevant quote from David Frawley (Hymns from the Golden Age, pp. 26-27 Motilal Banarasi das, Delhi, 1986).

"Gau— is symbolically a cow. Generally it is anything that comes from a cow, Is made from cow or is somehow cow-like? From the cow as the basic wealth of the ancients, it meant wealth; nourishment and value generally-The cow is the Divine word-wisdom at the heart of the soul, which yields all boon. As such the cow is the Goddess, who inwardly consciousness is outwardly the sky. The dappled cow can be a general term for the Gods as the powers of light and wisdom-word.... The cow is the basic archetypal symbol of reality that is the beneficence of consciousness. The word Cow or gau (if not used properly) reduces and violates the actual usage of the term, ignores many deeper implications and etymological word plays."

The author continues to explain that like the term gau, other mantric terms have to be used correctly and in a proper context. For Instance, In the Rgveda 1.135.8 &1.161.11 cows are given to mean wealth, which no thief can steal; in Rgveda 1.147.3 cows mean philosophies - mundane as well as spiritual; in Rgveda 1.160.3 cow is abadh i.e. someone which is not to be killed; in Rgveda 1.164.6 cow is used for earth; in mantra 173 as intellect, in Rgveda 1.174.8&1.186.4 dhenu or cow is used for speech. Read this Rigvedic 1.164.26 hymn.

"I invoke the milch-cow (the cloud) that is easily miked, that the handy milker may milk her: may the creator accept our libations" etc.

Of the some more meanings of the term it was used as 'mix Soma with milk.' In the latter day meaning of the text Gauh also means milk when its root is derived from mand etc. Controversies like: whether or not the ancients ate beef are irrelevant for the majority of the Indians. Raking up such controversies means that these individuals are playing politics with the term and that too in an out of context manner. I argue simply. If one read the text of the Vedas one would discover that the ancients were obsessed with the term cow. They used the term in different manner in a variety of contexts. The very people who mention repeatedly about the cow being a badh and aghanya- not to be killed, how could they eat it? Those that are obsessed with the term cow, why would they, name an animal with this name and how could such people even think 01 eating it? The question is: provided they ate the cow: Which cow did they eat? The word cow that means intellect, speech, cloud, earth or something else, which one did they eat? In most cases the term gau/cow stands for earth and surely one does not eat earth. Why don't these people undertake some well-meaning, positive research?

The Vedas constitute divine knowledge (because no such knowledge existed before the Vedas) therefore the question of their being obscure or primitive does not arise. For our purpose whatever be their periodicity they have a social as well as personal message to convey. Above all they offer knowledge the variety of which just about amazes us because we have not moved an inch beyond what they already had. While the details will follow in the subsequent chapters I shall merely mention a few bits of knowledge where we in 2010 or there abouts are as well informed as these ancients were. For instance, they knew keeping the environment clean; knew that rivers should not be polluted (Yajurveda XXX. 8) or forest guard bent upon burning down forests (see XXX. 19), are punished; Similarly they knew about Time and its divisions like, Year, months, days etc. and gave us names that we are using even these days. They gave us methods by which eclipses and the movement of earth, sun and moon could be predicted without hitch. The functions of the physicians; astronomers, researchers; shipbuilding; cars and airplanes for going to high and low places; see Yajurveda XXX.14 and arithmetic in which how to calculate billions are given. Read the Yajurveda XVIII. 23. & 24 etc.. Yajurveda Ch.1. 22 and other hymns talk of the reasons of performing the yagnas.

# Chapter - 2

# On Understanding the Vedas

"The One who deserves everyone's prayer, that venerable Being-God, is responsible for the birth of all the four Vedas – Rgveda, Yajurveda, Samveda and the Atharvaveda. These Vedas are the source of all the knowledge that is spread across the world. Therefore, God alone is the original teacher of all Knowledge." Yajur/31/5.

There are reasons to believe that despite all the advancements in our historical knowledge there are numerous aspects in India's past that remain shrouded in the cover of its antiquity. *The more we try to be accurate the more inaccurate we become.* The real problem does not lie in what we pretend to know but in what we in reality do not know. For instance, the archeological discovery in around 1920s of Harrappa and Mohan Jo Daro put a definite date to India's known civilisation that had previously been only guessed. In the year 2010, besides China we are the only other most ancient living civilisation in today's world. What has remained hidden in the shallow waters of the sea near Bhet Dwarika thus far might some day force us to revise our history books completely. The archaeologists believe that what lies beneath the seabed is a highly well planned urban habitation of far greater antiquity than known to the mankind. This may not bring about any significant change in our attitudes toward the Vedas themselves but one thing is more than evident. "Aryans had lived in India for a considerable period before the composition of the Vedic hymns" (Prafulachandra Basu, Indo-Aryan Polity, p. 40). In fact, on close examination of the Vedic text everyone would endorse Basu's statement.

It is commonly believed that the Vedas do not contain any history. But what has never been denied is that the similes and metaphors used in the Vedas do reflect contemporary societal norms. For instance, when they talk about a gambler's plight or describe a marriage ceremony or give an outline of the behavior of a gentleman or recommend medicines for most of the diseases humans are commonly afflicted with do make us conclude that the rsis were no recluses and kept their eyes wide open to events or environment around them. Even their likes and dislikes-their love for begetting a male child, hatred for their enemies, disapproval of a bad student, the liking for a good scholar-teacher, their understanding and appreciation of a virile man (whose male organ is both proportionate and erect), their appreciation for frolicking women during sexual engagement *(rati-kujita etc.)* become ever so evident as one goes through the Vedic text. It would appear that the Vedas are generally treated with so much reverence that we are constraint to read only liturgy in them. While there is no need to dispute the contention of the majority, it does no harm to accept that the scope of the text is much wider than believed. Being products of the society it is only logical to hold the view that the rsis did not neglect the society they came from and neither did they forget that the function of the religion is to offer guidance to society and not to neglect it or turn one's attention off it.

"The Vedas enshrine the cosmic vision and vitality of our ancestors and epitomise a living legacy of divine inspiration, intuition and insight. The glory of the Vedas is their universal and timeless quality. The subtle and symbolic in vocations of the Sruti and the mystic and melodic music of the celestial hymns have hallowed human consciousness through trackless centuries with a sublime glow. The Vedas exemplify a carefully nurtured and elaborately systematised oral tradition, which is unrivalled in the annals of civilisations." Foreword, Rigveda Samhita, Veda Pratishthan.

We need no further proof than already available to state that the Vedic people knew more about a host of professions, running a polity and the ways to keep their women happy by getting them a tremendous variety of jewellery than we know of these days. The ancient women folk seemingly had similar weaknesses, as they tend to exhibit today. The ancient males too had almost all our modern day afflictions and weaknesses such as: greed, covetousness, jealousy, enmity, sexual preferences and lust. They knew all about elections and the possibilities of misuse of power. They definitely knew about the advantages of education or else why would they have insisted upon everyone to get educated. For them education meantone-fourth of one's normal lifespan. This was obviously equally applicable to both girls and boys. They wished to live for 100 years with all their physical organs and senses intact. But they welcomed the prospects of living much longer than even 300 years. They were cautious about girls receiving education alongwith the boys in the co-ed. institutions. They did not pretend to teach everyone free. The mode of payment of fee could be different according to one's ability to pay but everyone was enjoined upon to pay fees. It is ridiculous to suggest that the teacher didn't expect any payment or guru-dakshina They knew the difference between bad and good teachers. They taught their children in well-built school buildings and knewall about mathematics i.e. geometry algebra, and arithmetic. They knew not only zero but also their knowledge of mathematics helped them in calculations of sums and multiplications running into billions. It is usually said about the Mahabharata that what is not in it does not, or even may not, exist in the world. Some one could as well say the same about the Vedas.

I wonder whether the final editing of the Vedas during the Pandava rule has anything to with this fact. It would however be in correct to even suggest that modem day technology could have existed then, but at the same time it wouldn't be too much to say that without their help it would be impossible for us to reach the present stage of all-round development. *Theirs may have been only the first few stones in the foundations of modernity but their efforts to improve the quality of our existence are certainly beyond the scope of any dispute.*

We must remember that knowledge *perse* belongs to humanity as a whole. No nation should claim it to be its monopoly. The Vedas are griversal heritage; it would be very unwise of anyone to declare it otherwise. They carry message for all and not for any specific group. We in India are lucky that they were composed/revealed in this country. But it is the scholars across the globe that has made them known and helped in their worldwide dissemination. The labor put in by innumerable scholars from the West and the East in the translation and interpretation of the Vedic text should be gratefully acknowledged. We in India have been a Iittle narrow-minded and have therefore interpreted the Vedic message parochially. The added misery has been that for a certain class of people the ritualistic part of the Vedas alone excited their imagination. They failed to benefit from the all-rounded knowledge available in them. If only our scholars had taken a little care the Vedas could easily have served as the foundation blocks for multi-faced advancement.

It is our good fortune that others have taken care to correct this perception. We must express our gratitude to these numerous scholars both Western and Indian. We must always remember that veneration by itself can be extremely dangerous unless it is tempered by knowledge. *The veneration of an ignoramus can easily become fanaticism.*

I am not interested in any controversy that relates to the composition/revelation of the Vedas. For me they exist and therefore I would like to read them. If as I read them I find that they ought to be read and venerated by others too I think I have the right to say so. of the several ways to interpret them if I add one of mine own I do not think that will harm anyone. As of today numerous scholars for varied reasons have attempted writing on them. If there are Western scholars like Max Muller whose sole aim of translating the Vedas was to denigrate them and establish the superiority of the Holy Bible over them, there have been native scholars like Sayanacharya too who took them to be liturgies to Nature gods.

In his lectures to selected ICS Max Muller however corrected himself (1879) by recording the following: "The true history of the world must always be the history of the few; and as we measure the Himalayas by the height of Mt. Everest, we must take the true measure of India from the poets of the Veda, the sages of the Upanishads, the founders of the Vedanta.." (India: **What can India teach us**?, Munshi Ram Manohar Lal, 1961), Aurobindo comments on his work thus: "For if ever there was a monument of arbitrarily erudite ingenuity, of great learning divorced, as great learning too often is from sound judgment and sure taste and a faithful critical and comparative observation; from direct seeing and often even from plainest common sense or of a constant fitting to the text into the Procrustean bed of pre-conceived theory." He goes on to add, "Sayana, not unlike the Western scholars minimises the psychological and ethical value of the hymns, because his theory of Vedic discipline was not ethical righteousness with a moral and spiritual result but mechanical performance of ritual with a material reward."

In the Vedic vision of human society, man in his relation to man was not predatory, aggressive and oppressive as in the Hobbsesian nightmare, which conjured up *homo homini lupus.* The Vedic ideal was that man was under obligation to protect and preserve and to comfort mankind everywhere. "O King! Honor that learned person who discharging arrows from the bow-string and protecting the arms of his master and extirpating the opposing foe from all sides, rains all with enjoyable objects, like the clouds and guards all industrious persons, knowing his duties properly." Rg. 6.75.14.

It was the philosophy of freedom and fearlessness. "O Almighty God! You are able to be victorious in the effort of attaining wealth, in the manner of encounter in gevils in connection with combating the army in the battle, in acquiring gain and fame on the rivalries of rivals." Atharvaveda 19.15.7. The Vedic vision has no place for a fractured and fragmented world. On the contrary they view a world of togetherness. "May you move together, speak together in one voice; let your minds be of one accord; and like the ancients ages, may you enjoy your assigned share of fortune." Rgveda. 10.191.2

Over a long period of time numerous ways were evolved to interpret the Vedas. Here are a few ways in which they have thus far been interpreted:

1. The Nairuktas-the ones who go by philology of Yaska's Nirukta. This is the most acceptable scholarly way of understanding the Vedas:
2. The second method is historical according to which the Vedas supposedly refer to names of kings, rivers and territories. This method earned the displeasure of many Vedic scholars because it seemingly overshadowed the Vedic truths.
3. The mythological in which supposedly historical events or truths were embellished with fanciful stories. Though attractive

and appealing these old wives' tales failed to earn any credibility or respect.

4. The scientific method wherein explanations are based on physical-scientific truths. This method is both difficult and abstruse.
5. The fifth method is intuitional in which truths are felt and communicated but they cannot be logically explained or demonstrated the way others can.
6. The ritualistic in which a Vedic passage is explained in terms of rituals that is apparently being described. For instance, if at the time of a child tonsure a prayer to God is being said, this prayer is then converted into a ritual for all others to follow.

Swami Dayanand Saraswati affirms that the truths of modem physical science are discoverable in the hymns. Like me several others too believe that there is nothing fantastic about the idea that these hymns contain both, scientific as well as religious/spiritual truths. Where I differ from most is that I hold the view that the Vedas also record certain contemporary occurrences and places.

The method I have followed is a mix of both historical as well as scientific methods. I have gone by my logic according to which the Vedas do make references to their contemporary society. They do suggest the presence or absence of certain ground realities. If they were way ahead of their historical period in mathematical knowledge, scientific truths and if they reflect a far advanced society than what we wish to believe they ought to have been in, then the fault lies with us and not with the Vedas. Fed as we are on Western history it is not possible for us to believe that Indian sages could have experienced a superior civilisation and scientific advancement than that of the ancient Greeks. Will it be easy for a modem man to replicate the Egyptian pyramids? It is more a question of our mind-set than any fault with our culture or scientific knowledge. If the Vedas talk of binary system, use of steam in machines and talk of aeroplanes whose fault it is? All these could as well have been like the designs of Leonardo da Vinci - a futuristic reality-something far ahead of the contemporary knowledge or information.

Although for my purpose I did not think it necessary to fix the dates of the Vedic writing. But the evidence at our disposal suggests that they were revealed around 1500 years before the Mahabharata. Ved Vyas had done the fourth and the last editing of the Vedas. The most interesting part of it all is that they were revealed to more than 407 families of the rsis and that too over fifty generations or even more. These are but *tentative* conclusions. There are several Vishwamitras and Vashishthas, Therefore, there is lot of confusion about who actually said what. A school of thought claims that there are no proper nouns in the Vedas. They assert that how could a single hymn of mere 24 words be composed by about 100 rsis? It is therefore only logical that these names are accepted as generic in nature- something that does not suggest any specific individual. One can never be sure whether a single hymn was revealed at a stretch.

The contradictions that one notices in their text carry their own meaning. There are scholars who have suggested that a single Sukta may have multiple authorships. For some it may appear sacrilegious to say that even a single hymn could have been thus written. I take it that the composition of a complete Veda may as well have taken around a thousand years or even much more. Since all of us know that neither Time nor society could ever be frozen, changes would always occur. Nor can any one force these changes to be uni-dimensional. To my mind one could trace contradictions in the Vedas to contemporary societal impact. If a volume takes ce-nturies to compose, contradictions will inevitably occur. Afterall, poets and writers are difficult to remain immune from societal influences. The other possibility is that during the course of editing the choices of the Suktas reflected individual preferences. In that process the logic of arrangement failed to take cognizance of chronology.

My information is based on an extensive survey of Vedic literature and the Vedic text. I have had the honor of consulting some of the well-known names in this field. For instance, I have had access to books written by persons like Padmashri Professor K.D. Dwivedi whose book Vedic Sahitya and Sanskrati was brought out by Vishvavidyalaya Prakashan, Varanasi in 2000; Professor H. R. Divekar-Rgveda Sukta Vikas, Motilal Banarasidas, 1970; Dr Suryakant Bali and Dr R. K. Sharma, Historical and Critical Studies in the Atharvaveda, Nag Publishers,1981; The Religion of the Vedas by H.D. Griswold, Motilal Banarasidas, 1971; The History of the Dharmasastras by Bharatratna

P. Y. Kane etc. I did consult S.A. Dange, Rahul Sanskrityayayn and scholars like D.P. Chattopadhyaya also. The list is long and varied but one must remember that all these authors are eminent scholars in their own right and have earned recognition in their own ways. Their approach to the textual interpretations has been very individualistic. In analysing the Vedic text they have, at times, been ruthlessly frank and uncompromising.

One must also remember that scriptures and logic seldom work in tandem. If forced to live in a given mould they tend to create fanatics. In analysing a text nothing is to be accepted as sacrosanct. Luckily the Vedas are not Holy Scriptures in the sense Bible, or the Koran is. They can always be subjected to logical analysis without arousing any bitterness among their admirers. The reason is simple. Unlike other texts of similar nature, they preach no religion. They contain divine poetry and therefore being poets they are armed with poetic license. Whether revealed or not, a Book is a Book and it aims at giving some message. But even for that one must be able to understand the text first. These great scholars I have consulted have done just that.

The question I need answer is: What is the great idea of my writing on the Vedas or about its subject matter when I claim no originality or possess any urge to declare my self very different from all others?

The only novelty in my attempt, if it can be so called, lies in strict adherence to the text and support of all major contentions with relevant citations there-from. I propose to present a portrait of Vedic society in all its myriad forms without bothering to hide its warts or foibles, if any.

Let us not forget that a question was once raised [see, Preface, Vedic Sahitya, by R.G. Trivedi (1950) Bhartiya Gyanpeeth, Kashi, p. 21] when all the rsis are gone who shall then be our guide or who will be our rsi? Prompt came the reply: "Logic" shall guide you. Today when no rsi is around, let Logic be our guide. I have gone along with my logical norms and standards unmindful of who says what. G. K. Chesterton once wrote, "The modem man of science who writes down a fact in black and white is not more but less accurate than the medieval monk who wrote it down in gold and scarlet, sea-green and turquoise." (GB. Shaw by G K. Chesterton; Guild Books, London).

Let us not forget in our zeal for objectivity that it fails to measure up to the intuitive truth. The reality is that science does not answer all questions and logic has limited solutions. We have left behind us the times when Satpath Brahman could claim: "The gods are two types; one, the real ones and the other Brahmins-since they know by heart all the mantras. They teach others and therefore in the shape of humans they are divine beings." We no longer subscribe to rituals because by now we have come to realise their real worth. Indeed so scientific have we become that like Bertrand Russell we deny even the existence of God. For the majority of us the Vedas are our most revered ancient books but beyond this statement this section of the society too finds it hard to move.

We have become asur *(na sura iti asura)* since we have the power of logic with us. Perhaps we do not deserve more. Therefore, I write for those who may like to go beyond their self-imposed restrictions and boundary-line.

**The Vedic Text**

We should remember that it is extremely difficult to fix the date of their composition. Max Mueller had found it diflicult to date them. But what they contain is of considerable interest to us all. Therefore, I am attempting to introduce the reader to the Vedic text. But before I do that it would be in the interest of all to remember that by the time Yaska wrote his Nighantu the language of the Vedas had become uncommon. He wrote his workaround 700 B.C., which to say the least is that the composition/ revelation of the Vedas must have taken place way back in time. Those that can follow Yaska's work will appreciate that the real key to the understanding of the Vedas lies in Nighantu. What Yaska wrote around 700 B.C. continues to be valid. The book Yaska wrote- the Nighantu, containing 12 chapters is a commentary on a traditional list of Vedic words known as the Nighantu. It is generally agreed that opinions differed about the exact derivation of this word even during Yaska's times. Yaska says, while justifying the need for his compilation, "Former rishis had direct intuitive insight into dharma, and Brahma (Veda) made itself manifest to them. They handed down by oral instruction (updesha) the hymns to later. generations who were destitute of direct insight. The later generations, declining ill powers of upclesha, compiled the work (i.e. nighantu) in order to comprehend the meaning." (1.20)

**Traditional View of the Vedas**

The traditional view is given in the Vishnu Purana. According to it the original Veda was revealed to the rsis. It consisted of 1 lakh verses in four divisions. With time these divisions got mixed up. In the beginning of the Dvapara Age, Krishna Dvaipayana resuscitated the Vedic study and classified according to the four ancient divisions– the Rk, Yajus, Sama, and Atharvan. For the perpetuation of their study he gave Rgveda to Paila, Yajur Veda to Vaisampayana, Sam-Veda to Jaimini, and Atharva-Veda to Sumanta. This reclassification constitutes the ancient tradition. All scholars by and large believe this view to be correct. Each of these main divisions has three divisions–samhitas or mantras, the Brahmanas and the Arayankas. The Brahmanas are mostly inprose containing detailed descriptions of the sacrificial rites and the modes of their performance. According to Sayanacharya eight classes of topics, viz. itihasa, purana, vidya, Upanishad, sloka, surra, vyakhyana, and anuvyakhyana i.e. history, old stories, esoteric knowledge about meditation, supreme knowledge, verse, aphorisms, explanations and elaborations are contained in the Vedas.

The Rgveda is supposedly the most ancient of sacred literature. But over a period of time its oral character and four editions that it had to go through have forced scholars to try to piece together the underlying meaning they carry for the interested lay. At least one thing is certain. The entire composition must have taken quite some time to complete. Since it had to be committed to memory an elaborate system was needed to do so. Originally it was divided into five branches (sakhas) of which only one has survived. The five branches were: shakal, vaashkal, ashvalayan, sankhyayan, and mandukayan. Of these only the first has survived. According to shakal's division the Rgveda has 10,600 mantras or 1028 suktas. These suktas are then chapterised into 10 mandals.

It is commonly believed that chapters or mandals 2-7 are the oldest and therefore their content is also homogenous. Each of these mandals is linked with one rsi and his descendants. These rsis seriatim are: Gutsamad, Vishwamitra, Vamdev, Atri, Bharadwaj and Vashishth. In these mandals the first god that is worshipped is Fire (Agni), thereafter there are prayers addressed to Indra and other lesser-known gods. Interestingly, the number of suktas kept both increasing and decreasing with each mandal. For instance, whereas the second has 43 suktas, the third has 62, fourth has 58, fifth has 87, the sixth has 75 and the seventh contains 104 suktas. These six mandals supposedly constitute the core of the Rgveda. These mandals are called 'family books" because the seers for these mandals come from a single family each.

The eighth mandal also to an extent belongs to the family grouping because the principal family connected with this mandal is that of Kanva and his household. However, it is different from the earlier group in as much as that it has only 92 suktas and its meter too is different i.e. it is composed in pragatha and is a mix of jagati and thristub. The mantras in this mandal do not start with prayers addressed to Agni. In fact, it has links with the first mandal because Kanva and his family is associated with the first mandal too and the same meter is found in the first as well as in the eighth. Also a few mantras are common too in both mandals.

The ninth mandal also seems to have some link with the other mandals although it is distinctly different from the rest. A few of the mantras and suktas are composed by the rsis of the other mandals as well. Most of the mantras in this mandal are devoted to somras. The other major distinction lies in its priests because it is not hota who presides over the ninth mandal but udgata.

The tenth mandal seems to have been the latest composition because on all counts it is different from all others in terms of size, subject matter and the language. This mandal carries a few of the earlier suktas too. In terms of its content it deals more with the subjects that concern society and individuals than with the gods as in the other martdals. Looks as though by then the society had settled down to carry its secular burden rather than remain confmed to performing its devotional duties.

Towards the end of chapter eight 12 suktas have been added which are called Balyakhilya suktas. These suktas too are supposedly the oldest lot but no one knows the reason for their placement.

**The Vedic Gods**

The number of Vedic gods is 33 who are divided into three groups of 11 each-these groups being allotted to each of the following groups:

terrestrial, inter-space and heavenly. For example, Fire is the god of earth, Indra belongs to middle or inter- space and the Sun belongs to the Heaven where he receives maximum attention. The Rgvedic gods generally come in groups; for instance, the *maruts* or the *adityas.* Goddesses too find themselves occupying pride of place in the divine pantheon. Usha is the main goddess followed by Saraswati and *vak.* Indian scholars have recounted certain characteristics of the Vedic gods.

The Vedic gods look like humans because they too posses human organs like eye, ear, throat etc. They too carry arms like any common mortal. For instance, their armaments include—the bow, arrows, spear, bajra and they mount chariots driven by horses. They too are fond of milk and milk products just like humans.

Secondly, each of the Rgvedic gods is supreme, because the seers found each god deserved to be worshipped as the greatest of all. The third characteristic of the Vedas is that here the priests occupy center stage. It looks as though the Vedas were composed for the priests.

But the best characteristic is that the Vedic religion is not pessimistic or insular. It regards 'hope' to be light and pessimism as complete darkness *(aasha hi param jyoti nairashya param tamah).* Their religion is pragmatic. For instance, while the priests prayed on behalf of their clients they expected material returns for the service rendered. What characterises the Vedic religion is the fact that while the ancients had full faith in their gods but they needed no idols or buildings for worship (temples). This is one reason why the Vedic people worshipped gods but they accepted them in the form of Nature's forces. They accepted the whole world to be a family and therefore prayed on behalf of all to be both happy and prosperous without being afraid of anyone' The type of degeneration that we notice in the later period had no sanction of these sages.

Three suktas in the Rgveda are important from the point of view of understanding their philosophy and also for appreciating their world view. These suktas are: Purush Sukta (Rgveda X. 90); Hiranyagarbha (Rgveda X.121) and the Nasadiya Sukta (Rgveda X. 129). I have referred to these suktas in detail at appropriate places. The Vedic people believed that at the time of death the physical body is burnt but as the soul reaches Heaven. It receives another body, which is refulgent.

Interestingly enough they believed that there are three types of Heavens–the best, a little less than the best, and the third of poor quality. The concept of these three categories helped them define human conduct. While they praised and admired good conduct they were critical and condemning of bad deeds.

By and large the Rgveda contains (as already pointed out) prayers to different gods and goddesses, still they are not quite sure which one of them rules the roost. Therefore, a few of their prayers are in the form of questions reflecting their ignorance/knowledge about the Ultimate Divine Being. They pointedly ask about the god they must worship? *(Kasmai deva havisha vidhemam).* If this question reveals their doubt about their knowledge of the deity they should Pray, it also shows that they wished to get assured about their present and future. They disliked doubt and uncertainty.

There are several stories, which get prominence in their hymns. These hymns are called dialogue Suktas. For instance, X. 95 deals with a dialogue that took place between Pururuva and Urvashi or X. 10, wherein Yama and Yami enter into a heated discussion over sex between siblings or a dialogue between Shuni Sarama and Asura Pani (Rg. 10.130). There are about 20 suktas that deal with secular subjects for instance X. 97 deals with medicines, or X. 163 deals with tuberculosis and its cure and there are 5 suktas that deal with the funeral rites. There are 4 suktas that deal with subjects that are edifying in nature. For instance, X. 34 deals with a gambler's lament, which to say the least is morally uplifting. It deals with a highly self-destructive human passion for a game and the resultant consequences.

There are two suktas (for instance Rgveda 1.164) that contain extremely difficult riddles and there are 30 suktas that resemble Atharvaveda's abhichar (magic and supernatural subjects) suktas. For instance, 10.58 deals with recall of one's soul or 7.1 0 that deals with how to get rains to come on demand. These two suktas viz. 10.58 and 10.60 are mantras that can save a sick person from death. There are several suktas that deal with contemporary political, social and economic conditions and talk about rivers and mountains. Therefore to say that the Vedas are purely liturgical is not supported by the Vedic text.

In political terms the Rgvedic society was divided into five parts. The lowest rung of society was family (household or kula), the next in the hierarchy was village. Then came Vis or the region, followed by Jan or the conglomeration of several Vis and lastly the nation. The heads of each rung were called grihapati, gramni, vishpati, janapati and the king. The functions of each unit were neatly demarcated. There were several military states called vrat or gana. At the time of war people sang patriotic songs. These however must have taken time to time to develop. The Vedas refer to military comprising of foot soldiers and the chariot-driven senior warriors. There is no description of horse-mounted fighters. However, there are references to metal-headgears (shirastrana) and Armour besides skin-shoes *tvatudarinapada)* covering the leg from knee to foot (1.133.2). They normally used arrows and bows but additionally they could employ poisoned arrows, spears and spades. They had iron-forts and used extensively stones and boulders. There is a particular reference to Indra destroying 100 stone-forts. Surprisingly enough, there is an indication that they had mobile iron-forts *(puracharishnu)* too. (See, Rgveda 1.189.2 &1.166.8). It is safe to conclude that these people knew how to fight as well.

**The Caste System**

In support of the caste-system Purush Sukta of Rgveda (X. 90), Yajurveda's Chapter XXXl. Il and Av. XIX; 6.6 are usually cited.

The Brahman became His mouth,

Of both His arms the rajanya was made,

His thighs became the Vaisya..

And from His feet the Sudra was born.

But everyone is not agreed on the interpretation of these hymns. A few scholars suggest that this hymn defines various functions in life. Broadly speaking the four functions as implied in the afore-cited hymn are universally performed by certain class of people such as, the priests, warriors, businessmen, agriculturists and others for which the most impoverished are willing to come forward. The term Varna has been used in the same sense as *'class'* is used in the *West. It is the nature of work that defined one's class.* It is a historical reality that over a period of time the class changed into caste in India and got fossilised. In the Vedas caste and class are indistinguishable. There are numerous references in the ancient literature that caste mobility was fairly common and the two primary castes/classes continually changed their caste-groups to undertake each other's social obligations. If Vishvamitra could become Bramharshi, so could others. There is a reference in which King Bharata (son of Shakuntala) who asked Bharadvaj II–a Brahmin by birth to take over the reins of his empire which he accepted gladly on the condition that his progeny will be entitled to retain its original as well as the assumed caste. This gave rise to the birth of a caste category called *kshatropet* Brahmins. It has been pointed out that interdependence of the priest and the ruler was a necessity. When either of the two wished to show total independence, it created tensions. This explains to some extent why open hostility and dissensions between the Kshatriyas and the Brahmins would come to the fore at the slightest pretext. This caste rivalry was largely due to the question of primacy in society. which eventually led to the birth of organised religions like Buddhism and Jainism. These religions accorded no special place to the Brahmins. Indeed they ignored the Brahmins completely and faced their backlash. Even so for a very long time caste mobility remained a recognised fact of ancient life.

"Thus spoke Lord God,' Humans! These benefit-granting language of the Vedas that I am giving to the Brahmans and the Kshatriyas; it is meant for the Vaishyas, Aryas and the Sudras too. *I make no distinction between ours and theirs*'." Yaj. */26/2.*

In the Atharvaveda too there is a specific mention that God makes no distinction between either castes or gender.

The teachings of the Vedas are universal. "Yajurveda 26-2 clearly enjoins all learned persons to preach Vedic truths to all, the Brahmanas, the Kshatriyas, the Vaishyas, the Shudras, the Chandals, the degraded and the forlorn. Dwijas, the twice-born alone are not entitled to study the Vedas. The Shudras and even women are equally entitled to read the Vedas. Persons like Kavish Aylush (the seer of R. Y.X. 30) a Shudra by birth, vide Aitraiya Brahmana 11-19 and women like Lopmudra were the seers who explained the Vedic texts and their names are from times immemorial attached to the Vedic verses. God is not partial to any one caste or a section of people."(See, Introduction to Yajurveda, p. 6, Devi Chand. M.A.)

## Marriage

The Vedas contain no references to child marriages, which became so common during Muslim rule and still continue despite all kinds of law. We have made a detailed reference elsewhere to the marriage ceremony *perse*.

### Food Habits

The ancient Indians enjoyed all kinds of milk products, fruits, honey and other beverages like some juice and alcohol. They ate barley, all kinds of lentil such as moong, urad, and masoor. There is no mention of wheat and arhar and also of rice although it would appear they did eat rice of some kind.

### Dress

The ancients wore both upper and lower garments but there is a mention of under garments too. They wore head gear called turban. The women folk used silk and zari. golden peshash (hiranyapeshasha).

### Enjoyments and pleasure activities

They loved to drink hard liquor (sura), and their convivial normally included gambling and group participation in which couples took part. Singing and dancing were common. They played on veena and flute besides drums were also commonly played.

### Economy

The ancients depended on agriculture but they also traded across the seas and knew boating in the rivers as well.

They built brick houses and knew all about vaastu sashtra. They also used bamboo, stones, and wood in their house-building activities.

### The Samveda

Among the Vedas the Samveda occupies the next rung of the ladder immediately after the Rgveda. This only means that although the Rgveda contains the core of the Vedic knowledge but its poetic 1 musical rendering with necessary cadences is given in the Samveda. The Samveda is the first *source book of Indian music.* It contains the base of all the ragas and raginis that later on developed in the sub-continent. Even without being aware of how this phenomenon prospered the Indian classical music grew out of the Samveda. It is generally believed that the meaning and potency of a Vedic mantra is determined by the manner in which it is musically rendered. The sound vibrations in the atmosphere inject potency into the content. The root of the word I sound saman means the one that destroys all hurdles; also, that which satisfies god through mantras. A few scholars have suggested that it means song. In fact, when the Rgvedic mantras are sung they are called saman. Therefore, scholars suggest that the root meaning of sam is 'beautiful, pleasant statement'.

Today only three branches of the Samveda are known to exist. It is immaterial how many branches it earlier had. These three currently popular branches are: (a) kauthum, (b) jaimaniya and (c) ranayaniya. These branches are more popular in specific regions; such as the Kauthum branch of the Samaveda is popular in Gujarat, the Jaimaniya (it is also called tavalkar branch) in Karnataka and the Ranayaniya in the Maharashtra. Currently the Kauthum branch is more popular in the entire country.

The Samaveda has two branches-Purvarchik and Uttararichik. Both parts put together contain 1875 mantras. A few of the mantras have been repeated therefore the basic mantras are 1549 only. Except for 75 richas the rest have mostly been taken from the Rgveda's ninth mandal. A few have come from the first and the tenth mandal too.

The reason for taking most of the rich as from the Rgveda lies in the fact that they were put together for the priest called Udgatha. The job of the priest sang Rgvedic richas set in different musical cadences as liturgies in the honor of different gods. It is thus obvious that the original base of the Samaveda is the Rgveda. In Brihadaranyaka Upanishad the Rgveda and the Samaveda are called husband-wife because the identity of the wife lies in her husband.

The meters (chhandaas) of the Sarnaveda are largely set in gayatri and jagati-the root of both these terms lies in gai meaning 'to sing'. In Purvachik 650 mantras are divided into six parts. The first part of this division is devoted to Fire god. From part 2 to 4 are devoted to Lord Indra. The fifth part consisting of richas that have all been taken from the Rgveda's IX mandal are addressed to Soma. The sixth section is called *aranyagana*- i.e. the songs sung in the forests. The Uttarachik contains in all 1225 mantras. They are divided into 400 songs. Occasionally a song consists of \two to three richas. In some places the Uttararchik is divided into nine sections. It has 21 chapters in all and the number of the suktas is 400 in all. However, in comparison with Purvarchik the Uttararchik is given less weightage. In fact, saarna means *swar or cadence* and this is the soul of the Samaveda. This Veda is the fountain of Indian music. It is commonly agreed that this Veda may not have much literary value, but it certainly enjoys tremendous religious esteem.

**The Yajurveda**

In the Vedic hierarchy the Yajurveda occupies the next rung immediately after the Samaveda. The term 'Yajus' has several connotations. For example, it is synonymous with the mantras intended for performing Yagnas. It also means uneven ending of a sentence. The third meaning is 'mantras in prose' that are different from the Rik and the Sama. In other words, the meaning of the term Yajus is worship and the yagnas. The Yajurveda is meant for the adhvaryu priest just as Hota invoked the Rgvedic deities and gods. Adhvaryu is the conductor and the organiser of the yagna. He is the sole authority of the yagna. While the Rgveda is knowledge-based and the Samveda is emotion or feeling-based; the Yajurveda is action-oriented.

These days the Yajurveda is available in two parts called the Krishna and the Shukla Yajurvedas. The underlying reason for this differentiation is that while the Shukla Yajurveda contains only the mantras, the Krishna Yajurveda carries within its text the meaning of the mantras and methods of their use. The other reason lies in the generally advanced theory that these are the names of the rsis attached to both versions. The Krishna Yajurveda is named after its principal rsi Krishna Dvaipayana and the other is known Shukla Yajurveda because Yagnvalkya received it after worshipping sun god, which symbolises light and brightness. And yet another explanation for this differentiation lies in the popularity of the both according to the regions.

While the Krishna Yajurveda is popular in south India, the Shukla Yajurveda is popular in the north. Personally, I think the last explanation is ridiculous and totally unacceptable. There are a few other reasons too that are advanced for this distinction. But since they are couched in myths they cannot be taken very seriously. For instance, there is a story that rsi Vaishampayana once got very furious with his pupil Yagnavalkya, who was then learning under his charge the Yajurveda. He demanded that whatever the pupil had learnt he should give it back forthwith. As a result he vomited the entire knowledge of the Veda, which was immediately eaten away by his classmates. Therefore, this vomit is called Krishna Yajurveda.

It is commonly asserted that there are 85 branches of the Krishna Yajurveda but these days only four are available. These four branches are Taittariya, Maitrayani, Kathak and Kapishthal. The first one in this list i.e. (Taittaraiya) is very popular in the Maharashtra, Andhra, and south India as a whole. This branch has 7 sections and 44 sub-sections. Each sub-section has several versions of meaning and interpretations. Each sub-section has several divisions whose number is estimated to be 631. This branch of the Krishna Yajurveda is considered to be of immense literary value. The reason is that all the bramhnas, aryanyakas, Upanishads and the sutra literature associated with it are readily available. It not only carries mantras but their interpretations too.

Maitrayani branch is also called *kalap samhita.* It has four parts and 54 sub-sections.

Kathak branch, also called katha, along with Maitrayani were most popular before the emergence of the Taittariya branch. Patanjali has infact advanced this view. These branches were widely known around Ayodhya. The religious message contained in it was widely known across the region of Ayodhya. But with the passage of time however Taittariya branch of Krishna Yajurveda and Vajasneyi samhita of Shukla Yajurveda became popular and widely known.

The last branch called Kapishthal is available in parts only. It has 6 ashthaka and 48 chapters.

The Shukla Yajurveda (also called Vajasneyi samhita) is thus called perhaps because the sun having taken the shape of horse delivered the message through Yagnavalkya. It has 15 branches called Kanva,

Maadhyanindin, jabal, budheya, shakaiya, taapnis, kandis, paundravaha, aavartika, paramaavartika, parashariya, vainaisha, baudhaiya, yaudhaiya and galava. Of these only two are popular and they are: Kaanva and maadhyanindhin. And both these branches arealike. They havean identical serial order as well as commonality in the textual material. The difference at times lies in their content delivery and textual rendering.

While the Kanvabranchis popular in the South India the Maadhyanindhin branch has its votaries in the North.

**The Content of the Yajurveda**

Scholars by and large consider the Shukla Yajurveda more important of the two and hence it is being analysed for its content. "It has 40 chapters of which the first two are devoted to Chandra darshan (sighting of the moon) and full-moon yagnas. The third chapter details daily Agnihotrayagnas. Chapters 4-8 deal with Soma yagnas and animal sacrifices. Chapters 9-10 are about Vajpaiya yagna that are performed to honor the heroic performances of the Kshatriyas. Chapters 11-18 deal with selection of fire and the construction of the Vedis. Chapters 19-21 deal with Sautramani yagna. The prayers sung at the time of ashwamedha yagna are given in Chapters 22-25. The next 4 chapters recount the earlier mantras. Chapters 30-35 describe the rules for the new yagnas like the purushmedha yagna (human sacrifice) or shivasakalpasukta. Chapters 36-38 deal with pravargayaga-related mantras. The 39th chapter deals with last rites. The last chapter i.e. chapter 40 is called Ishopanishad.

It should be very clear by now that this particular Veda is all about the conduct of the yagnas. Yaska says that the Yajurveda contains rules and regulations for performing specific goal-oriented yagnas.

Western scholars accept only the first 18 Chapters as original and the rest 22 Chapters are later day additions. According to McDonald these 22 Chapters carry the same mantras as are available in the Taittaraiya of the Krishna Yajurveda.

Since the Krishna Yajurveda and the Shukla Yajurveda are not very different therefore any analysis of one would come pretty close to being the analysis of the content of the other as well. Incidentally, the religious attitude portrayed in the Yajurveda is no different from that of the Rgveda. Even so, we notice that Prajapati occupies much higher position here as compared with his position in the Rgveda. Also, we notice that Rudra is transformed into Shiva, Shankar and Mahadeva. Vishnu too gets promoted to a much higher position than he ever occupied earlier. For the first time the term asura denotes a devil or Evil spirit. This is quite a change from the pedestal this term had occupied in the Rgveda.

Yagna was an instrument to propitiate gods in the Rgveda but it became the sole way to do so. The place of Shakti (or spirituality) in the Rgveda gave way to Yagna (or action) in the Yajurveda. For the first time single worded prayers like Om Hri Sri or Om Bhu Bhuv Swah etc. came to occupy pride of place in the Yajurveda. We find that gods came to be addressed with varied names like shatrudriya and vishnu sahasranama etc.

Interestingly, it would appear that people came to forget that each god was invoked with a single name during times of begging the assistance. For instance, in the Rgveda Vishnu is invoked as Sun at the time of seeking assistance in agricultural growth or its protection because the root su stood for 'giving birth', and when it was supposed to be present almost everywhere then. He was addressed as Vishnu; when He occupied the Space in its entirety He was called Mitra. *This obviously means the names of the same god changed according to the occasion when a given help was needed.* But things changed in the Yajurvedic time. They seemingly forgot by that time the principle of specificity (the relationship between the occasion and the form of the god) and started giving omnibus powers to their gods and hence omnibus type of address/name. There are more spiritual riddles in the Yajurveda than in the Rgveda.

It is true that most of the mantras in the Yajurveda have been borrowed from the Rgveda but that does not mean that on its own it has no originality. The prose part of the Yajurveda is original. Besides, it records the birth of new deities/gods that were given birth for the sake of organising yagnas, This is even more original. For the first time basic principles of applied psychology were recorded here. For example, "Mitrasyaham chakshusa sarvani bhutani samikshe" (Vajasneyi Sarnhita 36.18).

This means that "Let us see all living beings with friendly eyes. It carries a command that humans should live for 100 years performing acts approved by the sashatras. (Vajasneyi Sarnhita 40.2)."

The greatest prayers (see, Vajasneyi Sarnhita. 18.48) is for the prosperity of all the four vamas according to which it is prayed "Let our Brahmans be illumined, let our Kshatriyas be resplendent and let our Vaishyas and Shudras be glorious and let me be glorious and resplendent too."

The Yajurveda is important for its religious attitude but it is even more so because it has recorded and reflects its contemporary society and customs. For the first time, the priests register their primacy in the society. It also records an increase in the caste rigidity. From literary point of view we get Taittariya and Shathapth Brahman. We also get Taittaraiya Aranyaka and Maitrayani Aranayaka. Related to the Yajurveda several Upanishads are also found. For instance, we get Taittariya, Maitrayani, Kath, Isha, Brihadarankya, Shwetash was warand Kaivalya Upanishads too. Eight shrauta sutras connected with the Yajurveda are also found. They are as follows: Kautyayana, Baudhayana, Aapasthamb, Hiranyakeshi, Bharadvaj, Manava and Kathak. Five dharma sutras viz. Haarita, Shankh, Baudhayana, Aapasthamb, and Hiranyakeshi and 4 shulva sutras - Katyayana, Baudhayana, Aapasthamb and Manava are also found.

One book related to Jyotish-astrology, too is found. One must understand that the three Vedas- Rk, Sarna and Yajurveda are mutually complimentary and interdependent. While in the Rgveda *Hota* sings prayers in the honor of the deities and gods, *Udgata* sang the Samavedi richas at the time of yagna-performance. Adhavaryu conducted the yagna; In this way we find that all the three Vedas are inter-related and their priests held the key to this connection.

It is a fact the Yajurveda holds the key for explaining contemporary social and religious transformation of India. It would therefore not be far-fetched to say that the Yajurveda is the foundation. for explaining the gradual movement in India's philosophical and religious traditions.

**The Atharvaveda**

The Atharvaveda is the fourth and the last of the four Vedas. For a few this Veda did not belong to the same class as the other three do. The reason is simple. The content material of the Atharvaveda is radically different from that of the others. This Veda has nothing to do with the yagnas. Acharya Kapil Dev Sashtri however refuted the assertion that the Atharvaveda was ever deniedits rightful place in the Vedacategory. He offered following arguments to suppor this standpoint: -

(a) In the Purvamimansa it is proved that the name *trayi* is given because of their content and is not dependent on the names of the Vedas. While in terms of style the Rgveda is poetic; the Sarna musical, the Yajurveda is essentially prosaic. In this sense the Atharvaveda is a mix of all the three styles.

(b) The Rgveda makes quite a few references to the Atharvaveda. In fact, this Veda is supposed to be the inventor of Fire and the originator of the science of the yagnas.

(c) Each Veda has its principal deity and according to the Rgveda Brahrna is supposed to be the divine-teacher of the Atharvaveda.

Still, it is generally known that the Atharvaveda does not find mention everywhere alongside the other three Vedas. The western scholars have given reasons for the non-inclusion of the Atharvaveda in the class of other three Vedas. Except for the last chapter in the Atharvaveda, which has something to do with the Yagnas, there is hardly anything to relate it with the yagyas. They therefore suggest that the last chapter is an add-on only for the purpose that it qualified to join in the rank of the Vedas. The mention of the Purvamimansa by the Acharya Dwivedi in support of his argument to get the Atharvaveda included in the category of the other Vedas is indefensible. The reason is that Purvamirnansa was written long after the Athavaveda. The word Atharva is very ancient in origin and it means 'priest'. This term is not necessarily linked with the Veda of the same name. Also, the fact that Atharva is the inventor of Fire occurs in the X mandal of the Rgveda but then this mandal itself was composed long after the other chapters had been composed. Therefore, its mention in the Rgveda by itself does not merit serious consideration. Also, the entire Chapter 20 (in praise of Indra) of the Atharvaveda is bodily lifted from the Rgveda without a single change. All this suggests a motive behind it. The idea was perhaps to get the Atharvaveda join the ranks of Veda class.

There are reasons behind the move to get the Atharvaveda upgraded. The Rgveda (the Samaveda and the Yajurveda cannot be treated separately as they tend to complement it) are connected with the upper class segment of society and the prayers contained in them are simply sublime and possess high ennobling quality. This is not true for the Atharvaveda. It relates with the common man and thus its content material addresses the problems of the proletariat. The proof of the usefulness and efficacy of the Rgvedic mantras lie in the performance of the yagnas, but the mantras of the Atharva veda are inherently power-embedded and need no extra help. The other reason is that while the Rgveda reflects refilled tastes and highly cultivated ideas and manners, the Atharvaveda -trades in the beliefs of common people-like magic, hidden spirits and supernatural powers and lists cures for some 99 ailments through ordinary herbs and roots.

The Rgveda too has some 30 suktas that deal with magic and superstitions-the themes that constitute the principal part of the Atharvaveda. This means that the rsis of the Rgveda were familiar with magic and superstitions but their knowledge was not very deep or vast as the rsis of the Atharvaveda had. Also, they intended to address a different class, taste and subject as compared with the rsis of Atharvaveda Like the Rgveda the Atharvaveda took long time in its composition therefore at some point in time the rsiso fone Vedamust have interacted with the risis of the other. Societies are not static by nature. They change and in the cycle of change many things get added or deleted from their repertoire.

The Atharva veda is so named because some 1768 mantras have been contributed by the *rsi* Atharvan. It has according to Patanjali's Mahabhashya nine branches. But currently only two branches viz.. Pippalaad and Shaunak are available. Out of the two Shaunak branch alone is currently more acceptable. The Shaunak branch of the Atharvaveda has 20 chapters (kaand) 730 suktas and around 6000 mantras. As already pointed out, the last chapter of the Atharvaveda is made up entirely of the Rgvedic mantras. It is believed that the last two Chapters (19 & 20) are later day additions. In the Atharvaveda the number of mantras in each Sukta, keep on increasing. For example, in the first chapter (kaand) the number of mantras in each sukta is only four. In the next chapter the number of mantras goes up to five each. And this process goes on until we reach chapter 6, which has 3 mantras to a sukta. In the 7th chapter the number of mantras in each sukta is reduced to 1 or 2 each. But from 8 to 12 the suktas have large number of mantras each. The content of these suktas is also immensely varied. In the 9th chapter the details of madhukasha medicine are given. The 12th chapter is devoted to intense love for the nation. From 13th to 18th the number of mantras is large but the subject matter remains identical. Interestingly, chapters 15 and 16 are in prose like the Brahmanas.

Atharvaveda's content analysis would reveal that it deals with a vast variety of subject matter. For instance, the first two chapters deal with several types of ailments. The third deals with hypnotizing techniques of large armies and with dairy farming and animal husbandry. The fourth chapter deals with poisons, brahma vidya, coronation ceremony, and invocations for the rains etc. the fifth chapter deals with the importance of the Brahmans and methods to deal with enemies. The 6th chapter deals with frightening dreams and the ways to handle them; the 7th relates matters concerning soul, and conquest in the battles etc. The 8th chapter talks of Rgvedic meters (chhandas) and the 9th deals with the medicine named madhukasha, the tuberculosis, and with welcoming guests. The tenth chapter describes brahma vidya even as the eleventh describes the importance of celibac. The 12th contains bhurnisukta and the 13th deals with spiritualism. The 14th chapter details the mantras for the conduct of marriage. The 15th describes the greatness of Brahma. The 16th chapter contains mantras to overcome miseries *(dukhmochan mantras)* and the 17th carries vashikaran mantras (or mantras that can be taken recourse to while trying to cast a spell on others). The 18th chapter describes the funeral rites. Astrology finds mention in the 19th chapter and the last is all about coronation ceremony and the *rajsuyayagna*.

Going though the content of the Atharvaveda one can safely conclude that this Veda deals with the contemporary conditions of a rising society in all its multi-phases. There is hardly an aspect of social life that has been left out. A glimpse of what this Veda is all about can be had from the following citations in the write-up that follows.

**Medical science-related suktas**

These suktas are related with several health problem. Their cure is possible only when the asuras are overcome that cause diseases. The Atharvaveda deals with the cures of some 99 diseases. These mantras offer the methods for cure. A few of the diseases are like fever, common cold, cough, leprosy, impotency, snakebite, poisonous insects etc. see, e.g. "This Rama Raiani, the dusky Rajani, Krishna Rajani, the dark colored Rajani and the Asikri Rajani; the black Rajani (three kinds of Curcuma Longa), springs up at night and removes the ashy spots and leprosy." Atharvaveda, 1.23.1 or see, mantra CXXXVIII.1. "This medicinal plant (Tvam Virudha.) is heard to be the best of all the herbs. Let this make now my impotent man potent."

**For Longevity**

See, Atharvaveda 8.1 .7, "The heavenly region has raised you from death, the earth and the herbaceous plants like the soma, have rescued from death."

**Prosperity and security**

"O Celibate Disciple! Come hither, climb on the stone, and let your body be strong and constant like stone. May all the physical forces prolong your life for hundred autumns." Atharvaveda, XIII. 4

"I dispel away these diseases with mental prowess. 1 drive them away by intent and 1destroy them with the power of the Vedas. We banish these diseases with the proper application of the branch of Ashvatha tree." Atharvaveda VI. 8.

**Nation's Solidarity**

"The stable earth is like cow that provides for all without any distinction in their languages or religions." Atharvaveda, 12.1.20.

We should read the Vedas because they contain a kind of knowledge that is impossible to find elsewhere. There is however no need to compare them with other religious texts the way Max Mueller tried to rank and equate them. They indeed are a class a part-absolutely unmatched for their import and embedded guidance.

The question about the time when the Vedas were composed will continue to bother scholars. It is however generally agreed that they must have been composed around 1000-1500 B.C. It is commonly agreed that Yaska's Nighantu got written around 700 B.C., and the reason why it had become necessary to write the same was because the traditional meaning of the Vedic words were gradually becoming unintelligible. It is therefore only logical to subscribe to the belief that the Vedas were revealed/composed anytime between 1000-1500 BC. They took long time getting revealed/composed.

Who composed the Vedas? On the basis of Philology B.K. Ghose *(The Cultural Heritage of India,* Ramakrishna Mission publication, 1937) suggests the Seers who composed them must have been living in India 'long before' 1000 B.C. because 'a work like the Rgveda is not the first, but the final result of a long, uninterrupted, and homogeneous cultural life. Though nothing but a collection of hymns to the gods composed by several priestly families, the Rgveda clearly reflects the picture of a highly complex society in the full blaze of civilisation, ruled by constantly warring petty princes, but dominated most potently by priestly classes, through whose prayers the gods were persuaded to confer favors on the devout Aryans. Even literary culture had achieved a high degree of perfection already in the Rg-Vedic age, and had entered a stage that in modem parlance would be called 'decadent'. (p. 137). We have elsewhere in the book discussed the relationship of Mohen jo-Daro civilisation with the Aryans therefore I am not going to cover the same arguments all over again. I am however in agreement with Dr Ghose that the Rg-Vedic seers disliked Rudra/ Shiva and the worship of phallus. There is a suggestion that the name of Shiva (Rudra) occurring in Rg-veda(11.3.1) has deliberately been mispronounced in Aittareya Brahmana (III.3.9.10) as Rudriya. It would appear that Rudra/Shiva/phallus worship etc. is foreign to the Aryans therefore neither is acceptable to them. But thanks to the strong roots in the native culture all the three survive and intact over a period of time have even become much greater than the other gods to whom these Seers appeared feelingly devoted. Today there is hardly any Hindu who shares the Vedic dislike for Lord Shiva with the ancient Rgvedic seers. Does this reality not suggest that over a period of tirne, all Aryan and non-Aryan gods have become friendly with each other and do not mind living in harmony?

# Chapter - 3

# The Vedic Society and Culture

"O God! Keep aside a hunchback bent on destruction; a dwarf given to carnal pleasures; a blind man from sleep; and a deaf man devoid of righteousness. O God, create a physician for purifying our body with the eradication of disease; an astronomer for the advancement of knowledge; an inquisitive man full of craving for knowledge; an extra inquisitive man for desire of extra knowledge; and a question-solver for establishing moral law!" Yajurveda XXX. 10

Like any other society the Vedic people also had family structures just like what we have these days. They lived by the values they thought were of paramount importance. On the basis of those values or even independent of them they too wished to possess virtues. I am quite sure they too like us were afraid of evil be that in Nature or among the human beings. They must also have desired to live long lives. In brief, how could that society be so very different from ours? After all, everyone on earth if he is normal would want to have a home, family, food, some basic comforts and freedom from both disease and enemies. They would also have dreams to fulfill. I cannot think of any society that would be very different from the one that we live in. I am quite sure even the aborigines will have essentially similar expectations with in their habitation, culture and life.

I have attempted to build a real society on the strength of the Vedic text. It is generally believed that the Vedas contain no history and since they were revealed very little of the society is to be discovered in them.

"It is clear from the nature of this vast literature that it can give us a fair idea of only there ligion and religious practices of the period. Nothing but a superficial view can be had, from occasional allusions in the texts, about the secular aspects-political and social institutions, material conditions, domestic and civil life; position of women, occupations, recreations, and the like." This is what C. Kunhan Raja writes in the book The Cultural Heritage of India, on p. 202- a 1993 Ramakrishna Mission publication.

The Vedas have been cited to give an idea that the ancient Indians were no monists; instead they worshiped Nature in all its myriad forms. The fact is that they were pantheistic and did not hesitate to express their true belief. I cite the following hymn to let the rsis themselves speak on the theme.

Of the several methods adopted to read and interpret the Vedic text, I have evolved one of mine own, which I call socio-historical method. I invite readers to read text and interpret it in the light of the original matter being quoted. The Vedas have been written in a style which is very close to the dialectical method in which two sides of an argument are given and the conclusion as a synthesis of the same. Here we have both sides of an argument and the conclusion has to be drawn by the reader.

## The Creator- The Only One

"It is He who has created the entire Universe. The Universe itself has assumed His form. He has weaved the entire Universe with his divine, thread and sustains it through a unified law." In the Atharva Veda (Av. X.7.1-44) in a fairly long hymn called the Skambha Sukta it is given that God is the sole support of the entire Creation consisting of the terrestrial and celestial regions as well as of the interspace. It also states that God alone is the sole and ultimate Reality. In the Mahapralaya i.e. total destruction, nothing but the primordial matter alone shall survive devoid of all forms and name. The Supreme Being alone will be a witness to this annihilation. If this is the end of a cycle of Creation and destruction we have a description of how all this had begun. In the Nasidiya Sukta (Rg. X.129.1 -4) we have a very graphic description of the beginning of the Creation: Interestingly human mind and ingenuity has not reached these height seven today that the Vedic rishis had reached without any of the laboratory tested techniques. Herein lies their superiorit.

"What was the state of Creation like during its complete annihilation (maha pralaya)? What was the Principal Cause of Creation and what served as its Principal instrument? There was neither a sat (non-existent) nor sat (existent); there was no air, nor sky beyond it, what was shrouded in, and by what? Who was the Protector? Did only the deep seas exist? There was no Death and neither was there any Life. Even the division of Day and Night did not exist. The lone Creator breathed without any life-breath by his own will. Apart from Him nothing else existed.

"In that utter Dark existed the unrnanifest Nature like seamless water. All that existed then was void and formless. By the power of the great Tap (deep meditation) Nature gradually started manifesting itself.

Thereafter, rosedesire (Kama) in the beginning, Desire, the primal seed and germ of spirit. The Seers could thus realise that God was latent in the Evil even as light exists in the darkness. The Creation rose out of the unmanifested Nature. Slanted bright rays spread out of these three- God, Soul and the Nature. What was below was as amazing as the one's that could serve as receptacles for that energy up above.

Who, really, knows and who can say whence it was born and whence comes this Creation? The gods, the sun and moon all followed there after; who knows then whence it first came into being?

The One who created the universe is its sustainer. One who presides over it is the Creator Himself. Should any one know the Truth? Only He does.

Before the Creation the Supreme Being known as the Hiranyagarbha alone existed. Nature itself was in His womb. Because of divine consciousness both in its living and the non-living forms the Nature manifested itself.

The Supreme Being alone is, in the entire cosmos, the sole protect or and God Almighty. He carries with in Himself the entires tellar systems. Let us surrender before Him."

Nothing could be farther from the truth than to say that the ancient Indians believed in numerous gods and were even pantheistic. They lived firmly by the dictum *ekam sad vipra bahuda vadanti.* But what seems to have happened is that the abstract form of the Divine Being or the lack of clarity surrounding. His manifest form is too much for an ordinary person to rely upon in his/her day-to-day life situation. I am quite sure people wish to have a personal God and not someone that is abstract and unapproachable. People desire to have some one superior than them and also a deity with whom they could relate themselves both in times of distress and happiness. The later day birth and evolution of gods such as Brahma, Vishnu and Mahesh could as well have been a response to that human desire. These three gods are much more than the mere symbolic representations of the three forces latent in the Almighty viz. creator, sustainer and the destroyer that Nature's cycle needs for its manifested powers. Indeed, it would appear that the ancients did not feel satisfied with only these three gods. Instead, they needed seven i.e. four more being added to their ranks. They are Shakti, Bhairava, Sun and Ganesh. Whatever that may mean to the secular rationalist, this wonderful creativity of the Indians has served the later day generations well in making their existence sufferable. Of course, the subsequent generations have added many more forms and names of Divinity to this list. The truth however remains unquestioned. Human beings do need some one to rely upon in times of distress or otherwise for guidance and companionship. Most Hindu gods are companions and friends who respond to calls. I do not think it is too much to understand this simple truth. In creating a god or goddess of our choice with whom one could communicate, we have continued to be very creative. This trend has continued unabated. Each decade finds Indians adding a Seer or a Devi to this list.

It would be interesting to go through the type of concepts they had of the society in general and the family in particular. A clear view of both these should help us appreciate the nature of their ethical and material development. In the past couple of years in India we have witnessed a kind of obsession about moral and ethical values. As part of our study we might as well have a glimpse into this aspect of that ancient society's moral concerns. All this constitutes, in my opinion, their world view. But before I digress let me make it clear that I, like many others before me, do not subscribe to the viewpoint of the

Europeans who perhaps for lack of comparative, intensively reflective. studies thought that Indians have. down their history. been both backward and barbarous.

Consequently, they at one time doubted openly whether the ancients were in reality capable of such magnificent books as the Vedas and ideas as subtle as they contain and poetry so magnanimous as the one finds written in them. Several scholars have challenged this disbelief in the past but none surpasses the criticism of Aurobindo. He wrote:

"But this conception, supported by misleading European parallels, really explains nothing. Such profound and ultimate thoughts, such systems of subtle and elaborate psychology are found in the substance of the Upanishads; do not spring out of a previous void. The human mind in its progress marches from knowledge to knowledge, or It renews and enlarges previous knowledge that has been obscured and overlaid, or it seizes on old imperfect clues and is led by them to new discoveries. thought of the Upanishads supposes great organs antenor to Itself, and these in the original theories are lacking. The hypothesis, invented to fill the gap, that these ideas were borrowed by barbarous Aryan invaders from the civilised Dravidians. is a conjecture, supported by other conjectures. It is indeed coming to be doubted whether the whole *story of an Aryan invasion* through the Punjab is not a myth of the philologists." (Aurobindo, Vol. X. p A)

For me it is unimportant that such myths were created at one point in time and that they continue to haunt us even now. The fact that we today have the Vedas with us as a result of both Western and Indian scholarly efforts should be enough to make us feel happy. What more could we desire? However, it is important to remember that lots of. controversies that are floating around the Vedic text and its interpretations are classic examples of human failure to appreciate the serious message they intend giving. It is in the nature of the hymns that one who IS not capable of rising above his physiological limits or finds no time to get into their true meaning would find them beyond her/his hurriedly assembled abilities. It has been correctly stated that the Vedic hymns are "multipurpose in their essential nature... Sometimes, in one and the same hymn, one is instructed with the ephemeral and materialistic aspect, and then in subsequent verses in the same hymn, one is elevated, step-by-step , through stages up to the highest transcendental knowledge."

Aurobindo has also commented on these phenomena, more especially in the context of the interpretations given by the ritualistic and traditional Indian pundits and the Western scholars, in the following words:

"Both of them present one characteristic in common, the *extraordinary incoherence* and the *poverty of sense.* which their results stamp upon the ancient hymns. The separate lines can be given, whether naturally or by force of conjecture, a good sense, or a sense that hangs together, the diction that results, if garish in style. if loaded with otiose and decorative epithets, if developing extra ordinarily little of meaning in an amazing mass of gaudy figure and verbiage. can be made to run into intelligible sentences; but *when we come fa read the hymn as a whole,* we seem to be in the presence of men who, unlike the earlier writers of other races, were incapable of coherent and natural expression of connected thought. Except in the briefer and simpler hymns the language either tends to be obscure or artificial, the thoughts are unconnected or have to be forced and beaten by the interpreter into a whole. The scholar in dealing with text is obliged to substitute for interpretation a process almost of fabrication. We feel that he is not so much revealing the sense as hammering and forging rebellious material into some sort of shape and consistency." (Aurobindo, Vol. X, p. 3)

It has been said that if the hymns of the Rgveda can be justifiably called "obscure and barbarous compositions" *then* they have the most splendid fortune in all literary history to have been the source of some of the profoundest and the richest religions of the world. For the past thousands of years they have been worshipped as the sole source for being the most authoritative and true that has been written in the Brahman as. The coherence and profundity of what is written in the Vedas can be appreciated only if one went through the entire procedure delineated for it. For example. it is necessary to take the help of Yaska's lexicon called Nighantu and the commentary called Nirukta that constitutes one of the six vedangas. In this connection one must also rely on the Ashtadhayi of Panini and Patanjali's Mahabhashya, Needless to say what requires lifetime of study and meditation cannot become suddenly available with meagre efort.

It becomes therefore all the more necessary to try visualising the society that produced them. We have quite a few indicators that reveal the nature of the ancient society and its contemporary existence. For instance, the type of occupations that society pursued is just one of those indicators. The other would be its material development. What kind of dress did they put on and what ornaments, if at all, their ladies preferred? Did they have a script? Did they know, for instance, how to count and if they did what was the last number that they knew? Did they know any arithmetic or geometry? What was the type of ornaments that their women folk wear? Did they have diamonds? Did they have liars, thieves, petty criminals and band its or was it an ideal society something distinctly different from ours, where all manner of crimes and nefarious practices abound?

The purpose of writing this chapter is precisely to do just that. I intend describing in detail the nature of Vedic society on the basis of the textual material available in the Vedas. I have no particular thesis to prove. I intend only to present the reality as it existed without any apology or pride. If my claim is correct and if it can be so called, I shall write nothing for which I do not have textual support. Let the reader also see for proof the textual material and check with the original. In terms of method I have followed the socio-historical method.

"A learned man, who has got passion for battle, exertion for prosperity, tact for acquirement, practices yoga for knowledge, arranges for money for habitation, teaches the knowledge of time to the utiliser of days, practices non-attachment, uses truthful, friendly language for the confused and the master of the decadent knowledge, renders sound advice to the vacillating and the most degraded, gives correct lead to the low-born and friend of humanity, uses respectful language towards the leader of men, preaches the art of administration to the ruler, and reveals kingly statesmanship to the guardian of his subjects is an excellent politician." Yajurveda XVIII. 28.

The action that with exertion removes evil propensity, lends determination.

Concentration of mind gives strength, Perseverance leads to various efforts.

Increase in prosperity leads to independence,

Emancipator from this world is worthy of adoration.

Air is useful.

Space in which reside different objects is full of light.

Food worth enjoying is acceptable

Brilliant fire is acceptable.

Speech gives enjoyment.

The mental attitude that after hearing makes us understand the religious books serves as our mentor.

Acquisition is the result of exertion.

Service of the learned is worthy of resort.

Life is synonymous with independence.

Means for prolonging life are exercisable.

Emulation is laudable.

Enterprise is praiseworthy.

Removal of obstacles is the bringer of happiness.

Conquest of affliction demands strength.

Independence is splendor.

Arithmetic is a useful science.

Yajurveda XV. 5.

The Vedas and the Vedanta sutras acknowledge God as the source of Knowledge. In the Vedanta sutras Brahma is regarded as the first cause of creation, its sustenance, and dissolution, and He alone is the source of divine knowledge.

From the Great Yagna, or Supreme Lord, richas (the Rgveda) hymns were born. Therefore, the chhandas (the Atharvaveda) were produced. The Yajus (the Yajurveda) had its birth from it.

(Rgveda X.90.9; Atharaveda XIX, 6.13)

It is believed that one cannot read the Vedas without the proper study of the vedangas. The reason given for this assertion lies in the fact these were given proper form by the Rishis.

In this chapter, however, I intend citing the Vedic text to support the statements I have thus far made. But before I do that I should also like the reader to know the nature of the text that that the Vedas contain.

*We already know that the Rgveda deals with the spiritual and mundane matters and also a model code of conduct. The Yajurveda deals with the Karma-kanda. The Sama Veda deals with prayers and chants.* But the Vedas do not believe in rigidity. In all the four Vedas we have all these three categories of subject matter. The Vedas were not primarily meant for the purpose of performing certain rituals or ceremonies. Therefore, its text covers almost all aspects of human life since the Vedas do not believe in demarcating boundaries between the empirical, ephemeral or the mundane matters, and the world of Absolute Reality, transcendence and spiritual existence. Whatever is born-movable or changing and the eternal - the Supreme Reality pervades everything. The entire text exists within Him, and His extensions. The Vedic text has been interpreted in several ways but the actual text remains eternally unaffected. Of the three ways in which this text has been interpreted viz. cosmic, spiritual and the social my choice of interpretation is purely social.

The Vedic literature consists of the four Vedas. Each Veda in tum is divided into the Sarnhita portion, containing the original texts of the Vedas and the Brahrnana portion, containing interpretation of the content of the original texts. This latter is again divided into the Brahmanas proper, dealing with interpretation of the rituals, the Aranyakas, dealing with worship and contemplation, and the Upanishads, dealing with philosophical questions. All these are called Sruti.

The Vedangas are works needed for understanding Vedic text. They are six in number-Shiksha (phonetics); Kalpa (rituals); Vyakaran (grammar); Nirukta (etymology); Chandas (meter); and Jyotisha (astronomy). Kalpa is sub-divided into Srauta-Sutras; Grhya-sutra; and the Dhannasutras dealing respectively with sacrificial rites, domestic rituals, and social rules. The Pratisakhyas, which contain phonetics, grammar and meter; the Anukramanikas (indices); and the Charana-vyuhas (branches of the Vedas) also must be brought under the Vedangas. They however have never been placed under that category.

Of the Charana-vyuha only a few are extant. The Rgveda has only one, the two Samhitas of the Yajur are a black (Taittariya) and white (Vajasneyi) and have four (Taittariya, Kthaka, Maitrayani, and

Kapisthala) and two (Madhyandina and Kanva) recessions. The Atharvaveda has two-Saunakiya and Paippalada.

Society is the eventual inspiration for all types of text therefore one must examine the texture of social formation and its material development. There is nothing better to succeed in doing so than to analyse various terms used for by these Sages.

The following mantra from AV. VIII.4 also known as address to Indra-Soma reads like this:

O Indra-Soma, against the sinner and his sin let heat boil up like kettle glowing with the flame;

Against prayer-hating, raw flesh eating, dreadful-eyed Kim din, keep hostility, unceasingly.

Read carefully this mantra which suggests the presence of some people in their midst who had different food habits than those of the Rishis. The gods are being invoked here because it would appear that it is not easy to handle them easily.

Whatever one, O Agni, tries to injure

The substance of our food, steeds, kine or persons,

May such thief, robber, trickster go to ruin,

Sink to destruction both himself and his children.

In the Rgveda X.34.2-6, 10, 13-14 we have a beautiful description of a lamenting Gambler

She wrangles not with me nor is she angry:

To comrades and me she was ever kindly,

For dice that only luck less throws effected

I've driven away from home a wife devoted.

Her mother hates me, she herself rejects me:

For one in such distress there is no pity.

I find gambling man is no more useful in

than is an aged horse, that's in the market.

Others embrace the wife of him whose chattels

The eager dice have striven hard to capture;
And father, mother, brothers say about him:
"We know him not, lead him away a captive."
When to myself I think, "I'll not go with them
I'll stay behind my friends that go to gamble;"
And those brown nuts, thrown down, have raised their voices,
I go, like wench, straight to the place of meeting.
To the assembly hall the gambler sallies,
And those asking "Shall I win?" he quakes and trembles,
And then the dice runs counter to his wishes,
Giving the lucky throw to his opponent.

Grieved the gambler's wife grieved by him abandoned,
Grieved, too, his mother as he aimless wanders,
Indebted, fearing, he desiring money,
At night approaches other peoples' houses.

'Play not with dice, but cultivate the tillage,
Enjoy thy riches deeming them abundant,
There are thy cows; there is thy wife, O Gambler'!
This counsel Savitar the noble gives me.
Make friends with us, we pray, to us be gracious,
Do not bewitch us forcibly with magic;
Let now your enmity, your anger slumber,
Let others be in brownies' toils entangled.

Rgveda IV, 5.5 offers a description of wives that do not hesitate to trick their husbands.

Roaming about, like brotherless young women,
Of evil ways, like dames that trick their husbands,
As such being full of sin, untrue, unfaithful,
They for themselves this place have created.

And the placed too here is Hell in these words:-

O Indra-Soma, dash the evil-doers down
Into the pit, the gloom profound and bottomless,
So that not one of them may ever thence emerge;
Such is your wrathful might to overpower them.

The Vedas do not primarily deal with mundane matters. At the same time they do not cast an iron wall around the subject they deal. They accept life as it comes to them. If their lyrics achieve heights, which it has not been possible to scale, the reason lies more in the clarity of their vision and transparency of their large hearts than in the inspiration alone. This may primarily be the reason why the Vedas do not exhibit signs of pessimism. But for the hymn addressed in the honour of the Ushas (Rgveda. 1.11 3, 10-11), which sounds pessimistic, there is nothing that even remotely deals with this human failing. In his book the Religion of the Rgveda H.D. Griswold (Motilal Banarasidass, 1971) on page 332 cites MacDonnell that this Veda contains two types of religious poetry. On the one hand its poetry deals on the higher side with praises of gods and generally accompanying the sacrifices offered to them and on the lower side consisting 'in spellsor charms directed against hostile powers, and accompanying them some domestic practices of a magical character.' This statement does not support the view that the Rgveda does not deal with magic. In fact, MacDonnell goes on to suggest that monogamy may have been practiced but the Sages knew how to control rival wives. The following verse reflects the triumph of a Rishi,

Vanquished have I these rival wives,
Rising superior to them all,
That over this heroic man
And all his people may I rule.

Kidnapping seems to have attracted the attention of the Rishis in several Rgvedic verses. See for instance Rgveda 1.117 records,

A helpless girl glorifies you when saved from the clutches of kidnappers, as if a quail is rescued from wolf. You carry the devotional prayer to the top of the mountain in your triumphant chariot and slay crooked mischief-mongers with deadly poisonous weapons.

See again in Rgveda. 1.119

O twin divines; you provide the cows belonging to old peaceful persons with milk, when they implore you for help. You also liberate innocent kidnapped girls from the clutches of kidnappers (as if a quail from the mouth of wolf) and you also give, as it were a new leg to a chief town administrator.

O twin-divines, you both give to our infantry brilliant, foe trampling, foe defying,

Loudly roaring high-spirited, strong-bodied vigorous vehicles, capable of acquiring a thousand treasures in exploits.

The normal questions all of us ask agitate these sages too. For instance, Bound at three places- knowledge, action, faith-and entrapped in dark ignorance, the helpless man has been praying to the divine powers for protection. Ultimately, the great Lord would hear his voice and indicate to him the path of liberation. May I know why this, 0 earth and heaven?

*The desire to lead a healthy and happy life afflicts these Sages too.*

I have obtained the self-driven car (body) of the food- bestowing twin-divines, and with the help of this I expect to procure wealth in abundance.

May this wealth-bearing car increase my prosperity and may delightful car carry luxurious sweet drinks.

God assigns hundred autumns to us in the midst of our passing existence subject to old age and decay. Those who are sons today shall be fathers tomorrow, and therefore, may be have no afllictions or infirmities in the midst of our lifespan.

We invoke for our preservation, the head of state, the people in charge of social welfare, justice, militia and the preceptors. May these bountiful people save us from all distress just as a chariotis rescued from a difficult ravine. (Rgveda 1. 119)

May the goddess of learning, along with other teachers and the learned, be vigilant for our protection. (Rgveda, 1.106)

These Rishis seem to be quite intolerant of those who do not have the same or similar forms of worship or gods. For instance, see Rgveda 1.121.26

O glorious resplendent sun, may you stop your yellow horses, which drag the wheel of your chariot in the opposite direction, - the one of back gear, drive them away to the opposite bank of navigable rivers where the non-worshippers, the infidels, reside.

O resplendent God, with adamantine determination, may you preserve us from this affliction that is so difficult to be destroyed.

The resplendent God humbles the non-believers and punishes those that turn away from noble deeds, whilst He encourages the virtuous. Rgveda. 1.51.10

Cow killing may be a point of debate in certain **circles** but read this. Rgveda. 1.115.4

O Lord of heroes may the cow killing or man slaying divine-weapons of destruction be kept far away from us. May the facility granted by you be ours; may you, the owner of mighty two realms (mundane and the spiritual), be gracious to us in granting prosperity.

This is what they declared were the sources of wisdom. Read Rgveda. 1.73.10

The seven channels (two of eyes, two of ears, two of nose and one of speech) full of wisdom flow from the inner most illuminated region. The wise persons have known the door of the inner cavity where the treasure of the divine knowledge is concealed. For you, the divine consciousness has discovered the milk of knowledge, furnished by the sense organs (the kine) with which the mankind is ever nourished.

Yajurveda / 18/30

Let us forever continue to praise the mother-like grain-growing land. On this land has God given birth to all the living beings. He may give us the inspiration to perform acts of Dharma.

Rgveda/5/39/2

O Gurudev, equipped with glory and knowledge, teach us about the desirable Dharma and the illumined knowledge so that we become accomplished scholars.

Rgveda/10/21/4

O eternal, powerful and glorious God! The riches that you regard the best give us that knowledge for universal happiness, and for performing good deeds.

Atharvaveda/4/16/2

The omnipresent and just God is watching all whether one is sitting, cheating or torturing in a secluded place, or when two individuals take joint decisions.

Rgveda. 1/94 /15

O the indivisible God! To whomsoever you give good wealth and inspire him for his well being and happiness that individual becomes completely void of sin. 0 God! Let us too receive such wealth and become good.

Atharvaveda /7 /115/2

O the inspirer of all, Savitadev! The wealth that will take us downward, the wealth which we may not be able to utilise and which is likely to exploit us like the creeper (amarbail) that first gets on to the trunk of a tree and then sucks out its life-sap, kindly send it away from us. You are the owner of heart-pleasing glorious riches. Kindly give us that wealth which may stay with us and enable us to possess all means of comfort.

## Man and Society

"create an elephant-keeper for deep walking; a horse keeper for speed; a cowherd for nourishment; a shepherd for manliness; a goatherd for enhancing keenness, a ploughman for growing more food; a preparer of Soma for obtaining essence of medicines and food; a house-guard for weal; a possessor of wealth for well being; and an obedient attendant for supervision". Yajurveda XXX. 11

On the nature of society in which both good and bad live cheek by jowl.

"O God create a Brahmana who knows the Vedas and God, for propagating the knowledge of God and the Veda; a Kshatriya prince for the safety of the kingdom; a Vaishya for rearing the cattle; a Shudra for hard labor and service. Cast aside the thief, who steals in the darkness; the destroyer of heroes; who passes his life injail; the eunuch mentally disposed to licentiousness, the dacoitbent on looting and harming people; the harlot full of lust; and the bard disposed to abuse." Yajurveda XXX.5

The next hymn says:

a God, create for dance a bard; for song a public dancer; for duty who administers justice; for sweetness a panegyrist; for pleasure a wife-loving husband; for dexterity a car builder; for firmness a carpenter.

Cast aside, a debauchee who indulges in conversion with a dissolute; a ridiculer fond of derision; an illegitimate virgin's son, addicted to carelessness.

The Vedic verses depict a picture of a highly developed concept of family and Its life. Somehow, there is nothing evolutionary or anthropological in this concept. It would appear that whatever concepts the Vedas cany they appear in variably in their polished and highly evolved form. It is only logical to assert that no society could produce the Vedas Without any literary tradition and knowledge creating systems. We all know that the Gayatri meter constitutes the opening hymn of the Rgveda. We also know from a contemporary folklore that the author of this meter was Rishi Vishwamitra who was denied the status of Bramharshi by Rishi Vashishth and his cohorts. After a long stretch of meditation Vishwamitra had taught himself the art of writing hymns in lyrical form. On his return from his deep hibernation he faced Vashishth and challenged him to write in a meter like the one he had developed. Since it was beyond the abilities of Rishi Vashishth he was forced to accept Vishwamitra a Bramharshi. It incidentally also reveals that there existed during the pre-Vedic times castes and the Brahminshad arrogated to themselves a higher status than that of the kshatriyas. This reality stand ssupported by other corroborative evidences too. This was in fact a *casus belli* between the two communities. But for that discussion we have to wait a little. To continue with our subject let us talk of the content of the Vedas.

The Vedas contain *three* kinds of verses–the details of rituals, philosophy and material progress. While too much stress has been laid on the rituals by the priestly class who usually wield tremendous influence in all societies, but the philosophers have been attracted by the philosophy they contain. Except for some attempts where the Vedas as such have been examined for purely sociological reasons independent of their spiritual content, generally no meaningful studies are available of the Vedic people and their society. Interestingly, the Vedas lay a great store by learning. Numerous references can be cited to support this statement.

See for instance, this hymn in Yajurveda XXI. 14, "Just as a learned person, lustrous like fire, immortal by nature, supreme, fit for eulogy and research, divine, guarded by vital breaths, laudable for his knowledge; and just as Anushtap-metre with praises, attains satisfaction–and intellectual mind, so should all do."

It is this aspect alone I wish to concentrate on. References to their other aspects are, however, not possible to be blocked out completely. Creating a very tight division in the content and interpretation is neither possible nor desirable. Societies should always be seen in their totality. Even the most decadent societies have aspects that do not wither away in isolation. Certain rituals are common to the entire human race. Being part of social existence they provide greater insights into social life than any other reference one could think of From the time of conception, birth of a child to starting its acquaintance with tetters, marriage and to the last journey of one's life etc. represent events that furnish details or collective living. They could be ignored at one's peril because the end-result in that case could easily be highly distorted or partial.

In the Rgveda Book X Hymn 85 and in the Atharvaveda, Book XIV there is a description of a divine marriage, which symbolically represents a model that many of us follow to this date. Except in matters of detail the description of the marriage ceremony of Savitri Surya - a rsika or the inspired interpreter of the hymn, with Soma could have taken place anywhere or at any time in an average Hindu family. The common features between today's marriages among the majority of the Hindu families are strikingly similar to the description given here. The steps followed here are so similar that it makes one believe that the passage of time hasn't counted for much since the days when the ancients lived and their so-called modern-day descendants. Savitr gave Surya to a worthy husband. Soma, being highly accomplished, is a worthy brahmacharin. He is fully matured for the married life; and so is Surya, his fiancee. In enlightened societies marriages take place between two mature individuals because it is a serious business after all. Here is the description of the marriage ceremony, with which we are so familiar.

The first stage is the introduction of the bride and her groom.

> Earth is upheld by truth; heaven is upheld
>
> By the sun; the Adityas are supported by sacrifice (yajna)
>
> Soma is supreme in heaven.
>
> Vishnu is the guardian of Soma, the maker of years and months.
>
> Raibhi was Surya's companion;
>
> Narasami her slave; Surya's lovely dress
>
> Was adorned by Gatha.
>
> Citti was the pillow, the eye the collyrium;...

Now the background is being described.

> Heaven and earth were the boss when Surya went to her husband.
>
> Hymns were the cross-bars of the car;
>
> The Kurira meter was the thong of the whip;
>
> The Ashvins were Surya's groomsmen;
>
> Agni was the leader of the procession.
>
> Soma was desirous of a bride; the Ashvins were the two groomsmen
>
> When Savitr gave Surya who was ripe for a husband, to Soma endowed with intelligence.

Here is the bridal procession being detailed.

> Surya's bridal procession, which Savitr dispatched, has advanced;
>
> The oxen were whipped along in the magha (constellations);
>
> She is borne (to her husband's house)
>
> In the Arjuni (constellations).

Behold the forms of Surya; the asana (the border cloth), the visasana (hand cloth),

The divided skirt (adhivikartana); of these the Brahmana relieve her.

This is what happens immediately before the actual ceremony.

Now the bride and bridegroom come to the place of the marriage and are felicitated by the assembly of guests and hosts.

Fortune is the bride; approach, behold her;

Having given her your congratulations,

Depart to your several homes.

This stage is most interesting. This custom is followed today as well, only its form has undergone some change.

The bridegroom receives the hand of the bride and repeats the verses with a characteristic solemnity:

"I take your hand for good fortune, that you may attain old age with me, as your husband; the Lord known as Bhaga, Aryaman, Savitr, Purandhi, has given you to me, that I may be the master of a household.

O Lord Pusan, May you inspire her who is most auspicious; in whom men may sow seed; who most affectionate may be devoted to us, and in whom animated by desire, we may beget progeny."

The married life becomes a nucleus of family, and the benedictions are showered on the new couples-Abide here together; may you never be separated; live together all your lives. supporting with sons and grandsons happy in your own home.

The conduct for the wife is being detailed.

Look upon your husband with no angry eye, be not hostile to your Lord, be tender to animals, be amiable and be very glorious; be the mother of males, be devoted to learned people, be the best ower of happiness, be the bringer of prosperity to our bipeds and quadrupeds.

Be a queen to your father-in-law, be a queen to your mother-in-law; be a queen to your husband's sister, be queen to your husbands' brothers.

In the following few lines the cohesive life of the family stands portrayed together with the blessings of all those that count. For the sake of that cohesive life and harmony the Supreme Lord and worthy people of society are also invoked. Thereafter, the last part of the hymn is cited to show how it inspires the entire society for concordance, love, humility, and well-knit affectionate discipline, which arises out of mutual respect, fondness and reverence and also,mutual understanding. Here is the remainder of the hymn,

May the Vishvedevas unite the hearts of us both; may the Apah, the Omnipotent Lord, and all the cosmic fluids unite both of our hearts; may the Matarisvan Dhatr unite the hearts of both of us.

Meet together, talk together, let your minds apprehend alike; in the like manner as the ancient people of wisdom concurring accepted their rewards in the social selfless sacrifices.

Common is the prayer of these, common be the acquirement, common the purpose, associated by the desire. I repeat for you a common prayer; I offer for you a common oblation.

Common be your intention; common be your hearts; common be your thoughts so that there may be thorough union among you.

The union of marriage leads to immortality if invoked with higher ideals.

For the sake of immortality, enjoying personal union, they (wife and husband) worship the gods.

The above scene as presented here should give the readers an idea that the Vedas contain material about all kinds of social and economic activities. This should be able to demystify the Vedas, which the priests have always portrayed as a religious document. We can find in the Vedas almost all the rituals that the majority of the Hindus even now engage itself in. For instance, the first haircut (Atharvaveda, 6/68/1-3), the name-giving ceremony (Yajurveda/7/29), the yagyopavit ceremony (Rgveda /5/82/1), or the ear-piercing ceremony (Yajur. 24, 40) etc. have all been written on in one form or the other. The ancients did not forget to suggest that finding a good teacher for the child was a primary 'duty of the parents'. They then went on to say that mother was the best teacher in the world. For the Vedic rishi woman is the natural teacher and the best must be always mentioned. Here some girls are praying to their lady teacher:

"O exceptionally brilliant and highly learned mother-like teacher, although we girl students have no special abilities, give us education and make us extensively competent." (Rgveda 6/61/6). Even a model lady teacher stands defined (Rgveda 2/41/16).

There is another hymn that says:

"O Scholars, O Teachers! Those that are not trained in the cultivated language, whose information is not chronological and is disorganised, those that accord precedence to body-building, those that are narrow-minded and mean, are as stiff as a stick is and also defame others among the low-breeds are unfit to be instructed. Such stupid persons may not be taught. On the contrary, those that venerate their teachers and are forward-looking they may be equipped with education." (Rgveda, 7/33/6)

Indeed, they even suggest that for better class of instruction a teacher ought to be "truthful, kind and compassionate besides being reflective." (Rgveda7/2/3)

In fact these Rishis appear to admire ladies and their special innate abilities. There is hymn in the Rgveda1/126/7 in which a wife is telling her husband to come to her to seek her advice instead of worrying, because she could resolve his problems. The Vedas function in most cases as guide to us all in most of the activities we feel interested in.

t-or instance. here in an example of the most mundane of the desires:

We invoke the resplendent Lord, whether He comes from this earthly region, or from the heaven above or from the vast firmament, that He may give us wealth. (Rgveda.I.6.10)

In the first verse of the Yajurveda, Lord God is invoked for providing food and fuel for the sake of nourishment and vigor. They have no wish to fall sick therefore there are prayers in the Vedas to keep them free from pain and sickness. Their concept of prosperity comprises being rich in progeny and cattle. Their God is also called *gopatau* - Lord of cattle. Their concept of marriage covers its twin well known functions viz. begetting children and also having the pleasure of prospective company especially when one is old.

"O people, just as in this world, the female teacher and preacher of lovely form, like two dawns of great brilliance, all immortal bright forces of nature, the Trisht up metre and the bull that carries the burden on its back, give us wealth and life, so should yet all acquire them!" Yajurveda XXI.17

Even when these rishis are praying for material wealth, fuel, progeny, cattle, and viands and similar other things they take one gradually on to higher planes or realms each of which in its turn has its own fuel and level of prosperity. The most abstract of the realms is the realm of vital forces, mental complexes, and finally of the spiritual one of the highest order. The materialism of the Vedas is capable of lifting one up in gradual step-by-step fashion to the highest mysticism from the childhood to the adulthood of each realm.

The spiritual mystic mounts up from the earthly region to the earth's mid-region i.e. antariksha, with the help of the Yogic exercises. His eventual goal is heaven. He therefore sings:

From the earth's mid-region have I mounted,

And from mid-air ascended up to heaven,

From the high pitch of heaven's cope I came into

the world of light. (Yajurveda, XVII.67)

**The Vedic community and its occupations**

I wish to remind the readers that the Vedic sages had their own concept of social organisation. They had an image of a very simple social setup. At least so it looks like. They apparently were very flexible in their, approach about the implementation of their own concepts. What we should remember while reading the Vedas is that it took more than a thousand years to finally compile them. In the process of editing its text four times the arrangement and the sequence of hymns must have also not remained static. During this long intervening period i.e. the time/date of its first version and the last it is only reasonable to expect that the society must have also witnessed numerous transformations. Along with the society the attitudes of people must have also not have remained static. The idea is that since societies change with time so do their preferences and material conditions. What was at one time a prosperous and high-ranking class can slide down in its status after a short while. If the position of the Brahmins was high in matters concerning certain rituals it does not necessarily mean that they enjoyed identical or similar status in all others pheres of social life. While engaged in woodwork no Kshatriya or Brahmin could match the skills of a carpenter. Several scholars have commented upon this aspect of social hierarchy. The Kshatriyas monopolised esoteric knowledge as well as political power while the Brahmins controlled and presided over ritualistic functions. In the Upanishads (Brihadaranyaka 2/l,6/2; Kaushitaki 4/1, 1/1; Chhandogya *5/3,5/11*) there are several references to the Brahmins inquiring from the Kshatriya rulers about the knowledge area called brahmagyan. The Brahmanic superiority or their social primacy is only contextually correct.

There are reasons to believe that caste is pre-Vedic or the story cited earlier of Vishwamitra and Vashishth would no longer be acceptable. R.K. Mookerji has attempted to count the number of Rgvedic Suktas written by Rishis that were members of different castes and declared that the maximum number of Suktas got written by Kshatriyas and not Brahmins. This finding endorses Dawson's assertion that Kshatriyas enjoyed social primacy. H.D. Griswold in his book The Religion of the Vedas (Motilal Banarasidas) says, "the highest level was reached by the Vedic nobility in the mater of strength, beauty, wealth and happiness. They were the favored class. Hence, most of the Vedic gods were patterned after the nobility. They were in fact glorified Kshatriyas." Let me mention in passing that all Divine Being srevered by the Hindus and others are Kshatriyas. Lord Buddha, Lord Mahavir J in, Ram and Krishna etc. are all blue-blooded Kshatriyas. It does not seem proper to cite a single hymn and declare that what has been mentioned in this for once alone is the absolute truth. We should not forget that truth is both contextual and relative. The only absolute Truth is the Almighty. Everything else is only partially true.

Humans contradict themselves. No statement ever remains uncontradicted. I have an example where one finds an illustration of the statement I just made. The case in point is the so-called the caste-system. The Purush Sukta of Rgveda (X.90), Yajurveda's

Chapter XXXI.II and Av. XIX; 6.6 are normally cited to support what is written below:

> The brahmana became His mouth,
> Of both His arms the rajanya was made,
> His thighs became the Vaisya,
> And from His feet the Sudra was born.

Since I am just going to cite another verse, which contradicts the concept normally popular I have my own guess about it all. Firstly, Indians have always been fond of symbols. It is possible that the above-cited verse may be merely a symbol of certain classification of occupations or of a hierarchy left undefined. Secondly, the time lag in the interpretation of the hymns could have caused this contradiction. Atany rate it is quite strange that what we would normally question first before accepting, everyone seems to have accepted it without demur. I wonder whether an analogy will be acceptable to my readers. The ruling class normally puts down other classes in the meanest of the terms once they have the opportunity. I find the class IV of Uttar Pradesh was made to put on a livery that was once the official dress of the Minister of Interior of the Great Mughals. The idea was to show contempt for a rank by downgrading it as a reminder to everyone that political downfall carries with it indignity, and to the others that it was both possible and necessary to be arrogant. Do we have here a case like that on hand?

Here is a quote from the Yajurveda, which denies rigidity of castes and the monopoly of one community against the other: The mantra is from Yajurveda. *126/2*

"Thus spoke Lord God, 'O Humans! This benefit - granting language of the Vedas that I am giving to the Brahmans and the Kshatriyas; it is meant for the Vaishyas, Aryas and the Sudras too. *I make no distinction between ours and theirs'."*

The rigidity, which became the bane of the followers/descendants of these ancients, makes a mockery of these far-sighted rishis (the visionaries 1 drishtas). If India's priestly class had only realised their folly that rigidity in a society can always be injurious to social health there was no need for numerous religions to arise as a protest against this malaise of rigidity and shortsightedness. I am surprised that even in the twenty-first century we in India continue to have persons who are a throwback to some dark age where humans could be distinguished on the basis of the accident of their birth.

The Vedic people wished to live long lives. Here is what a Rishi is praying to get:

"O God! The learned having acquired education and other abilities from you live up to the age of 300 years, similarly, we too by restraining our senses, disposition, intellect and the soul and by acquiring education and sciences may live more than 300 years."

To me this desire to live so long shows that they too seem to suffer from the common, human affliction of excessive love for life. Or else, why should they desire so unless they lived in the twenty-first century USA?

The ancients were quite clear in their mind that humans differ in their abilities and all this is genetically determined. To think that mere education could remove these disparities and bring the entire society to an identical level is little too much to ask. There is a very beautiful hymn to describe this distinction. Read this following verse from the Rgveda 10/71/7.

**Differing levels of understanding (Constructivism)**

Here one can see that a clear-cut distinction is being made between superficial and real knowledge. Therefore, they say that while "a few do not understand the secret of the language even *after reading* it, some others do not make out the reality even after listening as well but there are some to whom the language presents its true form and meaning even as a fully decked beautiful bride does, when she reveals her true self before her master/husband". Rgveda./10/71/4

The differences in pupils' understanding lie in their own potentialities and attitudes and not in the teaching of the teacher. He teaches them all the same content and in an identical manner. This incidentally is the first example of Constructivism in education wherein it is clearly explained how learning takes place and the same content could result in varying results depending on one's intelligence and the effort. In the present day context our present day emphasis on individual attention to a child's individual LEARNING was known to the Vedic people.

It is possible to say here that one can hardly come across a better description of intellectual differences among humans vis-a-vis their linguistic abilities. Incidentally, there is lot of confusion whether or not the ancients had a script because if they did not have one it would be natural for them to resort to memorisation to keep their literature from being forgotten. For me, with number of very clear cut indicators of a script having been present and repeated mentions of the same in the Vedas it looks rather strange that they did not readily write the Vedas down in it. Until an answer is found for this query the question of a neglected script it would always remain a well-guarded mystery.

There is yet another reference to script in the Rgveda 7/15/9

"O girl students! Just as intelligent teachers introduce *writing and reading* of letters with the help of fingers, you should know innumerable subjects and possess immeasurable knowledge."

Like the case of the absence of script or of a written word there is yet another myth that these ancients lived in the jungles or thick forests and had apparently no interest in life or its activities except to keep themselves remaining busy with deep meditation and ate only fruits and the tree roots etc. To me this appears a very questionable proposition because I now cite two examples to show that these ancients did not teach under the shade of the trees or in schools without walls.

Here is the proof:

## School Building

Atharvaveda /9/3/1 and /9/3/16

"It is a beautiful school building good in looks and built after proper measurements and it is good enough for all materials and mean. It has doors on all sides and is fully equipped with the best of the materials. Its masonry is perfect. We accept this building".

The design, which the master of all the four Vedas, Brahma prepared and the qualified engineers executed after proper measurements is a beautiful building; let that be protected by the provision of light and air by their twin deities.

"The building, which has been constructed after proper measurements, that which is meant to increase strength and valor and where there will never be any shortage either of milk or water and which is stocked fully with food items we wish to live there in love and without harming anyone."

It is possible that since all the Vedas were not revealed at one time, the rishi lived in the sylvan surroundings initially but gradually they advanced materially in all the worldly senses.

Atharvaveda carries number of hymns that reveal their interest–in the Vaastru sastra or in the science of building houses according to the configurations of the planets. There is a verse that says that God is present in the two, four or even eight room school building. So much is the insistence on the proper measurement of building that one has a feeling that some modern day faddist was assigned the charge of the school buildings. Also care is to be taken about the lighting arrangements and the quality of other equipments provided in the school. It looks as though someone is worried that the contracted money would not get paid unless proper work was done according to the satisfaction of the owners/government. The surprising part is that God Himself is present in all these rooms (Atharvaveda 8/3/1 & 9/3/11 etc.) I would like some one to suggest that these classrooms are some kind of symbol and since I have no clue about it at all. Let some one say that I have committed an error of judgment. But one must note here that these rooms are not only lighted, as all school buildings ought to be, they are also well provisioned.

**The Ideal Teacher**

The following quote from the Rgveda describes the attributes of a good teacher. Few definitions could improve upon it.

"A teacher should have the ability to buildup the students under his charge. He must never be proud of his knowledge. He should be as glorious as fire and possess qualities of leadership. He must be specialist of his branch of knowledge. Just as a cow collects milk in her udders after grazing grass, a teacher should collect knowledge through reflection and self-study. He should make teaching an enjoyable experience even as food items are made tasty and palatable before they are served. He should be popular among his students and be their benefactor. Sitting in the midst of his students he must look distinguished because of his knowledge. "Rgveda 1/69/2"

These ancients irrespective of their material advancement are very health conscious. They know that germs affect their health, therefore they say:

"Let us bring home contamination-free water, which may cause diseases. We wish our homes to be always equipped with materials like foodgrains, milk, ghee and fire to help us cook meals etc. that protect us against death". (Atharvaveda 3/12/9)

Before I take up other aspects of that society it would be appropriate to talk of their preferences for the type of governance they either had or elected really to have. We have here numerous references to a very democratic arrangement. One can find them stated clearly in all the three Vedas viz. the Rgveda, the Atharvaveda and the Yajurveda. In the Yajurveda one can see them mentioned in these hymns: 18/38/42; 10/2-20/8-10/27; 18/43 and also 9/40-41/1. In the Atharvaveda these can be seen' in 6/98/1; 12/1//; 3/15/4-8 and 2/19/41/1. In the Rgveda 10/125/3, -4. &6; 7/31/14, 2/41/11. On the basis of these references, it is possible to state unequivocally that they were a democratic people who believed in the process of election and took majority decisions in an assembly of elected representatives.

Here is what the National Assembly itself says in the Rgveda:

I, National Assembly, am the mistress of the entire nation. I alone make people receive moneys. I am the only principal body to consider all matters seriously and take final decisions. The people and scholars having given me lots of powers and assigned duties constitute in the form of their representatives.

In the Shatpath Brahmana there is a discussion on the dangers of a king trying to become a dictator, Meanwhile, here is another reference to the National Assembly from the same source, as above, in the Rgveda.

I, National Assembly, use arms against a tough enemy and also for the destruction of the violent and the criminals against their knowledge. I go to war for the welfare of the people. I use my powers to extend the territorial limits both in this world and the next.

Now the last part of the last sentence has a very significant message because it refers to the next world. It further says:

God commands: "Hey Humans! The arms of your nation should be admirable enough to defend your country. But the treacherous and the conjurers should not possess them.

That they are peaceful people should be in no doubt because they also pray in the Yajurveda 33/17.

O God! Let us have peace in the two worlds. We desire peace from the horizon, from the earth, from the medicine grown there in. Let the scholars give us peace and so should the knowledge, foodgrain and strength grant us peace. Let there be peace with happiness and not the one born out of fear.

The following is the first is part of an oft-quoted hymn in which the members of a family are shown to be engaged in different occupations.

"I am a karu (carpenter, or a singer), papa is a physician and mother throws cornson the grinding stones, various occupations, desiring riches we remain in the world like cattles in the stalls; flow Indu for Indra."

The Yajurveda gives us an idea of a highly cultured society in which people were engaged in hundreds of professions. Chapter XXX hymns 5 to 22 of the Yajurveda offers a list of these occupations. Indians are still pursuing most of these professions in their original or modified form. If this list is properly understood we find that such a society in no sense could have been living in the forests. Also, since the rishis are writing about them it is virtually impossible that even they too had either no urban contact or were in different to that kind of life. I find it totally absurd to even suggest that living in the caves of the Himalayas or on top of the snow-clad peaks they could visualise a society, which engaged in the activities totally unconnected with either meditation or renunciation. To me these rishis appear worldly-wise and extremely perceptive regarding human weaknesses.

The list of the Yajurveda includes: the learned, teachers and priests/ the brahamanas, the royalty, the defenders and the warriors/the kshatriyas, the businessmen, landowners, farmers/the vaishyas and the labor class, menial workers, or the economically poor/the sudras. Jmay mention here that this description is common knowledge in India that defines the nature of their ancient society. They know that the ancients had a hierarchy in occupations. But doubt if they also know that well that the ancient society of the Yajurvedic times had other occupations too, such as: the harlots, public dancers, gamblers, speculators, dealers in beverages, carvers, iron-smelters, jewelers, artificers, damsel's attendants, baby sitters, cane-splitting women, paramours, thorn-working women, women dealing in love charms, a yielding man (homosexuals), question solvers, astronomers, astrologers, elephant keepers, house guards, watchmen, female dyer, washerwoman, strife-makers, doorkeepers, high stewards, fire-kindlers, besprinklers, nishad, vratya, ointment-makers/chemists, goldsmiths, merchants, gamble managers and keepers of gambling houses, forest-fireguards, pole dancers, village headmen, watchmen, dancers, fish-catchers, hide-dressers, wood-rangers etc.

However, we also have mention of elder sisters! brothers remaining unmarried while their younger sisters! brothers were married. We have in this list included persons called dwarfs, eunuchs, robbers, thieves, blind and deaf individuals etc.

This list suggests a vast variety of occupations and the presence of a range of human beings of who all are neither healthy nor socially acceptable. At any rate it would appear that the ancient society too suffered from almost similar maladies as our contemporary society does.

They also knew about basal instincts and weaknesses. The only difference is that they did fmd out certain methods to overcome their worldly miseries. For instance, the Yoga or deep meditation orrenunciation of the world appears to be part solutions to human suffering.

**A few additional comments**

As we write about the Vedas, its content and form etc. we must also recognise the fact that such a huge volume of literature like the Sruti, Smriti, and the Sutra literature couldn't have been written in a single go. Since it took long to write, to edit what had been written and also to select what should be preserved for the posterity are some of those processes, which even otherwise are time consuming and therefore amenable to memory lapses. Scholars have attempted to explain away contradictions in various ways; for some they are so holy that the contradictions are made to look in consequential and therefore immaterial. Others a little more scientifically minded than the lot just mentioned would definitely like to explain these contradictions either as editorial lapses or the out growth of a society, which in the process of its own development forgot to sort them out. It is much more logical and sane to imagine that the ancient society also witnessed a tremendous amount of change over a time stretching beyond a thousand years or more to produce a literature like the one we have. Therefore, in their collective memory some useful concepts grew and were retained the others less relevant got either sidelined or gradually made to recede into oblivion. In a long history of the ancients we have numerous areas where it is possible to show that there did take place a kind of conceptual development. For example, what is the ultimate source of life? At one time the answer given was -Agni! Fire! In the next stage we find water being added to this list, which later on gets expanded to include foodgrains! *anna*. By the time we come to Rishi Raikva we have all the four main substances that sustain life other than ether. As we read the Vedas we are sure to notice this kind of development in ideas and concepts. Similarly, it is only natural to imagine that the ancient society grew from a certain materially underdeveloped stage to the scientifically and conceptually highly developed state of a mature and learned society. Scholars like Divekar and several others have suggested that the time when the first verse of the Veda was composed the ancients were already familiar with Soma and Homa! Yagna. They possessed bullocks and horses, agriculture and must have known how to water their fields, had canals and crops like that of the sugarcane, cereals and oil seeds etc. they knew the usefulness of the dog and the science and art of archery. But they were constantly on the move as they were expanding into the vast territory of the subcontinent. In support of their statement they offer an example. They moved from the source where the Soma was readily available to the place where its availability became scarce we are informed that the manner of the crushing the herb for extracting juices changed radically overtime. From the fresh stem of the plant! creeper when a gentle pressure by fingers sufficed, a time came when even ring-studded hands became inadequate for the purpose. The ancients still found it hard to forget the nectar of Soma and had to evolve and use either grinding stone or the pestle and mortar to drink it. To study this reference alone or to read about the development of cities and town planning, from building simple houses to building magnificent palaces etc. is a civilisation's march that requires appreciative understanding. This kind of growth and development of highly critical books on the Vedas that are regarded holy by the majority may be widely ignored. But times have changed. Such studies are gradually becoming acceptable that depart from the earlier practices. This I personally think is a healthy trend.

But let us remember that the methods of research should follow universal norms and writing a paper may not be attempted to either endorse or refute a personal predilection. In order to look at the complexities of social life of the Vedic people it is necessary to allow the text of the Vedas to depict the same without my intervention. Read on the following:-

Yajur Ch.V. 43 "Just as I gaze not at the sun, so should thou."

Yajur. Ch. IX. 20 "For the attainment of full knowledge, noble deeds; for the attainment of happiness, religious life; for the attainment definite object, activity, for the attainment of wisdom, the habit of reading and teaching, for retention of knowledge, truthful speech; for arithmetical measurement of the day, the science of arithmetic; for checking the waste of time in infatuation, a word of wisdom; for the fool, who revels in vice, a word of caution; for the degraded, wicked soul, advice to ward off evil deeds; for the strong person amongst the low and despicable, speech revealing the nature of things; for the attainment of God, the Lord of the universe, the knowledge of yoga; for the king, the knowledge of all affairs, are essential."

Yajur. Ch. X. 6 "In this world created by God, ye, male and female students, engaged in study lead a life of high morals."

Yajur. Ch. X.14 "0 king, ascend the zenith. May thou obtain the knowledge conveyed in the Pankti Shakvari and Rewati verses of the Sam Veda, the thirty-three-fold praise-song, three divisions of time, both seasons; Winter and dews, Arithmetic, the science of nine digits; thirty-three god, the study through Brahmacharya and riches. Castaside the head of thief."

Yajur. Ch. X. 19 "O royal skilled engineer, construct sea-boats, propelled on water by our experts, and aero-planes, moving and flying upward, after the clouds that reside in the mid-region, that fly as the boats move on the sea, that fly high over and below the clouds. Be thou, thereby, prosperous in this world created by the Omnipresent God, and flier in both air, and lighting."

Yajur. Ch. XI.62 "O woman, protect the valuable ancestral property of thy glorious husband, who loves thee, is the guardian of the people, and master of various nice foodstuffs."

Yajur, Ch. XI.78. "O king, devour the burglars, with both tusks, destroy the robbers with thy teeth. With both thy jaws, eat up the thieves and cheats."

Yajur Ch. XII.84. "Just as a thief steals into the cattle-fold, by breaking through the wall, as do all well-known healing plants come out of earth tearing it as under, and drive out from the body whatever malady there is."

**Qualities of a king:** Yajur, Ch. X11.33 "He alone is fit to rule, who spreads knowledge, and administers justice, kills the foes, roars like the lightening, protects the forest trees, wages battles on earth, is expert in statesmanship, and endowed with noble qualities, speedily preaches religion, keeps with his power under control, the Sun and Earth, and spreads aroundh is luster."

**On debauchery :** Yajur. Ch. VIII. 48 "O irreligious husband, I warn thee against cohabitation with the pure and noble wives of others. O evil-minded husband, I desist thee from approaching the tenderhearted wives of others. O ill-intentioned husband I keep thee away from going near the philanthropic wives of others. O unsteady husband, I censure thee again and again for teasing the delightful wives of others. O stone hearted husband. I separate thee from the company of sweet-tongued wives of others. O ignorant husband, full of virility, I prohibit thee from having sexual intercourse in day's light and sun beams."

**Service of maidservant/cook:** Yajur. Ch.XI.56 "O venerable, ever-happy wife, utilise the services of a maidservant who. full of love, with lovely looks, noble-minded, cooker of nice meals, places the cooking pan in thy hands."

**Suggestion not kill the cow instead kill forest cow (neelgai):** Yajur, Ch. XIII. 49 "O sagacious king, in this world, don't harm this bull, the giver of thousands of comforts, the source of immense milk, and worthy of protection. Harm not in God's creation, the cow, the giver of milk for mankind and innocent in nature. I point out to thee the forest cow. With her destruction add to thy prosperity and physical strength in the midst of vast space and under God's guidance. Let the wild forest-cow be put to grief by thee. Let thy foe, which we dislike, be put to grief."

**In the next hymn camel is allowed to be killed:** Yajur. Ch. XIII.50. "O learned king, don't kill the two-footed men and birds, and four-footed cattle, the source of comforts. Don't kill the sheep that covers our bodies with blankets, and is foremost worthy of protection among God's creatures. I point out to thee the forest camel. With his protection add to thy prosperity and physical strength. Let the wild, uncontrollable camel be put grief by thee. Let thy foe, whom we dislike be put to grief."

Their **dislike for predatory animals and mass violence is shown thus:** "Let injurious animals like the lions and others that eat flesh be destroyed. Let murderous crowds of men that destroy others like a powerful weapon be killed. Let virtuous rulers protect us from these animals and make us comfortable."

Reader can have a fair idea of **the complexity of the Vedic society** by going through the following citation from the Vedas themselves. Let the following hymns speak for themselves without my trying to forcibly giving meaning to hymns.

Yajurveda Ch. XIV. 9 defines **the castes/ status and qualities** thus: "The Brahman is foremost in the society, like the head in the body. His force lies in the protection of humanity through knowledge, religion and austerity. The Kshatriya is a class amongst men. His power lies in affording happiness in humanity through justice, humility and strength. The Vaishya is another class, who amasses foodstuffs. His strength lies in becoming the lord of riches. The artisan, Shudra is another class of men, whose strength lies in doing hard work." Yajur. Ch. XXX. 5 "O God, create a Brahman, who knows the Veda and God, for the propagation of knowledge of God and the Veda; a Kshatriya prince for the safety of kingdom; a Vaishya for rearing the cattle; a Shudra for hard labor and service. Cast aside the thief, who steals in darkness; the destroyer of heroes, who passes his days in Jail, the eunuch mentally disposed to licentiousness, the dacoit bent on looting and harming people; the harlot full of lust; and the bard disposed to abuse."

Yajur. Ch. XXX. 6 "O God, create for dance a bard; for song a public dancer; for duty one administers justice; for sweetness a pane gyrist; for pleasure a wife-loving husband; for dexterity a car-builder; for firmness a carpenter.

Cast aside a debauchee who indulges in conversation with the dissolute; a ridiculer fond of derision; an illegitimate Virgin's son; addicted to carelessness.".

Yajur. Ch. XXX. 7 "O God, create for penance a potter's son; for sharpening intellect an artificer; for beauty a jeweler; for welfare a sower; for arrows a maker of shafts; for destructive weapons a bowyer; for victory a bowstring maker; for control a rope-maker. Cast aside a hunter bent upon murder; and a dog rearer the helper of the murderer."

Yajur. Ch. XXX. 8 "O God, cast aside the vile man who *pollutes* the river; Nishad's son, hankering after libidinous women; a degraded arrogant man, friend of a person harmful like a tiger; an uneducated person attached to low dancing and singing women; the demented, given to the application of magical rites; an untrustworthy person who befriends the serpents and the tools; a gambler who acquires wealth by unlawful means; a non-gambler who creates unnecessary excitement; a woman who creates split among the Pishachas, the thorny woman who favors the freebooters."

Yajur. Ch. XXX. 9 "O God, cast aside a lover, who cohabits with another's wife, a paramour having illicit connection with a domestic woman; an unmarried elder brother suffering from the pangs of passion; younger brother who has married before his elder to inherit the property; the husband of a younger sister whose elder sister has not been married for ulterior motives of greed; a licentious adorned woman who pretends for penance; a lustful go between woman bent on arousing passions; a by-sitter for garrulity, an obstinate man who insists upon acceptance; and him who offers presents in the shape of bribe, to gain strength."

The type of people the Vedic people did not like are listed here. The references given above clearly show the variety of occupations they had and also their likes and dislikes. These citations also show the variety of animals they had was also tremendous.

# Chapter - 4

# The Vedic Community and its Occupations

O God, create a wood-bringer for Light; a fire-kindler for brightness; a bes prinkler for horse's path; a high steward for highest happiness, a master of all sorts of knowledge, for the sight of the learned; a distributor of knowledge, for the benefit of humanity; a magnanimous person who contributes to the happiness of all, a washer-woman for cleanliness; an affectionate wife for domestic happiness. O God, cast aside a wicked person bent on teasing, murdering, and offering opposition! Yajurveda XXX.12.

The economic activities and the occupations of a people for earning their livelihood are excellent indicators of the socio-economic level of any society. The Vedic community is no exception to this rule. There are several misconceptions and doubts in our minds regarding the material and social developments of the age long gone by. For instance, we are as yet not very sure of the time when the first Veda was actually composed. Similarly, we do not as yet know for sure how long did the Rishis take to compose all the four of them. Was this a simultaneous affair i.e. were all the Vedas written in a single go or they were written in a sequential order one after the other? Although now it is generally agreed that it took about a millennium and a half to complete the task but the surprise of the surprises is that a few devoted families could preserve such a vast literary effort through rote memory. Whether or not they had a script has been definitively answered. They knew about writing and therefore they had a script but for some unknown reason they did not write down their great works for a very long time. May be because they thought that mere writing is not enough if they had no idea about the process of its preservation. Therefore, they developed a very elaborate system of memorising and made their language suited for the purpose. One of the reasons why Sanskrit grew into being a perfect and amazingly scientific language could be ascribed to this requirement. Even otherwise there is a well-known saying that need is the mother of invention. People have been able to count the exact number of the Rishis along with their names who engaged themselves in this task of composing/revealing/memorising the hymns. But it remains a mystery how could such an extraordinary continuity in the ideas and diction be sustained for such a long while in order to accomplish their endeavors. The other part of the mystery is their ability to co-ordinate. Since all these things were humanly impossible in an age when written record keeping and meticulous training in lofty ideas and knowledge etc were absent one must logically and even otherwise declare that the effort was not merely superb but both *literally and figuratively divine.*

But as one reads the text of the Vedas as I do now, one would be constantly amazed at the perspicuity of these Rishis. One might safely conclude that the levels of culture and the civilisation that these Vedas suggest couldn't have been by any standard or norm less than urban. In almost all the Vedas examples of urbanisation are available To illustrate the point look at the complexity of certain occupations. It is impossible to think of a jeweler or a goldsmith who does not know the art and science of smelting precious metals. The very fact that a society had jewelry presupposes affluence and classes, the knowledge of mineralogy, the process of refining metals, designing and safe marts to sell these wares. There are references in the Atharvaveda (10.6; 19.46 and 7.14) about the type of jewelry available. It could be either studded with precious stones or be of pure gold. This clearly shows that these people were familiar with the science of refining and polishing stones as well. An uncut precious stone is nothing more than a stray piece of common earth. It may also mean that either they imported both the precious metals and stones or they had developed their own means of acquiring \them. But in that case one will have to concede the fact that they were a seafaring people, which would mean building long distance boats and the knowledge of navigation. Therefore, it would be easier to disbelieve or reject the very concept of such occupations than to deny that all the accompanying social and material infrastructure was too advanced and variegated to have existed in the primitive times as S.A. Dange has in fact suggested in his book *(india from Primitive Communism to Slavery).* Why would the ancient Indians talk of occupations like gambling (Rg. 10.34.13)and running of gambling houses if they did not know what gambling really means. The consequences of drinking or gambling are too well known practices to feign ignorance about. Therefore to say that gambling was more than an occupation and that gambling houses too existed would amount to possessing an extraordinary imagination if they were not a part of social reality in the ancient times.

The Vedas took longtime in getting composed therefore it is possible that developments in the contemporary society may also have got reflected in these hymns even without any deliberate effort. It would be highly immature to suggest that professions/occupations either grow simultaneously i.e. all at one time, or while writing anything literal, it is easy to ignore social realities.

The Vedas have given details about some 140 occupations a few of which are being referred to here. It would be interesting to observe the manner in which occupations got converted and fossilised into castes. The pursuit of an occupation and its becoming generally a sort of family tradition over a period of time led the ancients to accept the occupation itself as a sub-caste. This explains why while the broad categories of castes exist till this day but the sub-castes have continued to multiply. R.S. Sharma and several others have entered this fascinating research area and have found that the sub-castes increase with the growth and development of economic activities. Urbanisation by itself can also play a major role in the change of caste provided one changes one's occupation alongwith mobility.

Weaving appears to have been the most common and the most ancient of professions. The type of clothes and the materials to weave them finds mention in the Vedas. The Atharvaveda talks of the spinning and weaving of cloth through a beautiful symbol. It says a year is the spinning wheel and the day and night are men and women. Six seasons are the six hangers and while the night is the warp and the day its woof

(Atharvaveda 10.7.42), The Rgveda (10.26.6) classifies cloth into cotton, silk, woolen and the tusser. Special names are given to those who weave, sell and stitch them. Since most of this occupation was largely in the hands of women various names were used to address them. The details of the process are also given along with names of the instruments employed such as the spinning wheel, spindle, the warp and woof and the mechanism to stretch the cloth etc. to complete the job.

What must surprise many are references to buildings and the materials used for building them? Both the Rgveda and the Atharvaveda mention building activities. They go into the details of building rooms, their measurements, uses, names and also the science of building viz. the Vastusastra. In the Atharvaveda there are two mantras that give details about this branch of activity. The relevant references are as follows: Rg. 7.88.5; 2.41.5 and the Atharva. 9.3.12; 9.3.7, & 7.83.1. Herein one finds a description of houses with two rooms to ten in number. There is a mention of how a plot is to be measured and the construction started by deciding about the entry door first. This design is determined according to the definition given in the Vastusastra. There is an injunction in the mantra that the construction of these five rooms is mandatory. These rooms are storeroom for keeping rations; the kitchen and the place for the yagnas; room for the householder and his spouse, a drawing room and, a guest-room. In both these Vedas there is a mention of a mansion built of gold for Lord Varun alongwith a diamond-studded thousand-pillared hall.

In the Rgveda and also in the Yajurveda the method for building air-conditioned houses is also given. For instance, for the summer it is recommended that the house be constructed in the middle of a large pond with provision that the hollow of the walls be filled with layers office all around. During winters the ice may be replaced with heating arrangements. (Atharvaveda 6.106.1-3). The Vedic community had school buildings too, which we shall describe later.

There should be no doubt in the minds of those who without any evidence call the Vedic people and their times primitive. Their cities were called *pur.* The word *tri-pur* means the villages that had three protective walls around them. In one of the mantras in the Atharvaveda 19.58.4 the Seer wanted an iron wall to protect his township.

If there is a mention of the village councils, the designations of the office bearers are also given. Democratically elected councilsran the villages. They were independent self-contained units in every sense of the term.

Various terms are given for different items of furniture. A few of them come pretty close to describing modern day furniture. For instance, talp means an expensive bed, kashipu is a sofa set and asandi stands for a chair to sit on.

If one persisted to consider the Vedic community less than urbanised look at the utensil they used. If their earth enware consisted of water jars, pitchers and certain other utensils for use during serving meals, they had metal pitchers, service spoons, utensils made of silver and also various others that were made of wood.

For transport these people used horse-driven carts in which two to three horses could be yoked together. In the case of King Parikshit there is arnention of a ten camel-driven cart. (Atharvaveda 20/127). In the Vedas there is mention of the use of large boats or ships for distance travel on the high seas. Normally the ships were reserved for trade and commerce.

**Agriculture and the Animals**

Not unlike the present times the Indian economy was dependent on agriculture. It is therefore natural that they should have described the same in greater details and prayed for continued abundance of food grains, milk and milk products. This explains why they wanted each house including schools buildings to have storehouses.

The Atharvaveda declares King Prithu as the founder of the science of agriculture. He is supposed to have developed and might as well have discovered various kinds of foodgrains with the help of his knowledge of agriculture science.

In the Vedas there are several references to the activities that relate to agriculture and farming. For instance, in the Rg. 10.1 01; 4.57; Yajur. 12.67-71; Atharva. 3.17 etc. the following agriculture related activities have been mentioned. It is desired in one mantra that before sowing seeds the field should be thoroughly prepared. One must possess outstanding quality of bullocks and the plough and only the best quality seed must be sown. The sowing season must also be suitable even as watering should be done at the given interval of time. The crop may be cut only when it is properly ready. There is a mention of the ways of watering crops such as ponds, rivers, canals, small culverts and the wells. Grains of twelve varieties have been mentioned in the Vedas. They are: paddy, barley, urad, til, moong, gram, kanguni, rice, wheat, kodon, savan and masur. It is no easy task to find appropriate terms for all of them in English.

Though unexpected they knew all about the common diseases that afflict crops besides the harm the rats cause. They apparently had sufficient knowledge to counter these menaces to their agriculture and in a limited way used insecticides. They also knew all the terms concerning agriculture. The parts of the plough, the activities on the farm and the field were also mentioned. They knew about the yoke, the spur, and the sickle. For all these activities and functions, besides names, connected with agriculture have been given in Atharvaveda 6.91.1.

**The Animals**

Number of terms and activities concerning rearing and tending to the animals are given in the Vedas, especially in the Rgveda 10.101.4 and the Atharvaveda 2.26. & 3.14. The idea of a dairy farm was quite familiar to them. There is a special injunction that animals should be kept in a closed place (bara) for protection. Special care may be taken to keep them free from disease. In the Atharvaveda numerous mentions are made in different mantras/hymns regarding the care one must take of the animals in every sense of the term. Particular attention may be drawn toward these references: Atharvaveda 7.73.12; 7.75.1 & 2 2.26. 1-4 & 4.21.1. As one went through these hymns one would know the level of advancement of knowledge in this field that these ancient seers must have attained.

In the Vedas the killing of animals has been prohibited. In fact it has even been made a punishable offence. The cow has to be protected and not killed. Atharvaveda 7.73.8 bans the killing of the cow and in the Rgveda 1.114.10 the one who does kill a cow is to be declared an out caste and banished forever from society. 1 have the greatest regard for the only giant scholar India produced-Rahul Sankrityayan. He mentions in his book that beef was taken during the ancient times. But he does not tell us about the caste and class of people that took it. He also does not give the exact occasion for taking it. It is a casual mention totally unsupported by any textual reference. I am talking of the book called Darshan Digdarshan. But one could read:- Yajur. Ch. XXX. 18 "O God, drive away a gambler, friend of the dice-king; one who has evil designs for murdering cows; a cow-killer for gallows; one who for hunger goes to a man who is cutting up a cow; a leader of meat eaters bent on misdeed; the son of a depraved person befriending a sinner."

In a paper written by one Mrs Urmila Rastogi (see, Historical and Critical Studies in the Atharvaveda edited by Dr Suryakant Bali, Nag publication, 1981; pp.196-97) it is mentioned that in a yagna called Shatodan Sav an unfertile cow was sacrificed. This type of offering was supposedly much superior to the one offered in Agnishtom and Atiratra. Sayan has commented on this mantra (Atharva. X.9) and said that this cow itself was called Shatodana. The host of the Yagna was expected to put one hundred pieces of beef on the identical number of animal skin as an offering along with other offerings like a poop and purodash prepared from sweetened wheat flour. The entire process followed a well-laid ceremonial plan in which each activity was accompanied by a suitable loud-voiced mantra. Madam Rastogi concludes her discussion of the said ceremony firstly by stating that the host could eat both vegetables and the beef alike i.e. there was no distinction between the two and thereafter says, "the host could perhaps eat beef but no other type of meat." She then goes on to cite Kaushitaki Sutra 65.4-6 in support of her statements.

# Chapter - 5

# Vedic Knowledge: The Basics

The One who deserves everyone's prayer, that venerable Being-God, is responsible for the birth of all the four Vedas-Rgveda, Yajurveda, Samveda and the Atharvaveda. These Vedas are the source of all the knowledge that is spread across the world. Therefore, God alone is the original teacher of all Knowledge Yajur/31/5.

Just as my light of knowledge is valued by all, so should yours. The ignorant moving in the dark who are opposed to the learned and whom the learned disapprove for their antagonism to knowledge, should be brought round to the path of virtue by hundreds of means available and let restrictions not be removed till the enlightenment. May the wicked be not blessed with prosperity, and the pleasures of knowledge. Yajurveda Ch. 126.

Anyone writing about/on the Vedas should remember that interpreting them has never been easy. A large number of interpretations are already available both by Indians as well as the Europeans and each one could at times be both mutually contradictory as well as radically different. For example, read Aurobindo and Sayanacharya together and you will know the two thinkers approach the same Vedas with two radically different viewpoints. Or read David Frawley and Max Mueller together and see the difference. Any claim to declare one as superior to the other may not be advisable. Among the several under dispute the debate relating to the validity of anyone particular translation over all others is merely one of the many points of dispute The Vedas by themselves constitute contested terrain. On each issue there is some controversy or the other. The debates range from issues pertaining to their revelation/composition to all areas whether the same relates to worship or social behavior. Were the Vedas composed simultaneously or at different points of time? This question has also not been answered definitively. One of the things that interfere with these types of queries is the sacramental nature of the Vedas. They are worshipped and regarded by a vast majority of Indians as the final word of God. We all know that their devotees, who will accept whatever is offered as divine, do not always put questions. Instead queries come from those that have no such faith. I am not only struck by this genre of curiosity but I am also interested in answering such questions. My first answer to these questions would be that the Vedic text has undergone changes four times because of their editing. No one knows for sure when the revelation actually took place. If one knew. this fact or remembered that all efforts in this direction have failed thus far then most of irreverent questions will get automatically answered. We know that the Rgvedic hymns are repeated in the rest of the three Vedas, which have some new Suktas of their own as well. It has therefore made us believe that the Rgvedic hymns were perhaps composed first. Vedic scholars have repeatedly endorsed the view that originally there was only a single Veda-the Rgveda. At some later day the two other Vedas came into being the Yajur and the Sarna repeating some of the hymns of the original. The fourth Veda i.e. the Atharvaveda, compiled by Maharshi Angiras, carries quite a bit of magic since he perhaps loved exorcising, and therefore his specialisation is named after him. It took some time for the Atharvaveda to join the pantheon of the other Vedas but there are a few even now who refuse to acknowledge the fact that this Veda too ranks with the rest.

But there is a possibility that the reality might be very different from what we know until this day. For instance, the repetitions of hymns in the Vedas may have been merely part of the editorial prerogative. Be that as it may, at least that has made chronological writing about the social developments of those times a little difficult. The prevalent chronology of events has thereby become suspect. Trying to trace origins of any single concept and placing the same in a historical perspective has thus become all the more difficult. But that surely doesn't prevent us from attempting that exercise. Numerous scholars have suggested that the meaning of the Vedic text lends itself to several interpretations because of the metaphors and symbols used. For instance, one of the authors on these hymns has gone into great details into the symbols used in the Rgveda. The title of his book is Hymns from the Golden Rgveda by David Frawley published by Motilal Banrasi Das. We shall examine some of his observations at an appropriate time and place.

There are two questions one should like to address first. The first relates to the performance of the Yajnas. Why perform them at all. The answer to this query is offered in the Yajurveda. The Yajurved (Ch.1.24) says "By the impulse of God, the Given of Bliss, I perform the yajna free from Hinsa (violence), for the attainment of noble qualities and association of the learned, through the aid of life-giving breath, vitalizing air, and through the rejuvenating rays of the sun and moon. A yajna is the recipient of the rays of the sun that ripensa large variety of objects and is full of immense luster, and innumerable rays. Ayajna is the illuminating source of rain. With the aid of the yajna we should remove our miseries." This hymn, as one will notice, offers an explanation why yajnas are necessary. Besides having a secular purpose, the hymn reveals the ultimate scientific knowledge about the cause of rains. It incidentally suggests that Violence 111 the performance of the yajnas had no place whatsoever.

I cite here a sample of observations from the Introduction of the Vedic Samhita made available from Veda Pratisthan (see pages 99-100). "During the past 125 yrs., as a result of the labor of our Western scholars (also assisted by our own Indian scholars trained on the Western pattern), the interest into the Vedas, and the Vedic literature grew from an entirely different approach. This would be seen from the following observations: (1) Professor Wilson says; "To me, the verses of the Veda, except in their rhythm, and in a few rare passages, appear *singularly prosaic* for an era as that of their probable composition, and at any rate, their chief value lies not in their fancy but in their facts, social; (2) Professor Cowell says, The poetry of the Rgveda is singularly *deficient in that simplicity and natural pathos or sublimity* which we naturally look for in the songs of an early period of civilisation. The language and style of most of the hymns is singularly artificial..."Occasionally we meet with fine outbursts of poetry, especially in the hymns addressed to the Dawn, but these are never long sustained and as a rule we find grand similies or metaphors;" (3) To all these remarks, Griffith further adds: "The worst fault of all, in the Collection (Samhitas) regarded as a whole, is the *intolerable monotony* of a great number of hymns, a monotony which consists almost entirely of invocations of Soma Pavamana, or the deified Soma juice in process of straining and purification. The great interest of the Rgveda is, in fact, historical rather than poetical; (4) Griffith attached to the hymns of the Rgveda a fresh importance, for we find him saying, "As in its original language we see the roots and shoots of the languages of Greek, and Latin, of Kelt, Teuton and Slavonian, so the deities, the myths, and the religious beliefs and practices of the Veda throw a flood of light upon the religions of all European countries before the introduction of Christianity; and (5) In this connection, Griffith further says, "As the science of comparative philology could hardly have existed without the study of Sanskrit, so the comparative history of religions of the world would have beens impossible without the study of the Veda." Let me say that it is possible to be selective in these quotes. To remain objective and also be perceived as such is not easy.

I have no desire to enter into any controversy regarding the origins of the Aryan race, but even a casual study of the ancient literature will endorse the cotemporary scholarly opinion that our ancestors must have taken time to spread out in this sub-continent. I endorse in large measure the content of the following quote from History of Indian Literature by Albrecht Weber, (Trubner's Oriental Series, 1878);

"The reasons, however, by which we are fully justified in regarding the literature of India as the most ancient literature of which written records of an extensive scale have been handed down to us, are these. In the more ancient parts of the Rgveda Samhita, we find the Indian race settled on the north-western borders of India, in the Punjab, and even beyond the Punjab, on the Kubha or Kophen in Kabul. The gradual spread of the race from these seats towards the east, beyond the Saraswati and over Hindustan as far as the Ganges, can be traced in the later portions of the Vedic writing almost step by step. The writings of the following period, that of the epic, consists of accounts of the internal conflicts among the conquerors of Hindustan themselves as, for instance, the Mahabharata; or of the farther spread of Brahmanism toward the south as, for instance, the Ramayana. If we connect with this the first fairly accurate information about India which we have from a Greek source, viz., from Megasthenes, it becomes clear that at the time of this writer the brahmanising of Hindustan was already completed, while at the time of the Periplus, the very southern-most point of the Deccan had already become the seat of the worship of Gauri, the wife of Shiva. What a series of years, of centuries, must necessarily have elapsed before this boundless tract of country, inhabited by wild and vigorous tribes, could have been brought over to Brahmanism!"

These above citations have led us to the point where it has become necessary for me to explain their relevance. The first point in this regard is to note that the Vedas carry within them the seeds of India's early history. These hymns reveal the process of the growth and development of Indian civilisation. A large number of scholars have tried to present a coherent and meaningful history of ancient/Vedic India.

In the following pages I also intend doing the same citing (Vedic) text to support my standpoint. I believe that the pre-Vedic society was fairly organised (not necessarily on the lines suggested by S.A. Dange) and had developed considerably in areas like medicine, astronomy, mathematics, and contemporary warfare etc. In fact, compared with all other civilisations of that period this one had few unique characteristics. I refuse to believe that those who revealed the Vedas were unaware of cities or urban dwellings and the authors of the Vedas belonged to an uncomplicated life. Yet I do not subscribe to the thesis that they destroyed wholesale an urban civilisation in order to opt for a pastoral life. Firstly, unlike all others they developed an elaborate oral system to pass on their knowledge to posterity; secondly, their development was multi-dimensional; thirdly, few civilisations could boast of similar continuity or preservation. In that respect the Chinese are the only other living civilisation besides India that could boast of continuity in their culture and civilisation. Others like Greece or Egypt do have a glorious past but unfortunately their civilisation cannot claim to have similar continuity. It is possible to hazard a guess to resolve this puzzle. Howsoever much, we may blame our caste-system but it has proved to be a boon in disguise. The lamp of cultural continuity to glow on could be ascribed to the singular dedication, sacrifice and faith of the Indian in his peculiar caste Dharma.

All I propose to do is to show that whereas these Hymns contain so much of material about its contemporary society and history but what is actually being taught in our schools and colleges about India's past history is a puerile version of objective Reality. At times things are made to look (through purposive interpretations) considerably different from what they really were.

On the basis of what one learns about it in the course of higher studies one usually gets a general impression that the Vedas contain only esoteric knowledge and talk of a society, which lived in the sylvan surroundings, It all makes very difficult for us to imagine that such a society, if it really did exist, would in fact have any poverty, destitution and wherein fake mendicants abounded along with liars and cheats. The fact of the matter however is that the ancient and modern Indian has numerous social practices and beliefs in common. Indeed, it is possible to advance a viewpoint that not much has changed in this country since the ancient Vedic times. On given parameters we find, strangely enough, in place of advancement the quality of our contemporary life and thinking since the times when the Vedas were composed has in reality considerably deteriorated.

We know that knowledge perse has variety and can be presented in multiple forms. Philosophically knowledge is either valid or invalid. What can be cognised and proved is real or valid. This classification has no scope for intuitive knowledge-something that cannot be scientifically validated. For instance, logically there must be a First Cause. But we have consistently failed to give it a universally acceptable name or form. Like Bertrand Russell we cannot even prove that we live in a real world. Some day like him we might come to know that we have been dreaming all along in a world offantasy. Therefore to define knowledge or make an assessment of the same on some valid ground may never be possible. But we know for sure that there is one type of knowledge that does not change easily either with material or speculative advance mentin the society. This knowledge is foundational in character. If the quest for answers to queries regarding Nature is one such dimension, the spiritual or religious questions constitute yet another dimension of the same effort. The love and pursuit of knowledge characterises the Vedas. In the Yajurveda (Ch.I.26) it is stated:

"O Omnipresent Lord! The Giver of happiness, may we subjugate the wicked folk on this earth where the sages perform yajnas. May we associate with the learned and spread freely the system of education as propounded in the Vedic hymns. Just as my light of knowledge is valued by al, so should yours. The ignorant moving in the dark who are opposed to the learned, and whom the learned disapprove for their antagonism to knowledge, should be brought round to the path of virtue by hundred of means available and let the restriction on them not be removed till their enlightenment. May the wicked not be blessed with prosperity, and the pleasure of knowledge! 0 Ye dutiful may ye persistently follow the path of virtue." What needs to be noted in this hymn is that it goes much beyond the assertion that the Vedic people loved knowledge . It in fact records its displeasure against even the possibility of one becoming rich without possessing knowledge.

Even otherwise we find the Vedas contain two types of knowledge– (a) one that is eternal and is not subject to change. This knowledge is given to us as a finished product and is therefore higher; and, (b) the other which is lower changes with time and people. The knowledge they give us about the nature of humans-like, health, moral or religious code, philosophy etc. is liable to change either through deliberate efforts or Time. The reason is simple. Each age and Time defines its health, morality, and material requirements. But the constants like the need to work for a living, do business, undertake travel, evolve methods and modes of governance etc. remain constant with plenty of scope for redefinition in their form and content. The Vedas offer us a variety of knowledge most of it being eternal. They also lay foundation for apossible variety and scope for advancement. At the same time they are not always sure that their earthy sense of the real is definitive. They look for answers, and in certain cases they succeed as well. In this sense we are not very different from them. I cite below a few mantras from the Vedic (mostly Yajurveda) text and urge the reader to discover his/her reality against individual background and context. The greatness of Indian thought lies in its wide variety and largeness of heart. It is open to challenge. It loves to remain resilient. I have tried to present vignettes of Vedic life and thereby show the state of knowledge and prosperity they had attained. The fact that Indians had knowledge in several areas – a few of which continue to remain valid this day is amazing. The Vedas have been interpreted in several ways. But very little has been done to build a society on the basis of the text that is still with us and remains valid. I have tried to analyse their text of the Yajurveda and shown that there are areas in which the world has as yet to catch up with these people. The surprising part is that they had shown clearly that knowledge is acquired in various ways. Intuitive knowledge though not easy to verify is acquired without using labs and gadgets. Yet this knowledge is unquestionably valid and true. The rishis of the Vedic period acquired most of their eternal knowledge through this very method. Let me present the variety of knowledge they had from the Vedas.

**Social thinking**

"A rich owner of plenty of foodgrains, even after seeing a feeble person who has been struck by poverty and begs of him a handful of foodgrain, refuses to share anything with him. In addition, he even *starts eating delicious, rich meal in front of him;* such an individual is not likely to find a single person to help him when he needs it the most."

Rg. I 10/11 *7/2*

**On giving away food**

The stored foodgrain is inspiring me to be charitable. The havan off-rings in the yagna make all the deities clean and capable. May this charity of grain bring acclaim for my being a great donor. May I conquer all directions through this *charity of grain.*

Yajur, *118/33*

It is generally believed that the Vedic people lived in sylvan surroundings and that they had no concept of brick houses or shunned cities. Whether they had any large building structures has also been seriously doubted. One of their gods being Indra who is also called Purandar i.e destroyer of the cities, has helped modern day writers/ readers to conclude that the authors of the Vedas were not urbanised. It is also commonly asserted that these people had no script either therefore in their case any knowledge of writing was unimaginable. For the preservation of the Vedic hymns they therefore had to make an elaborate arrangement too and this made one to firmly believe that they lacked a script hence knew nothing about writing. But the Vedic text does not confirm these conjectures.

**Let us cite text to remove this conjecture**

"I resort to agriculture and craft for removing poverty and nurumizing happiness to all. May I feel happiness in domestic life. May our houses be sufficiently commodious, airy, fully comfortable, and built in the middle of an open space. May our life be in conformity with Vedic teachings. O Lord we pray unto thee to preserve and protect whatever gives us happiness." Yajurveda Ch.1.11

This mantra not only talks of a commodious house but of a house and built in airy place. This is obviously not an interpolation or written by a non-rishi.

They also talk of food being cooked and this is done for improving the digestive system. "I have prayed to the effulgent all sustaining God. May the Lord Father accept my prayer. Our digestive system digests food by means of gastric juices the food put into the stomach. In this universe, created by the All Blissful God I take that food through the qualities of attraction and retention, of inhalation and exhalation; and the forces of purification and permission of the invigorating air throughout through-out the body cooking my food in the burnt fire I eat with my mouth." Yajurveda Ch. 2. II

"May ye thriving, justice loving wise, learned persons, preachers of the knowledge of the Vedas, become supreme through knowledge. Let all seekers after truth, devotees of learning and action attain to happiness. Preach my noble word that brings all kinds of joys." Yajurveda Ch. 2.18

While these people did not like their war like enemies, they loved victory. They therefore desired to drive off men whom "you detest." "May I remove that sinful enemy by war like, military skill and equipment. May I achieve happiness through the impulse of the knowledge, used for gaining supremacy. May air and fire properly employed, drive off him who hates us drive off men whom we dislike. I purify this man with the light of knowledge." Yajurveda Ch. 2. 15.

**Scientific Knowledge**

These worldly wise men and women had known scientific truths that Europe took centuries to learn. For instance, while Europe learnt that the earth rotates round the sun sometime when Galileo told the world, these rishi already knew it. They even knew that the year has 12 months and each month has 30 days. Europe did have lunar calendar even as the Egyptians and the Babylonians had. The modern calendar was prepared in the Papal reign of Grepory. III and that could get over the discrepancies. Of course the Vedic people did not rectify the hours of the day as we can do now. But they were far advanced of anyone in the contemporary world about the division of time and the day and also the seasons. Let us read what they had to say on the subject.

"May the mighty space unite with oblation and butter. May it unite the 12 months of the year, and eight life giving agencies and vital breaths. May the Sun be harnessed with all rays. May pure water rain whenever duly consecrated oblations are offered.". Yajurveda Ch. 2. 22.

The 12 months of the year were named in the same mantra and they continue to retain their names until this day. All Hindu calendars have the same names of the months but Samvat is Saka or the one started by the Scythians.

Whether we are clear about the aims of education and the role education plays in our lives the Vedic rishis had this to say: "O God, the guardian of the primordial Vedas, make me, like the son of a learned man and, endowed with different capacities for the acquisition of knowledge, an interpreter of instruction, and a fulfiller of the aims of education." Yajurveda Ch. 2, 28.

These people wanted everyone to follow the Vedas and follow the laws of the Dharma, (Ch. 2.57) while they wanted to live long but they had no desire to die in pain. So the example they give for dying free from pain is like that of the ripe cucumber. "Through His Grace may we be released from this mortal coil without the agony of death as naturally as a ripe cucumber is from its stem. Yajurveda 3.60.

Look at the type of desires they had and try to imagine the difference in modern day Indians and in the Vedic people. At least to me there is no difference between us and them. Read:

"May we, on this earth, where reside happily all the learned persons be able to revere the sages.

May we acting on the teachings of the Rg, Sam, and Yajurveda end all our miseries. May we rejoice in food and growth of riches. These pure disease -killing waters be gracious to me. May the herbs protect me then the armed kings harm not the worshippers" Yajur, Ch. IV.I.

The next hymn says "May waters, like mother purify our bodies… May I advance in age through waters. Through celibacy and abstemiousness may I possess a body, healthy, comfortable, excellent, beautiful and strong."

Now read this hymn:-

"O learned person, may mechanical science perfected by the application of fire, the giver of light, bestow strength on me. It is the guardian of manifold objects, giver of happiness to the learned, the mechanic and the source of prosperity, make the crops produce abundant grain through aid. O learned person, depend thyself for advancement. Protect me from the misery of sin. Accomplish the yagna with the recitation of Vedic text." Yajur. Ch. IV.10

They knew all about diseases that infect us because of impurity of water. Read this:

"O men, the waters we have drunk, staying within our belly, give us peace, riches, freedom from consumption, disease, and pangs of hunger and thirst. They are strengtheners of the tree of our true knowledge, full of knowledge, full of divine qualities, and undying flavors. May they be pleasant to our taste!" Yajur. Ch. IV. 12

Here is something for the linguists:

"O Speech! Though art thought, Mind, intelligence, giver of knowledge and victory: thou art power worthy of worship, immortal, and double-headed. May thou give us comfort in the past and future!

May breath the strength–giving friend of time, advance in thee in knowledge, and guard the pathway for God whose eye is over all of us." Yajur. Ch.I Y. 19.

We should not forget that the Vedas took more than a thousand years to *compose l* reveal. The Vedas describe their contemporary realities. Therefore, it is possible a few scholars thought that these people had yet to urbanise. Urbanisation is a state of material development and since the Vedas directly mention urban dwellings therefore one could get this impression too. However, this view cannot be sustained for long once an individual reads the Vedas with some intent. Now let us infer their state of living from the hymns themselves.

We all know that the ancients had a great love for learning. This is perhaps one reason why they equated the teacher with the divine Supreme Power. The following (Rgveda /1/144/16) hymn has this to say on the importance of learning:–

What the blind cannot see the sighted can? "The learned women inform us that so can a knowledgeable man know that an ignoramus may not. The learned, all-knowing son acquires such a pure intellect that there is nothing beyond his ken. Being learned he is called his own father's father. Let all understand this."

These ancients knew the value of education and therefore had a great regard for their teachers. If on one hand they defined the characteristics of their teachers and could identify their attributes they also were on the other hand very critical of those students who failed to measure up to their expectations. Read: Rg. *7/2215*

"O my pupil! Who shuns practices in learning, even if you are ready for employment? I do not like your praise of me since you have failed to repeat the lesson just taught. You, who are well known among fools, I do not like your praise. I would much prefer if you received proper education and earned reputation. That most assuredly will enhance my reputation".

The Rgveda has a definite opinion about an unworthy student and go on to define the meaning of education.. In the Rg. 7/33/6 it is said "O scholars, O teachers! Those that are not trained in the cultivated language, whose information is not chronological and is disorganised, those that accord precedence to body-building, those that are narrow-minded and mean, are as stiff as a stick is and also defame others among the low-breeds are unfit to be instructed. Such stupid persons may not be taught. On the contrary, those that venerate their teachers and are forward-looking they may be equipped with education."

In fact they believed that for better class of intellectual activity the teacher should be "truthful, kind and compassionate besides being reflective." Rgveda /7/2/3. In another hymn they think that mothers prove to be better teachers than the fathers (Rg. 7/2/6). When learning becomes part of family culture and mothers happen to teach their sons that is a surefire success formula. This is what Shatapath Brahman says and so does the Rg. (7/43/3).

The names given to the first teacher are Acharya, King, Judge and God. This is what has created all kinds of complications for the Indian teacher. Even the most unsuitable ones love to be addressed as gods. In the Rg. 10/71/71 it is clearly mentioned that it is the child's own abilities and the aptitudes that make him learned or otherwise and not the teacher. Just as all students do not make worthy scholars, similarly all teachers are not equally competent or worthy of respect.

There are a few references to *script and the written word* too as distinguished from its spoken variety. If true that these seers knew the script then some one will have to explain why did they set a great store by the word of the mouth? In the Rgveda 7/15/9 the Seer says, "O girl students! Just as intelligent teachers introduce writing and reading of letters with the help of fingers, you should know lady teachers who know innumerable subjects and possess immeasurable knowledge." In case this is not enough then elsewhere in the Rgveda 10/71/4 they mention:

"A few do not understand the secret of the language even after reading it, a few others do not realise the reality even after listening to it but *there are others for whom the language presents her true form. as does a beautiful bedecked bride reveal herself before her husband.*"

I suppose if this proof is not enough to disprove the general notion that the ancients had no idea of the script they may add some more to list of evidences. On the demerits of gambling; the Rgveda(10/34/2);

says that the faces of the dice carried written symbols. At yet another place Rg. 10/62/7 the ears of the cows have the number 8 written on them.

Is it possible that even after reading all this and talking all along of the written word and even of the methods of its teaching etc. some one could still insist that those seers had no knowledge of any script whatsoever? There is hardly any need to be labor the point. Be that as it may, these ancients knew the value of language all Right. In the Rg./1/ 3/13 it is said "Language through its symbols explains the wide expanse of knowledge and is able to illumine all intelligence fully. Therefore, language should be put to good use."

What did the Rgveda say about the nature of the universe that we live in? According to it the universe consisted of three regions–the earth (prithvi), heaven (dyauh), and the intermediate world or the antariksha. We are familiar with the term earth, but not with dyauh because this is one term which was employed to denote the vault of the sky, from where the sun and the stars shine. They had an idea that there was an invisible world too where these stars and the sun retired after their daily ritual/duty was over. The Rigvedic hymns poradically mention the abodes of padam of Agni, (1.72.2), Indra Pusan (1 .162), Vishnu (1, 154,6) etc. In reality therefore, they thought the universe consisted of four regions. The name of the fourth region is Satya Lok. Read Rg. (1.35.2), which says "Causing immortal and mortal to rest, God Savitr returned (to his abode) by way of the Satya Lok (i.e. invisible) world; he comes on the golden chariot observing the worlds." The Satya Lok was considered the abode of Brahma, the Creator. The later day developments have only added certain more Loks to the list. Only as a passing reference I mention the seven loks that the Puranas talk about. From Bhu-lok upwards are Bhuvar Lok, Svar-Lok, Mahar Lok, Jan Lok, Tapo-Lok and the Satya Lok. Similarly, by that time the idea of seven 'nether' worlds had also grown and developed. They were called atal, sutal, vital, and patal etc. according to the depths at which different unwanted creatures supposedly lived.

Interestingly, the Atharvaveda carries a section on the Vaastusastra. Here a number of hymns talk of God being present in a three-room school or the eight-room school. One cannot imagine of a three rooms or eight rooms building without proper measurements and even building materials.

### School building

Like the animal heat in the body and foetus in the womb I, the master of the house live in the houses, which are built with two wings, four wings, six wings, eight wings, and are constructed in appropriate measurement.

Atharvaveda *19/3/21*

In fact, so great is the insistence on the proper measurement of the size of the rooms and the accurate mixture of mortar that one can seriously start thinking about the presence of the ubiquitous modem day contractor in that society too. I was amazed to read about the lighting arrangements necessary for a large room. The mention is of electricity and also of teaching aids. I must say I have failed to be specific because I do not know whether the light is not lightning and teaching aids something very elementary and highly primitive in character. These hymns in question are: Atharvaveda 91 3/1 and *9/3/11* and many more. The fact that God is present in all these classes of the school does suggest that schooling was carried on in built enclosures and not under the shade of the trees or in the hermitages only.

It may interest some to note that the term Guru is equated with both the learned and the divine being, the Absolute. These mantras can therefore confuse. It is not quite correct that all gurus had equal competence. But in terms of their respect the insistence was on respect. The impression that we have is that the Guru did not charge fees. May be he did not do so in the beginning. But no student could leave the residence of the teacher without paying the appropriate amount in terms of tuition fees/guru-dakshina.

### Pupil's return home

"O the best Guru! The restrictions that you had imposed on us regarding food, sensuality and travel, please relax them now. O luminous with knowledge, Gurudev! We shall continue to observe all the pure vratas, and shall continue studying with unbroken regimen, the Vedas". Yajur, 7 72/72

In fact, there is a mention that at the time of leaving the Ashrama or whatever else it was called the student does say that he would like to know what time does he leave the school and when does he invite the teacher home. Atharvaveda 11/5/26 describes how glorious the student looks on the completion of his education.

But here is one mantra wherein the teacher refuses to be admired by a student whom he regards to be a fool.

**Testing and examination**

"O you my pupil; Who shuns practice in learning, even if you are ready for employment immediately, I do not like your praise because you cannot repeat properly even those lessons that have already been taught. You, who are famous amongst fools, I do not like any praise from you. I would much prefer you becoming properly educated and earn reputation than what you are right now. That would enhance my reputation." Rg. *17/22/5*

Here is something, which defines the basic qualifications for receiving scholarship grants.

**The Teacher and his Disciple**

"Those who are well read and know the real meaning of the Vedas and those who are studying to accomplish that aim all such people are treading the path of well being. *Such persons alone deserve to be assisted by rulers.* They alone are beneficial for the nation for being helpful to all". Rg./7/22/9

Here is a description of a seeker of knowledge.

***Testing***

"O Gurudeo! Master of knowledge and fame, please tell with what words would you feel happy? Tell us when do we have to take the test for the lessons learnt? When can we add to our knowledge from your learning? And when can we come for the test again? Just as you had acquired your learning from your well wishing teachers, O Gurudeo!

We are anxious too to acquire knowledge from you. You are our teacher and father like well wisher and also a great master of premium learning. Kindly make us fully learned by your instruction. Rg. /7/29/3- 4

The other point, which has been generally laid stress upon, pertains to such mathematical calculations that require the use of zero in them. Some of the readers might recall the statement once made by Shakuntala Devi that her extraordinary gift for speedy numerical calculations is explainable in terms of what she learnt from the Vedic mathematics. Although we are not in a position to verify her claims there are numerous books on the subject that inform us that for the type of society it was and the requirements they had, they had a fairly advanced system of computation. Jagadguru Swami Sri Bharati Krsna Tirthaji Maharaja (Motilal Banarasidas, 1965; Revised 2002) has in, one of his books - Vedic Mathematics tried to demonstrate just that. While writing the foreword Swami Pratyagatmananda Saraswati referred to one his papers titled: 'The Metaphysics of Physics.' Herein he referred to Rg. X. 190 with a view 'to unveiling the metaphysical background where both ancient wisdom and modem physics may meet on common ground of logical understanding, and compare notes, discovering, where possible, points of significance or suggestive parallelism between the two sets of concepts, ancient and modem. That metaphysical background includes mathematics also, because physics as ever pursued is the application of mathematics to given space-time-event situation.' It is here that they examined the tapas as a fundamental creative formula whereby the Absolute emerges into the realm of measures, variations, limits, framework and relations. And "this descent follows a logical order, which seems to lend itself within a framework of conditions and specifications, to mathematical analysis. Ratri in the hynm represents the Principle of Limits. For example, rtanca satyanca stand for Becoming calana-kalana and Being vartana-kalana at a stage where limits or conditions or conventions do not yet arise or apply. The former gives the unconditioned, unrestricted how or thus of the cosmic process, the latter, what or that of existence. Tapas, which correspond to Ardhmatra in Tantric symbolism, negotiate, in its role especially of critical variation, between what is, ab initio, unconditioned and unrestricted and what appears otherwise, as for instance, in our own universe of logico-mathematical appreciation."

The ancients believed as we too do that the universe we live in must have a basic mathematical structure, and to know a fact or to obtain a result herein, to any required degree of precision, one must obey the rule of mathematical measures and relations. The ancients had developed six auxiliaries of the Vedas in each of which mathematical adroitness, occult or otherwise play the decisive role. The Sutras lay down the shortest and surest lines. The correct intonation of the mantra, the correct configuration of the yantra (in the making of the vedi etc. (e.g. the quadrature of a circle), the correct time or astral conjugation factor, the correct rhythms etc. all had to be perfected so as to produce the desired result effectively and adequately. Each of these required the calculus of mathematics. While the modem technician has his logarithmic tables and mechanics manuals, the ancient yajnik had his sutras.

In the same foreword a comparison has been made in the skills and competencies of the modem mathematician with those of their ancient day counterparts. There are classical cases of master mathematicians both modem and the ancients whose methods of analysis and solution have been regarded as marvels of cogency, compactness and elegance.

Some have been 'beautiful' as a poem e.g. Lagrange's' Analytical Mechanics'. The same logic and observation are extendable in the case of the Vedic sutras too.

One has merely to go through his book to realise the same feeling as expressed above. The book Vedic Mathematic contains 16 sutras and corollaries. It is not possible to discuss each sutra here. I am therefore merely citing the titles of the sutras for those interested in consulting the original text of the Vedas. These sutras are (1) Ekadhikena Purvena, (2) Nikhilam Navatascaraman Dasatah, (3) Urdhva-tiryagbhyam, (4) Paravartya Yojayet, (5) Sunyam Sarnyasamuc caye, (6) (Anurupye) Sunyamanyat, (7) Sankalana - vyavakalanabhyam, (8) Puranapuranabhyam, (9) Calana-kalanabhyam, (10) Yavadunam, (11) Vyastisamastih, 12. Sesanyankena Caramena, (13) Sopantya-dvayamantyam, (14) Ekanyunena Purvena, (15) Gunitasamucchayah, (16) Gunakasamuccayah and the corollaries for the first and 13 sutras respectively, are: (1) Anurupyena,

(2) Sisyate Sesamjnah, (3) Adyama-dyenantyamanatyena, (4) Kevalaih Saptakam Gunyat, (5) Vestanam, (6) Yavadunam Tavadunam, (7) Yavadunam Tavadunikrtya Varganca Yojayet, (8) Antyayoreva, (9) Samucchayagunitah, (10) Lopanastha-panabyam, (11) Vilokanam; and (12) Gunitsamucchayah Samucchaya-gunitah.

For those interested in these Sutras they may note that these are from the appendices of Atharvaveda. In fact, these sutras are the discoveries of the Author–Sri Swamiji Maharaj himself and need some additional effort to locate them.

I now continue with my narration. The following text is based on the available Vedic literature. For the construction of their Yagna Vedis they had an elaborate geometrical understanding and for their Vaastusastra they needed a system of measurement, which was also equally elaborate. Even to think that such people will lack knowledge of arithmetic or will have no zero is difficult to appreciate. For the benefit of those that have no means to read the Vedas, for them a brief reference or two will suffice. In the Yajurveda there are two references to a formula with whose help one can easily calculate additions like 1+2= 3 or 1 1-2==9etc. the hymn in question is *18/24* but the other one which is *17/2* carries the method of calculating numbers running into billions. Now this is not possible to do without the help of zero. Now read the hymn *18/24* and decide tor yourself.

"May my One and Three, and my Three and my Five" and my Five and my Seven, and my Seven and my Nine, and my Nine and my Eleven, and my Eleven and my Thirteen, and my Fifteen and my Seventeen and my Nineteen, and my Nineteen and my Twenty-One and my Twenty-One and my Twenty- Three and my Twenty three and my Twenty-five and my Twenty-Five and Twenty-Seven and my Twenty—Seven and Twenty-Nine, and my Twenty-Nine and my Thirty-One, and my Thirty-one and my Thirty-Three etc. increase or decrease by additions and subtraction.

It is to be noted that odd digits of Arithmetic have been enumerated e.g. 1+ 2= 3; 3+2= 5; 5+2=7 and so on. So 33-2=31; 31-2=29; 29-2=27; etc. this verse teaches us subtraction and additions in Arithmetic from which are deduced multiplication and, division, square, cube, square root and reduction offractions to a common denominator, described by Maharshi Dayanand Saraswati mentions addition, subtraction. Multiplication, Division; Square, Square root; cube and reduction of fraction to a common denominator.

The verse refers to Arithmetical progression with a common difference of 2 one has to read Ch. XVIII for the science of rearing cattle and Ch. XVIII for proper training of cattle.

Here the method is simple 1×10=10 and 100x10=1000 and so on. The president of the World Association for Vedic Studies Professor R.D. Shanna whose write Up on the Mathematics in the Vedas reminds us that the use of the terms like ekodash, dwadash or trayodash etc. in the Vedas clinches the issue without any need for further proof. But even so he goes on giving citing one Hymn after the other to stress his point there are evidences of the use of the symbols for the numbers like 1,2,3,4,5,10,100,200 etc. in the Brahmi script, which according to some is as old as 6000 B.C., but not so in the Vedas where these numbers have been used.

"O inviolable God, all knowing adorable God, you are our father. We are your kinsmen. May you grant us new life endowed with knowledge and happiness. Let us also acquire wealth and wisdom in hundreds and thousands. You are the defender of the persons performing noble acts, and you also favor those who are good and virtuous. Rg. 1.31.10.

Here is a citation in support of the knowledge of decimal system, which the ancients had.

### Education/Decimal system

"O light-like God! With your grace I have today bricks for building a mansion and for personal use cows: one, one × ten=ten, ten × ten=one hundred, and one hundred × one hundred = one thousand, and so on running into billions of burnt bricks and cows." (This is not the first reference to zero and the decimal. Yajurveda/17/2.

I have a question to ask those that doubt the advanced stage of this civilisation: Why did they need calculations that required the use of decimals? Why did they unnecessarily develop equations with whose help one could calculate billions? Why did they need to talk of riches when they knew nothing about currency?

## Education of Women

The ancient Indians knew the worth of women therefore they not only wished them to receive education and bring up a good progeny but also learn from experience that they (women) are infact better teachers than men. It would appear that the status of women during most of the Vedic stage was much higher than what they came to occupy later in the post-Vedic age.

There are hymns, which suggest that the education of the girls was not neglected. Instead a separate system of education was developed for them.

Here are several references to women's education and their natural talent for it. They are supposed to be better teachers as well.

Rg./7/34/2/

## Curriculum for Girls

Those girls, who can listen to the words of education like the sound of underground water, they should study the sciences related to sun and geological sciences.

Rg./7/15/9

## Methods of instruction

O girl students! Just as intelligent teachers introduce writing and reading of letters with the help of fingers, you should know lady teachers who know innumerable subjects and possess immeasurable learning. For your balanced development such an intelligent teacher will herself make all arrangements.

They were declared to be even better teachers than their male counterparts. The Atharvaveda has a hymn 11/15/ 8, which stands endorsed by Yajurveda in the hymn 12/54/;55. The Rgveda says the same in 10/1 09/4.

*On Girls' education* there is a hymn *Rg.* 1/ 164/ 41 which stipulates:

"The girl who wishes to practice a single Veda, or two or three or four or the 4 Vedas and 4 Vedangas besides being an expert in grammar can become herself a scholarly teacher *for the benefit of other girls.*

By becoming a learned scholar she can experience the sky-pervading Supreme Being and for educating other girls she can select clear statements like the sparkling water and remove their dirt-like ignorance.

74. Rg. /7/2/6

### Mother teachers

Like those that provide comfort similar to dawn and night or like cows that give plentiful milk, such knowledge-imparting mothers-who instruct their wards are the most respectable beings. Only such mothers inspire their children to attain heights of fame and glory.

Rg. 1/ 113/ 12

### Education/Model lady teacher

Even as the dawn drives away the dark, similarly, equipped with proper attributes and good education destroying mutual jealousies the lady teacher advances knowledge being the protector of Truth and Knowledge. Such a teacher adopting the policies of great scholars and being the upholder of the truths contained in the Vedas removes the doubts of her girl students.

Rg. /7/2/8

Those mothers who keep the company of learned women, and those who like fire can destroy the darkness of ignorance, such women brimming with knowledge elicit praise both from the ordinary as well as scholarly males. Such women alone by installing the trinity of the goddesses of culture, nationalism and learning can make their children able.

*Differences in individual abilities* and the current rage in India's School Curriculum viz. Constructivism have been noticed by these seers and mentioned in a variety of ways. For instance, the Rgveda says in 10/11/9.

"Though similar the two hands do not work alike. Born of the same mother two cows do not give equal quant it of milk. Even the twins have varying abilities. Two members of the same family do not give similar amounts in charity."

The following is the portrayal of a pupil's desire:

Yajurveda/34/1-6

Desire of a pupil

"The one who habitually keeps running away whether I sleep or am awake and which is the principal informer of the senses that mind I wish to always remain full of good wishes for all. Intelligent, active and patient persons take whose help in acquiring knowledge and with whose assistance engage themselves in the worship of deities, socialise and also give donations and the one which being venerable resides inside each one of us, that mind should always be brimming with happy and good intentions. That which is the best means of acquiring knowledge, that which provides consciousness to the senses, that which after having humans that intellect should forever remains full of good intentions. With whose assistance one recalls past events, that which is an instrument of present activities, that which helps making future plans and that with whose help five senses, mind and the intellect itself perform in the company of the seven Hotas good acts like they agnas, that mind should always be full of good intentions and wishes. Even as all spokes are joined together at the center of a wheel the basic elements of prayer along with knowledge and actron are present in one's mind. Where all knowledge is stored let my mind contain good thoughts, and feelings internalised knowledge retains its memory and that, which is a permanent flame of light in all. Just as a good chariot driver can rein in his horses, the mind can control senses of horse-like humans. That which is located in the heart and is beyond aging and that which is the fastest of all-that intellect should always have good thoughts and wishes.

I found the following as the best one of the hymns dealing with differences in learning and discriminating abilities:

"Of a group of persons, who go for a bath in a pond, each one takes his bath according to his liking and ability. Whereas a few while remain sitting on the rim of the pond feeling satisfied by touching water with their feet, others dare enter it to some depth. There are however a select few, who go to the center of the pond-and enjoy swimming in the deep waters. Although all students possess alike the eyes and ears but each one is different in aptitude and abilities.

Therefore, while some hear only the spoken word of the teacher without understanding it, others follow its meaning on hearing it. Some intelligent ones understand even the hidden import of the words. The differences in pupil's understanding lie in their own potentialities and attitudes and not in the teaching of the teacher who teaches them all alike the same content and with the same method of teaching."

## Family

The Rgveda refers to women without guardians going astray, but the perusal of R.V., X. 85 shows that the sanctity of the institution of marriage had already been recognised by the society and had grown into a formal ceremony. A.S. Altekar holds the view that the Vedic Society had no divorces but there is evidence to show that levirate and widow marriages did take place. Monogamy seems to be the general rule but III the case of the rich and the powerful polygamy was permitted. Polyandry was unknown. Marriage was not a secular contract but a religious ritual, which made the husband regard his wife as a god-given gift. Gandharva (love-marriage) was not uncommon, so were Ksatra (conquered), or rakshash (abduction) known. Atharva. XVIII.3.1. & IV.5; etc. but polyandry was unknown.

Child marriage was unknown. Girls were both grown up and trained to able to manage their house hold. R.V.X.85.46;A .VXIV.1 .43; in R.V.X.34.2 suggests that women were taken by their husband to gambling. This act however was condemned. Women had control on their parinaya (gifts and property received in marriage). Total absence of purdah; participation in public meetings, non-existence of segregation etc. (Rgveda.85.26).

We have been made to believe that teaching was essentially conducted under the shade of the trees. May be a few followed the system. But the impression that the schools did not have buildings does not appear to be correct. The mantras disprove of such a belief as already discussed above. As one reads them carefully one comes across a *mention of school building containing eight rooms* and of a *comparison between the written and the spoken word.* One may however legitimately ask then: where did that script go and why did It disappear? If! do not have the answer, it does not necessarily foreclose the argument or does not stop one to find a valid answer.

**On entering family life**

"O bride! I free you from the vow of celibacy which your father who as your well-wisher had tied you with. I, your husband, make you strong and grant you freedom from fear and ask you to enter the ground of truth and good deeds–this household."

Rgveda./10/85/24

It has also been commonly believed that the family life of the Vedic people was perfect and all members of such a family were indeed role models. It would be virtually a heresy even to suggest that children were forced to love their parents and more particularly when they became old. But that does not seem to have been a common practice. Hence, repeated in junctions to look after the old and the sick. We have been told that the caste was the creation of the Purush Sukta of the Rik. I somehow cannot subscribe to this view point because I find it hard to explain that caste functions got defined along with one's birth. As one thinks deeply and reflects on the implications of these mantras their value for a social scientist becomes evident soon enough. Indeed, it is doubtful whether the concept that all hum an beings are equal though they might belong to different castes is tenable. Be that as it may, the caste was an occupational reality and had nothing to do with birth. This somehow has been disregarded by the latter day social scientists.

The Yajurveda says in 26/2:–

Thus spoke Lord God, "O Humans! This benefit-granting language of the Vedas that I am giving to the Brahmins and the Kshatriyas, it is meant for the Vaisyas and the Sudras too. I make no distinction between ours and theirs."

In this following mantra God seems to contradict Himself Now, this type of contradiction is hard to explain.

Yajurveda /22/22

**National Education**

"O God! May our country be blessed with knowledgeable Brahmins, and brave Kshatriyas clever in warfare, milch cows, and strong bulls to carry heavy loads, and means of rapid transport like speedy horses. Let our women folk be clever in house hold work and the youth civilised, brave and victory-prone. O God! Let there be rains according to our need, and let our godowns be full with luxury goods, food grains and fruits etc. everything necessary for comfortable life. Let us make efforts to increase all these benefits and comforts".

Indeed, the Rgveda talks of the importance of education for all in another hymn as well. See, Rg. 1/144/16.

"Numerous references are made daily to the unusually wonderful understanding these Rishis had of the origin of the Creation, especially to the scientificity of their observations. For instance, the subject of Creation interested these Rishis immensely. The Rgveda talks of it in the Hymn 10/ 129/7 and Yjurveda in 10/129/3 etc. It does amaze one to imagine that even without the benefit of any of the modern equipments and gadgets they could be, at times, so precise in their observations. For instance, they say,

In the beginning there was nothing but darkness. It was the even state of Nature, which could drown all without a trace. That extensive nature, which is hidden in the Cause form, the same with the shinning glory of the divine God appears in the physical form as its effect."

In terms of scientific knowledge the Nasdiya Sukta is the best and most advanced. With all progress in science Modern Man has not been able to identify or understand the first cause of the creation. In these terms the following Sukta is a great surprise.

Read the Nasdiya Sukta Rgveda 10/129 i-v

What was the state during the Pralaya or total annihilation? Who is the Creator? What was the principal cause of Creation and what its principal instrument? During Pralaya there was no evil or good nor did the atoms fill the horizons? What was shrouded and by what? Who was the Protector? Did only the deep seas exist?

There was no death nor was there any life. Even the day and night had not taken birth. The lone Creator breathed without any life breath by his own will. Nothing superior existed beyond him.

In that dark existed the unmanifested Nature like seamless water. Everything looked small before Him. Nature gradually manifested itself because of the austerities of the Supreme Being.

A Desire superimposed what existed in the form of innerself during Pralaya. The seers could thus realise that the Good was latent in the Evil even as the light is in the dark. The creation could arise out of the unmanifested Nature. Slanted bright rays spread out of these three - God, Soul and the Nature. What was below was as amazing as the one who could serve as receptacles for that amazing semen above.

The Truth is who knows the REALITY and what could one say? How did the Creation take birth and how did the variety in it take shape? The gods, the sun and the moon all followed that Creation. Who really knows how this Creation itself took shape?

The One who created this universe is the Creator. One who presides over it is the Creator Himself. If anyone knows the Reality only He does."

I am quite certain that I am neither the first nor the last to say what I have to say. There shall be many in future as they have been in the past that would have been struck by the message these mantras convey. I am both amazed and virtually fulfilled with what I came across and I am quite sure that some one else like me would also enjoy reading and appreciating these Suktas. I think it is the function of each individual to look dispassionately at his own social and genealogical antecedents and to accept only what his reason tells him to. I disagree with those who think the Vedas are someone's monopoly or they could be associated with any form of crude religiosity. If one understood them properly *they are in reality a commentary on their contemporary society and a historical reality at the same time but* most of the time they envision something like a dream, a model that one should attempt to realise in a liberal society, which has nothing to do with a sectarian world.

I have my own views about the process through which knowledge is commonly acquired and how these Rishis must have come to possess it. Indeed, what I am saying is known almost universally. We know that the time one lives in and the environment that sustains him define knowledge, but its real understanding and exposition is an individual's own endeavor. For instance, the entire population of Delhi does not live in the twenty-first century-some do but the majority lives in whatever century they have opted for to live in. If my contention is correct and helps understanding my point then it should be correct universally and for all times to come. Only a small minority keeps pace with the change in time but the rest live or propose to live and force others too to live along with them in their cuckoo land. In this case the knowledge and beliefs of each individual define highly personalised life-styles. The Rishis must have constituted a very small part of their society and perhaps they alone had both understanding and a vision of the real.

Even as all poets and seers have attempted to answer a few of the eternal questions such as, who is the Creator, the purpose of life etc., these Rishis also attempted to grapple with them. The surprise is not that they did so but the most astounding part of this statement is that they did come up with amazing answers. For instance, they have an answer to the query regarding the Creation of this universe and it's Creator. There are a few pieces here in this selection but the best one is the Nasdiya Sukta. I doubt whether modem day science can improve upon it. To read the concept of Time and Space being non-existent in the beginning and the only reality being Darkness in which only the Supreme Being could and did breathe without air is really breathtaking. What I found amazing is the description in which the UNKNOWABLE Absolute creates Bramha. For us even He (Bramha) is unknowable. There is lot of loose talk about these Seers having innumerable gods and goddesses. Since majority of the Hindus regard the Vedas as Revelations and not written or spoken by any human being, therefore as a Hindu society they stand condemned for being pantheistic as against the ones who have only one God. The fact is that the Hindus too have only one God. They too are essentially monotheistic. They too say that the Truth is one, only the scholars have their own opinions. God is purely an abstraction of a creative force. Whose fault it is that this myth of pantheism has gained currency? Read the following hymn from the Samveda 111.31.

The suns, the stars, the oceans, hills

Are all flags that point to Him

The giver of Light, who kills all ills

And helps us to swim
Across the ocean of grief
Surrounding us from all sides.
God is Almighty, All-pervading
Omniscient Lord who guides
Wisemen meditating on Him
And gives them life and light
Day and night, they think of Him
And guide the world aright.
Or, read the following from the same Veda hymn 66
We send this eulogy to the Lord
To the Omnipresent God,
Who is worthy of adoration
Giver of bliss is His meditation.
We treat it as a chariot
Which we drive with intellect.
Let our intellect be pure,
Noble Mentioned and sure.
In God's company and friendship
Let's not suffer. Him alone we worship.

We seem to forget that everyone does not possess the intellectual capacity to think of an impersonal Divine Force. A personalised God with whom we can communicate during times of distress is an absolute necessity. We must have a father-like God who responds to our sorrows travails and shares with us our moments of happiness. I suspect this would be the sole cause of pantheism. The other possibility is that the Vedas are superb poetry. One cannot imagine that the risis would continue to address God with one single epithet. As we address our beloved do we always call her by one single name. If in daily life our love can force us to call our loved ones by different names what is so wrong with God being addressed with numerous names. The changing moods get reflected in our address.

The reason is that a simple answer need not be made to appear complicated. For the time being one may understand only this much. The hierarchy among the divine pantheon is not easy to understand and yet their multiplicity offers us with a choice. Other religions do not do so because they believe all have equal intelligence so also imagination. They limit the choice for their own reasons. For the ordinary mortals too much of abstraction is repugnant. Religion as distinctly distinguishable from the Dharma has greater appeal than an abstraction constituting an ideal.

The Original Cause is unknown; the guesswork is here to satisfy us. What exactly is Religion? Being faith - it refuses to stand to any rational examination. Therefore, the answer for the wise is Dharma and not Religion/Sect/Faith. Dharma, unlike religion can be defined and can vary with the status and capabilities of an individual. It means what one does as a duty. Hence, an individual can have several duties. This means an individual may have several Dharmas. One has a duty or Dharma as son, a husband, friend, as citizen etc. I think if only this part of the book was understood that would also be sufficiently worth one's endeavor. 'One can have several duties but not several religions or sects at one and the same time.

The emphasis of the Vedas is on one to be active, to be industrious and attempt to earn one's livelihood honestly. This need not make one either greedy or dishonest. All societies by their nature have weaknesses. People can be discouraged to appreciate these weaknesses but none can be fully protected or made immune to them.

The Rishis are aware of pollution and of the social inequality. But their obsession is health-both physical and intellectual. They do not want to have handicapped children and pray against their birth but once they are born they want them to be attended to both in the classrooms and also the home very differently. Indeed they feel concerned about them. They are very protective of their women folks and seem especially worried about their chastity. They want their womenfolk to work but within their bounds the parameters of which stand dearly defined. They want their children to be born to plenty especially the sons but for that they suggest industry. They have numerous obsessions and few of these continue to remain the obsessions of the present day Indian society too irrespective of the distinctions between religions and castes. This is the most surprising part of the Indian society as distinct from those of others. Briefly, the obsessions of that society are: family, sons, health, plenty to eat, sharing of Nature's bounty protecting the old. and the destitute and the pursuit of rituals. They have a desire, atleast so says the Yajurveda 3/82, to live long and even up to the age of three hundred years. Asking people to worship trees and rivers etc. is only to preserve and protect Nature's gifts against undesirable encroachments and harm, especially pollution. Apparently, rituals look like a cover to keep environment well balanced and help them live long, really very long.

Where the ancients may be faulted is in their attitude toward their women folk. For what Manu has been blamed is actually a Vedic injunction. It is expected that women shall never leave the protection and chaperonage of their men folk and remain always obedient to them, even when the latter are unjust, careless and irresponsible. This undue negative bias against them does not admit of the possibility of women having had much of a freedom to determine the course of their life. It is a strange contradiction that comes out reading the text of the Vedas. There are hymns that suggest that they had freedom to choose their marriage partner and yet at the same time there are hymns that deny them this freedom. What then does one conclude?

Rgveda/5/61/9

**Choice of a husband**

On reaching puberty when a girl expresses on her own clearly her desire to her parents for a competent, knowledgeable and renowned youth for a marriage; there after her guardians make a proposal to the bridegroom's side to confirm such an arrangement.

Rgveda/2/32/4

**A good wife**

Spreading happiness like moonlight, O Housewife! With the talents and grace you have by offering them to your husband you assist in the creation of riches, kindly inspire us too with your attributes and intellect. 0 the fortunate one! Kindly make us also strong by your knowledge.

The main function or role assigned to women is that of child bearing and that too of sons. Rgveda 10/85/25 says that "I place you in the house of your husband so that living with him you may become a mother to son", and of pleasing the mother-in-law. The Atharvaveda 9/3/21 says, "give comfort to your husband, be pleasure-giving to your mother-in-law." And without ever getting estranged with her husband, commands Atharvaveda 14/1/22, the woman must continue cohabiting with her husband says the Rgveda 10/5/27. Women appear to have very limited rights. The maximum she can ever do is either to give counsel to her husband, which he may or may not seek. The alternative is to become a teacher. In this respect the modern Indian does not differ very significantly from his ancient counter part. The proof of this similarity lies in the content and the intentions of the modem Parliamentarians when they seem to deny them adequate quotas of seats. There is, therefore, a legitimate ground for suspicion that many women may today find the import of several of the Vedic provisions irksome to accept.

Interestingly, the Vedas do not always talk of the esoteric subjects. Their interest in human well-being is both deep and comprehensive. One could easily trace the origin of rational medicine and the art of healing to the Atharvaveda. It is said that Vedic therapy was classified into four categories. Drugs made from the juices of the plants and herbs, mantra therapy or healing through chanting mantras, divine therapy through prayer besides yoga constitutes the bases for the wellness and healing The Ayurveda had eight branches of healing. Medical therapy, ear-nose-throat diseases, surgery, toxicology, psychotherapy, pediatrics, rejuvenation and virility formed the eight branches. While yoga has been noticed and is being practiced all over the world today, herbal medicines have as yet not been accepted as equivalents of Western medicinal products. The West has taken time to accept Ayurveda as an alternative form of treatment but its value has yet to be recognised. What has not been considered seriously in all this debate about the indigenous medicine, as being equal or unequal to some other system is the fact that Ayurveda's immense potential lies unsupported by a sustained, well-orchestrated and well-coordinated publicity? Somehow we have overlooked the material aspect of this knowledge. The Vedas are not simply scriptures, they are also great motivators and concerned with the material well being of the humanity as such. If on the one hand they pray for their worshippers to have long lives they also wish them to possess good physique and developed organs. Such is their concern for men to have "genital organ endowed with vigor" but it must also be proportionate to one's body. Read book VI. LXXII. 1&2. "As the genital organ of male made stout with the power of vital air, becomes capable of impregnation and as proportionate is the organ of well developed man so great stout proportionately be your organ, O Man of the household!"

**The Vedic Society and its people**

The Vedic people have a desire to travel but want their boats to be so constructed that they are both safe and comfortable. Whether one liked or not they wish their boats to be well lighted and to have proper seats. They approve of occupational differentiation hut disagree with the drawing up of perennial social or economic boundary lines. Instead, they wish people to live together in absolute harmony. For them no one is stranger or alien. All come from the same family, that means the entire human race is one therefore territorial division have no value. Forme the most important thing to always keep in mind is that the society that produced the Vedas was being by no means a primitive society. The ancient society had all the trappings of the modem age. There was poverty for which they devised charity as a means to alleviate it. There was greed so they suggested renunciation as a method to overcome it. The common affliction of attachment was frowned upon suggesting that such weaknesses do not behove those that have a spark of the divine in them. What is most interesting is the fact that human nature has remained the same over the period of time. Therefore, logically enough why not its solutions?

There are numerous dreams, which crowd the firmament of their desires. For instance, their dreams include the desire to have sons, their enemies, if any, destroyed, their women folk to remain chaste and faithful and marriages to always succeed. They pray to all elements to help them live in peace. Since everything in Nature is useful they want it never to go against them. This to my mind does not meet the requirements of Pantheism, as the two definitions do not corvey the same meaning.

The fact that the Vedas are a commentary on contemporary society makes them historically significant. Surprisingly, neither in beliefs nor dreams have we, despite a very long gap of time, shown any major change. We continue to dream the way they dreamt and desire to attain the same unattainable goals. Even though in appearance we may not have changed much but surely we have in practice become *degradingly mean, greedy, quarrelsome, fearful and jealous in human relations.* What do we call that?

Let the whole world be a witness to well-being and let all— parents, cows, both animals and humans alike be happy. Let this world be liveable and pleasure giving to all. Let us continue seeing the Creator or the SUD daily. Atharvaveda/ 1/31/4.

Rg. 1/13/2

**The original teacher**

Of all the eternal objects and beings one who is the most important of them all, we should know especially the name of that luminous divine Being. He alone, the divine God glowing fire-like, is capable of giving us eternal happiness by getting us Moksha or freedom from this mortal bond. He alone can grant us life after death so that we could meet our parents once again. He is the First Cause of all knowledge and the original Guru.

Yajurveda 1/2/

**Vow**

O Acharya! Radiating with the glow of knowledge, you know the Truth and are familiar with the vratas like Brambacharya etc., I solemnly take the vow today to follow the vrata of Brahmacharya. Bless me so that I may succeed in pursuing it. 1 for sake the untruth from this moment and accept Truth.

Rg./7/48/2

**Means of instruction**

Let us by living in the company of the intellectuals become intelligent, living in the midst of the best individuals acquire good qualities, and living with the strong possess strength. In the distribution of knowledge let us acquire knowledge from our teachers. By acquiring inner strength let us leave bad habits that are inimical to knowledge.

Rg./1 01117/8

**Social conscience**

One who happens to have one, wishes to double it, and one who has two wants it multiplied by three, and the latter desires to increase it fourfold but the one who already has that much would like to uplift the lot of the poorest in the queue.

Moral: having come to know that there is no end to the desires let the rich start thinking of others that are poor?

Atharvaveda/6/68/3

**Tradition (head shaving)**

The way the expert barber had shaved off the head of a mid-tempered, lustrous and well-behaved child with a sharp razor, in the same style O the Learned ones! Get this child's head too shaved off May this child too in future own cows and horses and be blessed with children.

Atharvaveda/7/50/6

One who offers his money for good work and does not hoard it due to greed he alone gets properties in various ways.

Yajur.724/40

**Tradition (ear piercing ceremony)**

Just as in a war the string in the bow reverberating like a lady secures victory, similarly, this friend-like ear may get connected from all sides with ear-piercing wire and assist the child develop under standing.

Yajurveda 1 34 77

**Foodgrain is life**

I worship the venerable foodgrain that gives life to all and that, which makes an army strong and that which has always been helpful in destroying enemies in the past, present and future.

Yajurveda 112/97

**Education/Medical Knowledge**

It is the duty of the Vaidyas to know, identify and use the herbal medicines like the ones that subside enhanced cough problem, piles, a variety of tuberculosis, mouth and skin diseases that enter the very pores in the skin.

Atharvaveda *115/9/3*

**Nation/The bases of the organisation**

One who is aware of the form of God, he becomes the secure refuge of the Nation, Defence Committee, the armed forces, and the Treasury.

The orthodox view holds that the Vedas were given to the man at the earliest stage of human history but then they carry a message for all times. They enumerate duties toward the conduct of various aspects of life, known as Dharma, and for the next higher stage too they provide *para vidya* or the divine knowledge. The first stage is of a para 1 worldly knowledge, which leads to abhyudaya eventually leading to para vidya-the knowledge of the Brahma. The people of that age developed their culture and civilisation on the basis of Vedic thoughts. They developed agriculture, domesticated cattle, discovered fire and its various uses along with domesticating other cattle discovered the benefits of owning a cow.

**The Vedic Cow or Gau**

There is a long drawn battle on the question whether or not the Vedic people ate Cow. While a few insist that they did others hold the view equally strongly that they did not. One can not be very sure of the of the result.

However, what one must keep reminded of is that Sanskrit words have several meanings. It is here that one learns about the exact meaning of words. We all know that each word has both a lexical as well as contextual meaning but we also learn that poets 1 authors can empower words to give additional meanings too That way all languages have their individual richness. The additional problem in Sanskrit is its extraordinary love for the use of symbols. In the following quotations one will come across the frequency with which these symbols have been used. To the unsuspecting eye these symbols hide their true import. For instance, the word "gau", which so frequently occurs in the Vedic hymns, has been interpreted as cow, speech, the rays of the sun, the sun itself, clouds, water etc.

R. Shamsastry said in a pamphlet published in 1908 that gau (cow), is nothing else but a name applied to the intercalary day, which being the product of four quarter days of four consecutive solar years is to be added to every fourth year making it consist of 366 days. Rg. 1.96.5 mentions that Kutsa Angiras is the first Rishi to have made this discovery. Here is the quote:

The night and day mutually effacing each other's complexion gives nourishment combined together to one infant. Gavam Ayana ceremony is vividly described in the Taittiriya Samhita (Krishna Yajurveda), seventh book, chapter V, and the Baudhayan Srauta Sutra. In the Asya Vamiya Sukta of the Rgveda, we have several verses, which obviously refer to astronomical observations, particularly concerning earth going round the sun.

The one sole (sun) having three mothers and three fathers, stood on high... The twelve-spoked wheel of the true (sun) revolves round the heavens and never tends to decay, seven hundred and twenty children in pairs. Agni, abide in it. (Rg. 1.164. 10-11)

The Vedic seers kept 21 days in each cycle of 4 years are also termed as three footsteps of Vishnu.

The first year after the fourth year of any cycle would commence in the evening and close at midnight after the lapse of 365 1/2 days; the second year would commence at the midnight and close in the morning and end at the midday of the 366th day; the third year would begin in the morning and end at the mid day of 366th day; the fourth year, beginning at the midday would come to a close on the usual evening of the 366th day. The first is called Kali or Ekta, the second year Dvapara or Dvita, the third year Treta or Trita, and the fourth year Krita (complete); Satya Rta, truth, i.e. that which has come into existence. The Vedic Yuga thus consists of four or five years. It is difficult to pinpoint the time when the concept of Yuga underwent a change and its life cycle got extended in terms of years. The Yuga that we know and talk of today, is very different from the Vedic Yuga because that is the creation of the Puranas. The following lines of the Aitareya Brahmana should be read on these lines:

The year Kali is lying down, Dvapara is leaving the bed; standing erect is Treta and Krita happens to walk here and there. (Aitareya Brah. VII. 15)

The knowledge of Vedic constellations can be accessed through Atharvaveda (XIX. 7, 1-5). Gargya is the author of this hymn. It is believed that he discovered these constellations for the first time. Originally these nakshatras were given as twenty-seven. But their number as well as their names and even the order underwent a change in the subsequent years. These changes are evident in their enumeration given in the Taittiriya Brahmana and the Taittiriya Sarnhita Citing the Rgveda X.65.6 Dayanand Saraswati produced evidence that earth rotates on its axis and revolves round the sun. The same concept (Rgveda VIII. 48.13) was later on worked on and explained by Aryabatta 1 in his Aryabhatiya. The planets, revolve round the sun under its directive attraction forces. It may be remembered that the Vedas have their own characteristic cryptic style of expressions capable of being interpreted on the cosmic, ephemeral and spiritual planes.

It would be interesting to read about the time when the earth took the present shape wherein humans could live along with others. The Atharvaveda VIII.21 offers an equation to calculate the time of all that happened 4320000000 years ago. This is one of those hymns, which took considerable time to yield its real import. This equation took time to shed its outer skin to reveal the truth. Read,

"O Man! For your mathematical operations, I, the Almighty Divinity make the one hundred years as one million (by sheer mathematical multiplication) and then place the numbers 4,3,2 before as digits having their value beyond the 'million' digitary zeroes. Let the all-pervading electricity, heat, and all other physical forces without any injury be convenient and comfortable for you".

We have dealt with the developments of mathematics in this write-up already. The developments of astronomy are dependent on mathematical developments. Mathematics is an aid to calculations, and calculations in turn depend on numerals, starting with kham/ zero and ending into Brahma (larger than the largest) i.e. the infinite MaxMuller in his Vedic Hymns, Part 1, p. 241, says that Aditi is "in reality the earliest name invented to express the Infinite, not the Infinite as the result of a long process of abstract reasoning, but the visible Infinite, as it were, to the naked eye, the endless expanse beyond the earth, beyond the clouds, beyond the sky. That was called Aditi, the unbound, the unbounded; one might almost say, but fear of misunderstandings, the Absolute, for it is derived from diti, bond, and the negative particle, and meant therefore originally what is free from bonds of any kind, whether of space or time, free from physical weakness, free from moral guilt. And thus, besides, the mathematical Infinity, God Himself is the Ultimate Infinity, an infinite similarity, and the soul, the lower self is also of infinitesimal dimensions."

Medhatithi gave the following verse (Yajur.XVIII.2) describes the numerals thus:

*"O Agni! May these bricks (ishtlkas), be mine own milch kine; one ten, ten-ten a hundred, ten hundred a thousand; ten thousands an ayuta; ten ayutas a niyuta; ten niyutas prayuta; ten prayutas an arbuda; ten arbudas a nyarbuda; ten nyarbudas a samudra; ten samudras a madhya; ten madhyas an anta; ten antas a parardha. May these bricks be mine dhenus (milch-kine) in yonder world and in this world."*

The numeral parardha is 10 raised to the power 12 is in fact a billion or million-million. It would be difficult to find a parallel to this enumeration in the entire ancient world. It is said that the Vedic texts are fond of describing abstract ideas in the form of numerals. They appear at times mystically cryptic. We have in a certain context an enumeration of the series 4,5,6,7... 19,20 etc. in the Atharvaveda (XIX, 23, 1-17). The numerals from I to 17 are given in respect of mantras and stanzas in the Yajurveda (Ix.31-34). The odd numerals 1,3,5 etc. are given in the Yajurveda XIV. 28-31 and XXVIII. 24. Similarly, multiples of 4 are given in the same Veda in Sukta 24. The very first verse of Atharvaveda refers to all types of combinations from 3 to 7/ or trisaptah.

The basis of geometry is to be discovered in the types of altars recommended for the various types of Yagnas. In the beginning the ancients used only three types of altars. These were ahavaniya, garhapatya and daksina. The ahavaniya altar was square in form. As the time went on, a few postulates were advanced, e.g. (1) the surface area, (A) of the altar should have a relation with the height (P) of the sacrificer (the yajamana), standing erect with arms stretched straight over the head; this unit of measurement was known to be a purusha; i.e.A=c.p. where c is constant a multiple or sub-multiple of the height of the yajamana; it is to the option of the sacrificer to construct the fire altar with square surface, or circular, but the area (A) in both options remain the same. It is easier to construct a square with the area A, but it becomes a geometric problem to construct a circle having the area A. In this context, the old Vedic geometers worked out a relation between the sides of a square (also of a rectangle) and its diagonal (Baudhyayan Theorem), relation between the diameter of a circle and its circumference (value of pi) and area of a circle and its diameter. The authors of the Sutras have given the details of the construction of the fire altars (the Manava Sulba Sutra, the Baudhyayan Sulba Sutra, the Apastamba Sulba Sutra and Katyayana Sulba Sutra). The units of various types of measurements laid the foundation of metrology in the Vedic age. The Vedic verses that inspired the birth and development of geometry and metrology are: Yv.XY.65; Rg.VII.35.7 and Rg. X.130.3.

**Mechanical and Engineering Devices**

As societies develop so do along with them mechanical devices. Human beings are born with only hands and feet but additional tools and devices are needed to make their lives comfortable. Traces of these developments can be seen discovered even in the earliest of cave paintings. This merely goes to show that human ingenuity knows no bounds. If the earlier devices were simple the later ones became both complex and refined. The development of mechanical devices presents a pretty good picture of the growth of civilisation. The Vedas fairly and extensively refer to this mechanisation. For instance, the Rgveda 111.29.1 refers to a simple "churning device to produce line. It was called the adhirnantha," Vishwamitra is the first Rishi in the human history to have introduced this mechanical device. The entire clan of the Angirasas specialised in the art of churning fire through wood sticks. Rishi Atharvan is believed to have written most of the Suktas of the Atharvaveda was the first to have discovered fire. Therefore most of the Vedic verses on fire are written by him. The others who took interest in the advancement of fire-culture are Mayobhuh and Grtsamada. (Yajurvda. XI.21; 22; 28).

The discovery of fire led to the development of fire rituals. These in turn led the development of primitive mechanical devices. Ishtikas or bricks started being used for the building ol'altars. (Yv. X11.21; 31;XV11.2; XXXY.) The Sulba Sutras give details of the sizes and the dimensions of the bricks used. The receptacle for the sacred fire Rg. X. 165.3; Y.27.3; XII.3.35) was known as Agni-dhana, Ladles and cups were known as sruk and camas; reservoirs or vats were known as dronakalasa, the pressing stone were known as gravana, pressing boards were adhisavana; and besides these we have numerous other simple devices too like: Idhma= kindling wood; Barhi = strew; Upvesha or Dhristi= shoveling stick; Sva-rava, Up-rava= sounding holes; Havirdhana = oblation holder; Parisasa= lifting sticks; Vayavya= cups and bowls; Sata= basket; Sthal = cooking pot; Ulukhala, khalva= grinding slate; Musala= pestle; Surpa= winnowing basket; Titau= sieve; Tarhana = bruiser; Carma or Krishnajina= skin or antelope's skin; Putabhrta = receiver of filtrate; Pavitra= strainer; Pinvan= milk bowl etc. (Yv. XVIII. 2021; XX.27; Av.lI.31.1;XII.3.19.iX.6 (1). 12-17; X.9.26) The interesting thing to note is that quite a few devices from this list are still being used in their original form and shape in most of rural India.

The society was inspired for the invention and creation of certain other devices as well. The references to these devices are being given along with their names. Anas or cart (Rg. III.33.9); abhri or spade (Yv. XLI0); asi or knife or razor (Rg.X.86.1 0); asandi or chair or throne (Yv. XIX. 16); itsuna or mat; isu or arrow, ukha or cauldron (Yv. VlI.61); kalas vat or beaker (Yv. VII.42; Av.IX. 1-6); kasipu or cushion of reeds (Av.VI.138.5); kasipu up-barhana or pillow covering (Av.IX.6.10); uparisayana or coverlet (Av.IX.6.9); ksuraor (Av.VI.68.1; Rg. 1.1 66 10) Khanitra or digging instrument (Rg. 1.179.60; graha or cups and ladles (Yv. XVII. 19-20) Jaya or arrow-string (Av. III. 19.8); tantra loom or warp (Rg. X.71.9); tantu or thread (Rg. X.134.5); tantumetam or out spun thread (Yv. XY.53); mayukha peg or pin for weaving tasara, or shuttle for weaving (Rg.X.130.2); dama or string or thread (V.36.1;

1.162.8); also rajju or rope, rasana rein or bridle, sandana bond or halter for horses or coursers.

The sacrifice which is extended on every side by the threads spread out by the worship of the gods for hundred and one years, these our progenitors, who have preceded us, weave it, weaving forwards, weaving backwards, they worship when the world is woven. (Rg.VI.162.8).

The first man spreads out this web, the first man rolls it up; he spreads it above in this heaven; these rays have sat down on the seat (sacrifice); they have made prayers serve as shuttles for weaving. (Rg. IY.37.4)

**Carts, ships and even aeroplane**

The Vedic verses make references to numerous mechanical devices that the ancients either really evolved or they had an idea about. The important thing is an idea. I suspect ideas are responsible for the creation of material goods and services. I have already made a reference to this hunch elsewhere. I now come straight to the actual Vedic text.

The road transport was dependent on carts driven either by horses or bullocks. "Vajins! You are borne by stout horses or coursers mounted on a brilliant car" (Rg.IV.36.3) Vaja is related to the Visvedevah (all-gods), rbhu or ribhksin, to Indra (dealing with space crafts) and Vibhu, or Vibhvan to Varuna (dealing with water ships) (Rg. IV. 33.9). Rbhus are said to construct the firm-abiding, wheel-conducting car (Rg. 33.8). The car made by them traverses the firmament without horses, without reins. (Rg. 36.1). It is this reference, which has been taken as a reference to the planes with which we are familiar. It is also suggested that It was perhaps intended to refer to heavenly bodies moving with tremendous speed in the space.

The water-ships are in fact boats or *nav* as we even now call them. It is possible these boats were of large sizes as well. They carried both passengers as well as cargo.

"Come as on ship, to bear us over an ocean of praises; harness, Asvins, your car. (Rg. 1.46.7)."

Another description of a ship is like this:

"Three nights and three days, Nasatyas, have you conveyed Bhujyu, in three rapid, revolving cars, having one hundred wheels and drawn by six horses, along the dry bed of the ocean to the shore of sea." (Rg. 1.116.4)

The Vedas are not only most venerable religious scriptures but they also contain secular literature containing voluminous and encyclopaedic materials concerning Man and his world.

"When O God (Agni)! Thou, living, vert born from the dry (i.e. wood) then all gods followed thy will. They obtained divinity, the name, serving the immortal Satya-lok-dweller in proper manner. The praises are for thee- the Satya-lok-dweller; the hymns are for thee the Satya-10k dweller. The god made longevity for thee, they performed works. Confer thou wealth, knowing, on him who makes offerings for thee, who is willing to conform to thy laws." Rg 1.68.3-6

Rg. 10, 140, 6 "Generations of human tribes, men, have, with praise, made thee, divine Agni, their purohita for the sake of blessing, thee whose ears hear (all prayers), who are lord of Satya Lok, strong, most great, a lovely sight for all."

Rg. 4, 19, 7: "He filled the dry rivers, which (then) made an outcry like maidens (when being ravished); he saturated deserts and fields which were thirsting; Indra procured milk for the sterile cows, he made married women pregnant."

Rg. 4, 19,7 The adjectives used are agruvah, vakvah refer to the sounds known as manita and rati-kujita made by youthful women at the time of union with their men.

Rg. 9, 101, 2 The Soma juice that, being pressed in the filtering current runs round and forward, is like a horse that decides the victory.

Rg. IV 5.6 "O purifying divine-Agni! Feeble and innocent as I am, you have boldly given a heavy burden to me of exceedingly profound, enjoyable, deep, mighty and tangible wealth of seven elements (metals). These are gold, lead iron, ayam, shyam, silver, and tripu, five tame animals: cow, goat, sheep, horse and man."

Rg. IV 24.9 A man bids small price (his material gains) for an article of great value (spiritual). Lord, the seller, speaks to the buyer; this is still un-purchased and you can have it. But he insists to get full price of he article. The purchaser, however, does not raise the offer, the seller sticks to his demand. And the purchaser on to his offer; both look to their own interests whilst milking the udder. Comment: the reference is to the knowledge of bidding (and auction) in an open market.

Rg. V 62. 7 Their chariot is adorned with gold; its pillars are of iron, and it glitters in heaven like lightening. The sacrificial altar has been established in an auspicious place along with all devotional requisites. May we share the wealth that loads the car seat'?

**Definition of a home** (Rg. VI. 49.7): Be pleased and bestow upon us comfortable home, flawless and impenetrable to wind and rain, and grant us felicity."

"Spacious habitation for our comfort" Rg. VI..50.3

May you, 0 Dawn! Bring me opulence. Unopposed you carry riches, as if on oxen, at your will and pleasure for worshippers. Rgveda VI. 64.5

"Praise lords of cosmic resplendence and plasma, renowned for all glorious energies and enjoyments; one of whom slays evil with his punitive justice, the other, and intelligent by his might, comes to the aid of the pious when he is in difficulties. Rgveda VI.68.3

O radiant Heaven and Earth! The asylum of created beings, you are spacious, manifold, water yielding and lovely. By the decree of the venerable Lord, both of you stand parted, each from each. You are uri-decaying and rich in creative elements. Rg. VI.70.1

Rg. VI. 75. 2-4 "Armed with the bow may we subdue all hostile countries" 2.

"This bow-string, drawn tight upon the bow and making way in battle, repeatedly approaches the ear as if embracing its friend (the arrow) and proposing to say something sweet and loving, as a woman whispers.." 3

May the two extremities of the bow act consentaneously, like a wife and sympathising (with her husband) uphold (the warrior) as a mother nurses her child upon her lap. And may they move concurrently, and harassing the foe scatter enemies." 4

Rigveda VI. 75. 6-9 skilful charioteer guides the strong horses wither-so-everhe wishes.

The horses raising the dust with their hoofs rush on with the chariot, and utter loud neighing. They do not retreat, but trample with their forefeet upon the enemies and destroy them. 7

The guards of the chariot, reveling in the unsavory spoil, are distributors of food, protectors in calamity, armed with spears, resolute, beautifully arrayed, strong in arrows, invincible, of heroic valor, robust and conquerors of numerous hosts.. 9

It is **the whip,** with which the skilful charioteers lash the thighs and scourge the flanks of the steeds, may it urge the horses in battles to march on. 13

**The hand gloves,** imparting protection from the abrasion of the bow-string, surrounds the forearm like a snake with its convolutions: 14

I cover your vital parts with armor. 18.

When the rain, the sustainer of all, is sent down by you, and the young rivers, the maidens, un-dried, diffuse fertility around without obstruction. Rgveda VI. 67. 7

May You; 0 Dawn! Bring me opulence. Unopposed you carry riches, as if on your oxen, at you will and pleasure for worshippers. Rig 64. 5

Rg. VI. 53. 3-5-0 resplendent nourisher, urge even the niggard to give us liberally, and make the heart of the miser grow soft. 3

O resplendent nourisher, make the roads comfortable for the passage of the provisions; drive away all hurdles and obstructions, so that our holy works may be accomplished. 4

O wise Nourisher! Penetrate with an awl the hearts of the avaricious churls and so render them complacent toward us. 5

May you destroy the voracious instinct of greed, for verily, it is wolf. Rg. VI. 51. 14

Rg. VIA7.20 We enter the life-desert, where there is not a single footprint of the missing cattle. This vast earth has become the savior of the murderers.

Rg. V1.47.23 From the Public Treasury Officer we have received ten vehicles, ten purses of coins, garments, ample food, and ten lumps of gold.

The chief of the Trust has given to the civic guards ten vehicles with extra horses, and to the preceptors a hundred cows. Rg. VI.47.24

Rg. VI.39.4 This radiant sun illumines the non-radiant worlds. He pervades many dawns with true lusture. The Sun, the benefactor of men, moves in a chariot drawn by horses, harnessed by praises laden with riches.

Rg. V1.28.3 Let not the cows run away from us, let no thief carry them away; let no hostile weapon fall upon them. The entire Sukta 28 is about cows and their welfare, upkeep ownership etc.. Also see Rg. 1.135.8 cows as wealth that no thief could steal, 1.147.3 cows as philosophies-both mundane and spiritual; 1.160.3 as abadhya 1.160.6 cow as earth, 1.173.2 cow as intellect 1.174.8 cow as speech or gau 1.186.4 cow as speech or dhenu.

Rg. VI. 28.8 0 Lord revered, all-pervading, the sovereign of all, on both of us, rich and poor, seated in chariots may you bestow charming divine damsels, and twenty divine cows, a gift hard to assure from any other source.

Rg. VI.25.6 Amidst the two disputants, that one acquires wealth, whose priests invoke Lord at worship in conflicts against powerful adversaries or in contention to gain dwellings among one's own relations.

Rg. 1.162.9 health and hygiene 1.191.10 cleanliness! washing of wounds! medicine etc. 1.191.10 sunrays as anti-dote of poison,

**Fear of being left out**

Rg. VI.1. 19 Relinquish us **not,** 0 adorable Lord! To the group of persons neither devoid of courage; nor to deficient clothing; not to such destitution; leave us not to hunger or to a fiend; expose us not. 0 observer of truth, to evil, whether in the house or in the forest.

**Family values (Rg. VIIA.7)**

Wealth is competent to the acquittance of debt; may we be masters of our permanent possessions. He is not real offspring, who is begotten by another (for verily, he would like to return to his own house Rg. VII.4.8). May you not give a long rope to a blockhead.

**Ceremonial halls with measured pillars**

Rg. VII. 35.7 May the moon be the source of our happiness; may the prayers promote our happiness; may the clouds be source of our happiness. May the sacred work and worship be source of our happiness. May the sacred work and worship be source of our happiness; may the measured lengths of the pillars of ceremonial hall be conducive to our felicity; may the well-grown herbs be our happiness; may the altar be raised for our happiness.

Rg. VII.35.14 May the cosmic suns, the cosmic winds, and the planets of abode be gratified by this new hymn, which we now repeat; may all the divines of celestial and terrestrial worlds, progeny of cows and those, who perform worship, hear our invocations.

**Religious fanaticism**

Rg. VII. 93. When two large defiant hosts, emulous in corporal vigor, contest, may you destroy the godless in favor of the god-fearing and in favor of the person who pours out devotional sentiments?

**About tradition of learning**

Rg. VII. 29.4 These ancient sages, whose praises you have been listening to, are verily, gems among common men.

The phallus-worshippers are taken to be unchaste, lustful,. and non-bramhcharis. Reference to phallus worship are to be found in Rg. X.99.3; 1.105.8; X.27.19; 33.3.

*According to* Nirukta. IY. 19 the word shishna/phallus is derived from sooth: meaning *to pierce.*

**The shape of the chariot**

Rg. VIII.I. 24 Chariot wrought of gold and yoked with two horses, peacock-tailed, white backed, may you come-O God.

Chariots were driven both by horses and bullocks. Rg. VIII. 48.5

It would be interesting to enumerate how many types of metals they used or were familiar with. Similarly, what was their knowledge about the precious stones, the jewellery, and the variety of clothes they wore and what their preference sex-wise of these clothes was?

# Chapter - 6

# Vedic Knowledge: Vignettes for Self-Interpretation

'O learned man! Follow the Veda and the law of Dharma' Yajur ch.3./57

"O Lord of resplendence, were there a hundred heavens or a hundred earths-not even a thousand suns could be equal to you at your manifestation nor could both the worlds of heaven and earth be equal to your splendor." Rgveda VIII.70.5

"May the five types of men, born to offer (the butter of) affection, and eager to perform the sacrifice, be pleased with my discharge of the function as an invoker; may the earth preserve us from the troubles that come from heaven.

"May you, spinning the thread of divine knowledge, follow the splendid light of the illuminator, and protect the pathways well...

"The great river of life-conflicts flows alone, be alert; rise up, cross over, my friends; here let us leave those who are wretched and hence unhappy; may we cross over (this river) to secure auspicious boons." Rgveda X.54.5-7

The present write-up is addressed to those who have a very vague idea of how advanced the ancient Vedic society was. In the modern high-tech world people have little time and even less patience to go deeper into any text even when it might have enormous value for contemporary guidance. Indeed, it is no longer considered necessary to read scriptures or may be it is even considered un-intellectual, if not *infra dig,* to try discovering any particular sense in reading them. Perhaps it is the job of a priest who is paid for his services to read the same out in bits and pieces on ceremonial occasions. Indian historians too took time to discover meaning into them and that too when the Western scholars had started using the Vedas and their text for purposes other than those of scholarship. One must admit that it is the West that initially led the path back to our glorious past and furnished insight to find for us gems that had been lying hidden in the obscure homes of neglected venerable scholars. The Vedas are correctly regarded as repositories of all knowledge and acme of ancient Indian wisdom. In them lie the seeds (at times the finished products) of our modern knowledge. For instance, there is hardly any branch of knowledge viz. music, astronomy, physics, modern mathematics, yoga, alternate medicine, philosophical systems, literature, grammar and prosody etc. whose foundations cannot be traced back to them. Not unlike Greece in Europe all sources of Indian knowledge can be traced back to the Vedas. Not only the dimensions but the depth of human knowledge is readily available in the Vedic text. For instance; few know that the binary system, which gave birth to computer sciences, has its origins in the Vedas. The yoga and the alternate medicine which are the current rage in the West, can also be traced back to the Vedas. True, we have outgrown many of the discoveries and findings. But there are numerous areas of knowledge where we are still groping in the dark alongside the ancients. In some ways the contemporary astrophysics has brought us back to the Nasdiya sukta to compare notes. Two Indian scientists wielding sophisticated mathematics are busy dissecting and analysing the traditional meditation chanting sound "Om". The Om team has already published six monographs in academic Journals, which plumb certain acoustic subtlety *of Om* that they say is the *Divine Sound.* Be that as it may, we share with them the desire to learn and discover. Their papers are published in the International Journal Computer Sciences and Network Security. The researchers explain; "It may be very fast, several cycles per second, or; it may be slower, several seconds for each cycling of (the) Om mantra or it might become extremely slow, with the mmmmm sound continuing in the mind for much longer periods but still pulsing at that rate." The important technical fact is that no matter what form of Om one chants at whatever speed, there is always a basic Omness to it." These scientists belong to an Engineering College of Technology in Maharashtra. While one is the Principal and the other is Assistant professor but they apply a mathematical tool called wavelet transforms to a digital recording of a person chanting this mantra. One is named Ajay Anil Gurjar and the other is A. Ladhake. (Read HT. dated May 5, 2010).

The main question is that there are areas where the ancient knowledge is available in finished form ready to be used; while in certain other areas we have moved away from the original stipulations. It always happens with knowledge. For instance, Lord Bacon is known today not for his initial efforts in the area of refrigeration but for his incomparable short essays. Even his Novum Organum is less known and definitely not consulted for new information. The fact that Aristotle gave us his *theory* of Golden Mean will always be regarded as a solid contribution in socio-ethical behavior but in other areas his contributions have lost their sheen. In the case of the Vedas there are numerous areas wherein nothing has changed much and may be their value has increased by leaps and bounds such as the Yoga or the alternate medicine, but there are areas wherein things may have changed unrecognisably. Let the reader judge on the basis of a few select quotes the continuity of Vedic knowledge.

To me it is important that the Vedas contain so much knowledge but what appears to be even more so is the fact that almost unconsciously we have been living them. All the samskars, rituals and other practices that form the basics of contemporary Indian living can be traced back to the Vedas. If the Vedas showed us the way to remain healthy via yoga and Ayurveda they also initiated us into the fundamentals of logic and philosophy. I am surprised why a few well-meaning persons accuse the Vedic scholars of being sectarian and advocating partisan knowledge besides being narrow in their approach about a common inheritance. The Vedas are part of our common heritage. For instance, read a gambler's lament (Rgveda.) and note that all gamblers irrespective of their nationality or time meet the same fate as this Vedic gambler does. All societies condemn debauches and women of doubtful character and yet they are not able to change human nature. It is difficult to imagine of a society which is at once progressive and yet very ethical.

The Vedas have universal appeal and carry a message for the entire humanity. One must acquire the right attitude to discern both the overt as well as the implied meaning in the Vedic text. In his book An Interpretation of India's Religious History (New York; 1911) Robert A. Hume declares, *"Hinduism is too philosophical to be a religion"* and its philosophy "over weighted on the side of intuition because of its association with religion." While the Indians do employ logic for arguing their case, they do insist at the same time on the intuitive experience of the Reality.

An attempt has been made to delineate the ancient Vedic society in the words of the Rishis themselves. The interested reader is invited to read the Vedic text and interpret it himself without any guidance. The reader is expected to compare the modern Indian society with that of the past and decide in what respect we are different from those ancient people. Surprisingly, our contemporary society continues to tread the footsteps of the ancients even as the latter continue to be as modern as us.

The ancients regarded four basic moral values for all to follow—they are Dharma, artha, kaam and moksha.

In the beginning, there was the Divine Desire *(mallaso retalt pratltamam vadasit)* Rg. X.129. 4 see also Atharva. 3/29.7

Since then a host of desires have been added to the list. Examine the text.

**Desires**

Yajur Ch. 3./37 "O God, friendly to the wise, do Thou protect my offspring. O worthy of praise do Thou protect my cattle. 0 God above all suspicion protect my food. O God through Thy grace, in unison with the three life-giving winds Pran, Apan and Vyan May I be rich in offspring, well-mannered with men, a hero with the heroes and strong with wise and invigorating deeds..

Yajur Ch. 3/ 57 "We worship the Omnipresent... who augments our physical, spiritual and social forces. Through His Grace may we be released from the mortal coil without the agony of death, as naturally as a ripe cucumber is from its stem."

On Mukti Yajur Ch. XVIII, 29 "May life succeed through the service of God and the sages.... O Sages, May we, freed from the pangs of the birth and death attain to happiness of final beatitude.

May we become the true sons of God. May we be yoked to noble deeds and truthful speech!"

**On rebirth**

"I get back after rebirth mind, life, breath, soul eyes and ears" Yajur Ch. 4/15.

**Sexual union with women from other castes**

In normal circumstances any union other than the one approved through marriage was unwelcome. However, exceptions did exist.

Of the numerous examples, a few are:

Permission was accorded to those who indulged in sexual union with women from other castes. Examples, for instance, Vidur was worshipped, Mahabharata, sabha. 52.3; see Sabha, *19/9,* which says Mahatma Gautam had relations with a Shudra and from Kaushinari he had sons.

He embraces beautiful nights and with swift movements. He encompasses the universe by His mysterious power. Visible all over is He. "All desirous of his favor diligently offer Him worship three times a day (morning, noon, evening). May all adversities vanish." Rg. VIII. 41.3

The worldliness of the Aryans, "He gives us riches like our father. He is so powerful that He can make anyone sovereign at His will. He the strong and bounteous Lord, give us immense wealth, cows and horses." Rgveda. VIII. 52.5

**Victory over Enemy**

Yajur Ch. 2. 7/75 May 1 achieve victory like the victory of Fire and Moon. May 1 speed onward with the materials of war. May Fire and Moon, drive off him who hates us drive off the man whom we detest. May I remove that sinful enemy by warlike, military skill and equipment. May I achieve victory like the Airand lightening. May lachieve happiness through the impulse of knowledge used for the acquisition of supremacy. May air and lightening properly employed, drive off him who hates us, drive off the man whom we dislike. I purify this person by the light o knowledge,

### Proud Possessions

The proud possessor of riches displays them as: "Hundreds O bamboos, hundreds of tanned skins, hundred bunches of grass, and four hundred red-haired mares are in my possession". Rg. VIII. 55.3

Yajur Ch. 3/ 43 "May we in this world get cows, goats, sheep and abundant food in our houses. I come to you for safety and quietude. May I acquire mundane and celestial joy and felicity."

Rg. VIII. 46, 26 "He, the sun, comes speedily mounted on horses and invested with thrice seven times seventy (3x7x70=1470) golden rays of morning. He (the sun) comes to you, the Lord, with these healinig herbs; and learned priests offer our invocations to you, the acceptor of loving devotion, - bright and pure."

Rg. VIII. 46.31 "He calls hundred camels (to be donated) when the herd has been grazing in the woods, and two thousand white cows from the white herds."

Rg. VIII.48.5 "I have drunk these glorious drops of divine elixir which give me freedom. Closely they knit together my joints as bullocks drawing together a chariot falling in pieces. Let them protect my foot from slipping on the way. May they deliver me from sickness."

"He gives riches to us as our father. He is so powerful that He can make anyone sovereign at His will. May He, the strong and bounteous Lord, give us immense wealth, cows and horses." Rg. VIII.52.5

### God rewards His worshippers/devotees

Rg. VIII. 92. 8 "O wielder of bolt of justice smiter of enemies, truthful drinker of the elixir of loving devotion, we know the value of the reward, given by you to all your faithful."

Ch. VI. 2 "O, King, thou art our leader; thou put teth upon the path O rectitude, even the leaders of a high order. Know thou this art of government"!

"God, the Creator will rule over thee. Just as the state officials anoint thee with sweet juices and flower-laden herbs, so should the subjects do.

The first duty is to undertake the spread of knowledge and the administration of justice.

The second duty is to propagate religious truths. The foremost duty is to strengthen thy rule over the Earth."

**The Vedas (Yajur. Ch.VI. 12)**

Says "O learned person! The diffuser of delight, behave not crookedly like a serpent, or proudly like a fool or ferociously like a tiger. Food is ready everywhere. Tread on the path of truth and rectitude, just as shelterless persons without any conveyance feel happy when they reach a stream of water."

**When to marry?**

Yajur. Ch.VI. 13 "O girls just as women, endowed with noble qualities pure and highly educated are married to their deserving husbands, and serve them faithfully; and educated husbands are married to worthy wives, so should ye be married; and so shall be joined in wedlock."

Yajur. Ch.VI. I6 "O sinner, demons pay homage to you. Get out evil spirited, I stand before such a devil for dishonoring him, rather I chastise such a fellow with great disgust. I carry such a Satan with great disgust."

Yajur. Ch.VI. 20 "Just as Udan breath permeates all our organs, so do thou O general shine forth in the battle field leading all your warriors. Let thy diverse forces in uniform gather together in large numbers. O general, may all warriors behave friendly toward thee for thy protection. May the mother, father and relatives be pleased to see thee moving in the midst of warriors."

Now their ***travel across oceans***:

Yajur. Ch. VI. 21

"O disciple, a student in the science of government. sail in oceans in steamers, fly in the air in aeroplanes. know god and the Creator through the Vedas, control thy breath through yoga, through astronomy know the functions of the day and night, know all the Vedas through their constituent parts!

Through astronomy, geography, and geology go thou to all the different countries of the world under the sun. Mayest thou attain through good preaching to statesmanship and artisanship, through medical science obtain knowledge of medicinal plants, through hydrostatics learn the different uses of water, through electricity understand the working of ever-lustrous lightening. Carry on my instructions willingly. May the smoke of thy yajna and military machines reach the sun. and may the flames go up to heaven; and may thou cover the earth with the ashes, the residue of thy yajna."

Yajur. Ch. VI. 22

"O praiseworthy king, do not destroy canals, wells, tanks, corn fields and forests. Protect us at every place."

Yajur, Ch. XX. 45.

"He who rears the trees by erecting strong barriers round hem, creating contact with the soul, like one under orders, conduces to our happiness, fills the treasure of fame. as one fills the belly with sacrifice, performs sacrifice with edible objects like honey and butter, and tastes them well remains immune from disease."

**Why pay taxes?**

Yajur, Ch. VI. 30

"For me full of splendor, in a civilised manner, pay open-heartedly tax, which is highly useful, is levied on all your products, which conduces to efficient administration, which is utilised for the advancement of industries and improving the cattle breed. O my subjects, ye who take interest in the welfare of your king deserve to be welcomed by us. Please me by paying your taxes."

"O botanist, just as medicinal herbs, rendered fit for the yajnas protect all, so do we for sacrifice hail thee, the remover of diseases, and the assuager of aftliction." Yajur, Ch. V. 42

Yajur. Ch. 5. 43

"Just as I gaze not at the sun, so shouldst thou."

**On Education and Teacher Training**

Yajur. Ch. 3/28

"O God the guardian of the primordial Vedas, make me, like the son of a learned person, endowed with different capacities for the acquisition of knowledge, an imparter of instruction and a fulfiller of the aim of education."

Rgveda./8/4/15

O Guru! We wish always to remain under your guidance because it is you who impart that knowledge which improves our intellect. It is you, O most admirable teacher! Who is capable of removing all ignorance, kindly educate us.

Yajur Ch. XII.7

"Return to me, thou ever-returning learned person, with life, literary luster, progeny and treasure, with wisdom that explains all departments of knowledge, with intellect and abundance."

Yajur Ch. XII.4

"O Learned person thou hast action, contemplation and learning for thy head. Gayatri is thy eye. Brihat and Rathantra are thy wings. Rgveda is thy soul. Meters are thy limbs. The hymns of the YajurVeda are thy name. The vamdevya saman is thy body. The yagnas are thy hooves. Thou art high souled, and master of noble qualities; acquire knowledge and attain to high position".

Yajur Ch. XII.45

"O Learned persons, may all the aged and young living at present in the world acting as teachers and preachers impart spiritual knowledge to the disciple filled with noble resolve. May thy teachers grant thee a dignified position. Shun unrighteousness and follow Dharma, and stick to it particularly."

Yajur Ch. XII. 49 & 51

"O Learned person, with the light of knowledge thou duly sing the praise of waters beyond the light of the Sun and those that are beneath it here. Thou well preachest knowledge to the students who are experts in the art of eloquence."

"Teach him while receiving education praiseworthy eloquence, eternal knowledge of the Vedas and the Rgveda, granter of success in all our actions."

**On wives of the learned**

Yajur Ch XII. 55

"The wives of the learned persons, with beautiful bodies and tender limbs, having good cooks and servants to milch the cows being reborn with knowledge, cook well-prepared diet, in this beautiful domestic life. They observing the lives of the Brahmcharya give happiness to their husbands in past, present and future, in all pleasant domestic tasks and give birth to good off spring."

**Domestic life of the learned**

Yajur Ch. XII.61, "The learned woman, calm like Earth, preserves in the womb, like a mother, the healthy beautiful son."

Yajur Ch. V & 65

Yajur Ch. XII.

"O husband, calm like earth, I fasten on thy neck the unbreakable binding noose of pure married life The same do I fasten unto me for thee, I enter this life of longevity. Let no one of us disobey the law of domestic life, Eatthou Young man this food, which I eat. O wives, the embodiment of virtue, follow strictly the duties of married life. J give thee foodstuffs for thy prosperity!"

**On lady teachers**

Yajur. Ch. XXI. 54

"O Student! Just as mother, mistress, preaches these three ladies full of glow and knowledge, in this world full of wealth, for the soul aspiring after wealth accept as their pupils, the three girls, superior, medium and low in intellect, and just as teacher and preacher; laudable and earned ladies like energy and power in the middle of the navel; cultivate the mind, and just as all procure these things, so shoudst thou, be conversant with all transactions."

**Purpose of education & the Performance of the Yagna**

Yajur. Ch. VI. 25

"O virgins, just as we live with our husbands and perform havan so do yeo Just as we impart instruction unto you for mental peace, for discriminating between virtue and vice, for spreading happiness, and acquiring brilliance like the sun, so do you uplift the domestic life for the diffusion of all kinds of happiness!"

O disciples! Write pleasing verses, be innovative after proper reflection, build oar-driven boats grow a variety of crops and make lethal weapons for the destruction of your enemies, keep burning the yagnic fire, and continue performing deeds for the welfare of others.

Yajur Ch. XI. 2

"We, the Yogis, with full concentration of mind, according to our resources, in this world created by the Supreme Lord, should strive to acquire His Light, for our happiness."

Yajur Ch. XI. 3

'"The master of the Yoga having concentrated his mind on God, should with his intellectual tivate noble qualities, which spread the light of knowledge and add to our happiness. God guides them who advance scientific knowledge."

Rgveda /3/60/2

"May you the disciples! Extend the horizons of the intellect like the ones who with their intellect and *actions cause the rainy clouds to come by performing yagnas* and cover the earth with greenery; and like those intellectuals who after meditation having identified necessary qualities and attributes, invent."

Yajur Ch. IX.20 "For the attainment of full knowledge, noble deeds', for the attainment of happiness, religious life; for the attainment definite object, activity, for the attainment of wisdom, the habit of reading and teaching, for retention of knowledge, truthful speech; for arithmetical measurement of the day, the science of arithmetic; for checking the waste of time in infatuation, a word of wisdom; for the fool, who revels in vice, a word of caution; for the degraded, wicked soul, advice to ward of evil deeds', for the strong person amongst the low and despicable, speech revealing the nature of things', for the attainment of God, the Lord of the universe, the knowledge of yoga; for the king, the knowledge of all affairs, are essential."

Yajur Ch. 1.28 "O Almighty Lord! Thou hast suspended in space near Moon and Sun this Earth which is full of foods tuffs and producer of all life-giving substances for the living creatures. May the learned of refined intellect, full of happiness, residing upon it the well wisher of all, abiding by Thy eternal laws, conquer all foes waging severe tight with the aid of warriors and arms, and thus attain to power. O learned person! Just as from times immemorial the dutiful have been acquiring wealth, so do thou full of wealth worship God. Let evil be eradicated."

Yajur Ch. 2. 1

"O Yagna! Thou art being performed in a well dug place, thou are rarefied by fire and attracted by air. For the sake of Haven I consecrate the oblations agreeably rectified by ghee. Thou art an altar for taking oblations high up into the space; I erect thee and consecrate thee with ghee. Just as water in the space contributes to the purification of material objects, so do I carefully cleanse the oblations to be put into the fire ladles."

Yajur Ch. 26

"O Yagna, thy name is sky, thou art full of butter. Be confirmed in this decorated place with thy lovely glory. O yagna thy name is space; thou art full of water. Oh Yagna, thy name is Earth; thou art the giver of longevity .... May necessary articles be placed in the holy yagna. O God protect these articles. May Thou protect this yagna; may Thou protect the worshipper; may Thou protect me the conductor of the yagna!"

Yajur. Ch. X.6

"In this world created by God, ye, male and female students, engaged in study, lead a life of high morals."

Yajur. Ch. X,14

"O king, ascend the zenith. May thou obtain the knowledge conveyed in the Pankti Shakvari and Rewati verses of the Sam Veda, the thirty-three-fold praise-song, three divisions of time, both seasons; Winter and dews, Arithmetic, the science of nine digits; thirty-three gods, the study through Brahmacharya and riches. Cast aside the head of thief."

Yajur. Ch. XXI. 43

"Just as a learned person keeps company with the teacher and the preacher, who ever derive in a nice manner the useful things like milk and greasy butter from a goat, and surely eats them before they are snatched by the wicked, and asked for by a *chaste* beggar woman.. "

**On Engineering**

Yajur. Ch. X, 19

"O royal skilled engineer, construct sea-boats, propelled on water by our experts, and aero-planes, moving and flying upward, after the clouds that reside in the mid-region, that fly as the boats move on the sea, that fly high over and below the clouds. Be thou, thereby, prosperous in this world created by the Omnipresent God, and flier in both air, and lighting."

"O Soul, master of physical organs, thou hast fine speech, pleasure and restful peace. Thou art soft like wool. Skilled engineers, with the use of air and electricity, through their useful workmanship prepare conveyances that move in water, overshadowed by space. Just as learned persons amass wealth for the soul, that roams in space between the earth and sky, is contemplative and eager for supremacy; and obtain these good things, so shouldest thou, 0 sacrificer be conversant with all dealings."

Yajur, Ch. XI. 62

"O woman, protect the valuable ancestral property of thy glorious husband, who loves thee, is the guardian of the people, and master of various nice food stuffs."

**Dislike for the undeserving members of society**

Yajur, Ch. XI.78. "O king, devour the burglars, with both tusks, destroy the robbers with thy teeth. With both thy jaws, eat up the thieves and cheats."

Yajur. Ch. XIJ. 84

"just as a thief steals into the cattle-fold, by breaking through the wall, as do all well-known healing plants come out of earth tearing it asunder, and drives out from the body whatever malady there is."

**Qualities of a king**

Yajur. Ch. XII. 33

"He alone is fit to rule, who spreads knowledge, and administers justice, kills the foes, roars like the lightening, protects the forest trees, wages battles on earth, is expert in statesmanship, and endowed with noble qualities, speedily preaches religion, keeps with his power under control, the Sun and Earth, and spreads around his luster."

Yajur Ch. IV 34

"O learned man, Lord of the Earth! Thou art my gracious helper. Fly happily to all stations in our overhauled airplane. Doing so, let not thieves, robbers and malignant opponents meet Thee. Fall like a falcon upon such foes. Go to the houses of the religious persons, situated in distant parts of the world"

**On debauchery**

Yajur. Ch. VIII. 48

O irreligious husband, I warn thee against cohabitation with the pure and noble wives of others. O evil-minded husband, I desist thee from approaching the tenderhearted wives of others. O ill-intentioned husband are keep thee away from going near the philanthropic wives of others', O unsteady husband, are censure thee again and again for teasing the delightful Wives of others. O stone hearted husband, I separate thee from the company of sweet- tongued wives of others. O ignorant husband full of virility, I prohibit thee from having sexual intercourse in day's light and sunbeams."

**Service of maid servant/ cook:**

Yajur. Ch. XI. 56

"O venerable, ever-happy wife, utilise the services of a maidservant who, full of love, with lovely looks, noble-minded, cooker of nice meals, places the cooking pan in thy hands.

Cast aside *a debauchee who indulges in conversation with the dissolute;* a ridiculer fond of derision; an illegitimate Virgin's son; addicted to carelessness."

Yajur. Ch. XXX. 9

"O God, cast aside a lover, who cohabits with another's wife a paramour having illicit connection with a domestic woman; an unmarried elder brother suffering from the pangs of passion; younger brother who has married before his elder to inherit the property; husband of a younger sister whose elder sister has not been married; for. ilterior motives of greed; a licentious adorned woman who pretends for penance; a lustful go between woman bent on arousing passions', a by-sitter for garrulity, an obstinate man who insists upon acceptance; and him who offers presents in the shape of bribe, to gain strength."

Yajur Ch. XXX. 10

"O God, keep aside a hunchback bent on destruction; a dwarf, given to carnal pleasures', a bleary-eyes man as a gate-keeper: a blind man for sleep; and a deaf man devoid of righteousness. O God create physician for purifying our body with the eradication of disease; an astronomer for the advancement of knowledge; an inquisitive man full of craving for knowledge; an extra-inquisitive man for desire of extra knowledge; and a question-solver for establishing moral law."

Yajur. Ch. XXX. 13

"O God, cast aside a thievish hearted man bent on violence, a slanderer bent on homicide. O God, create a religious-minded man for discrimination; an ascetic as a wise counselor; a servant for strength; an observer of celihacy for plenty of progeny: a sweet speaker for affection; a cavalier for safety; a collector of taxing *for* enjoying full happiness; a talented man spreading knowledge for highest happiness."

"Yajur. Ch. XXX. 14

"O God, a mentally angry man, blasing like red hot iron; an invader full o fire; an assailant destined for grief; an embarrassed woman bent on violence.

Yajur Ch. XXX. 17

"O God, drive away a sweeper's son bent on ferocity; a dissatisfied person given to back-biting; a slothful person destined to poverty; a shameless person bent on losing wealth; a destroyer and splitter bent on violence."

Yajur. Ch. XXX. 18

"O God, drive away a gambler, friend of the dice-king; one who has evil designs for murdering cows; a cow-killer for gallows; one who for hunger goes to a man who is cutting up a cow; a leader of meat eaters bent on misdeed; the son of a depraved person befriending a sinner."

Read the following to take a decision whether or not cow was approved for killing.

**Suggestion: do not kill the cow instead kill forest cow (neelgai):**

Yajur. Ch. XIII. 49

"O sagacious king; in this world, don't harm this bull, the giver of thousands of comforts, the source of immense milk, and worthy of protection. Harm not in God's creation, the cow, the giver of milk for mankind and innocent in nature. I point out to thee the forest cow. With her destruction add to thy prosperity and physical strength in the midst of vast space and under God's guidance. Let the wild forest-cow be put to gnef by thee. Let thy foe, whom we dislike, be put to grief."

**In the next hymn camel is allowed to be killed**

Yajur. Ch. XIII. 50

O learned king, don't kill the two-footed men and birds, and four-footed cattle, the source of comforts. Don't kill the sheep that covers our bodies with blankets, and is foremost worthy of protection among God's creatures. I point out to thee the forest camel. With his protection add to thy prosperity and physical strength. Let the wild, uncontrollable camel be put grief by thee. Let thy foe, whom we dislike be put to grief."

**Their dislike for predatory animals and mass violence is shown thus**

"Let injurious animals like the lions and others that eat flesh be destroyed. Let murderous crowds of men that destroy others like a powerful weapon be killed. Let virtuous rulers protect us from these animals and make us comfortable."

**On the Caste/Varna.**

Dasyus or dasas and the Aryans were two distinct groups in the Vedic period. The non-Aryans worshipped phallus (Rgveda. 136) and differed in language also from the Aryans. The Aryans on the other hand were fire-worshippers.

The hymn (Rgveda. X.90; & VIII. 35. J6-18) deals with the caste/class; but there is no evidence to suggest that these were hereditary. The priest is referred to as kavi, vipra, karu, vedhas and the warrior as rajanya and not as kshatriya Professions were not hereditary therefore we get a hymn which implores Indra that he should be made a ruler over men, failing which a priest and failing that a rich man (Rgveda III. 43.5) marriages between different castes was common such as Atri was married to a Kshatriya princess. Agastya's wife Lopamudra too came from the Kshatriya family etc. However, this kind of marriage continued for quite sometime.

Yajurveda defines the castes/their status and qualities thus: "Ch. XI Y.9 the Brahman is foremost in the society, like the head in the body. His force lies in the protection of humanity through knowledge, religion and austerity. The Kshatriya is a class amongst men. His power lies in affording happiness in humanity through justice, humility and strength. The Vaishya is another class, who amasses foodstuffs. His strength lies in becoming the lord of riches. The artisan, Shudra is another class of men, whose strength lies in doing hard work."

Yajur. Ch. XXIX. 44

"Warriors with arms in hand, soldier, swiftly along conveyances, trample upon the foes devoid of friendship, with their forefeet."

Yajur. Ch. XXX. 5

"O God, create a Brahman, who knows the Veda and God, for the propagation of knowledge of God and the Veda; a Kshatriya prince for the safety of kingdom; a Vaishya for rearing the cattle; a Shudra for hard labor and service. Cast aside the thief, who steals in darkness; the destroyer of heroes, who passes his days in Jail, the eunuch mentally disposed to licentiousness, the dacoit bent on looting and harming people; the harlot full of lust; and the bard disposed to abuse."

Yajur, Ch. XXX. 6

"O God, create for dance a bard; for song a public dancer; for duty one administers justice; for sweetness a panegyrist; for pleasure a wife-loving husband; for dexterity a car-builder; for firmness a carpenter.

Yajur. Ch. XXX.7

O God, create for penance a potter's son; for sharpening intellect an artificer: for beauty a jeweler; for welfare a sower; for arrows a maker of shafts: lor destructive weapons a bowyer; for victory a bowstring maker; for control a rope-maker. Cast aside a hunter bent upon murder; and a dog rearer the helper of the murderer."

Yajur. Ch. XXX. 11

"O God, create an elephant- keeper for deep walking; a horse-keeper for speed; a cowerd for nourishment; a shepherd for manliness; a goatherd for enhancing keenness, a ploughman for growing more food; a preparer of Soma for obtaining essence of medicines and food; a house-guard for weal; a possessor of wealth for well-being; and an obedient attendant for supervision." "O God, create a yogi for the practice of yoga; an alleviator of sufferings for welfare; a mechanic skilled in running ships; car and aero-planes for going to high and low places; a thoughtful person for welfare of the body; a well-behaved wife of the noble deeds for a Brahmachari; a wealthy lady for accepting land."

Yajur. Ch. XXX. 16

"O God, create the son of a Nishada for managing small tanks; a dry fish - clearer for reed-beds, a celibate who controls passions for uneven impassable places; a boatman for crossing watery places; an engineer for constructing bridges over rivers."

Yajur. Ch. XXX. 12

"O God, create a wood-bringer for Light; a fire-kindler for brightness; a be sprinkler for horse's path; a high steward for highest happiness, a master of sorts of knowledge, for the sight of the learned; a distributor of knowledge, for the benefit of humanity; a magnanimous person who contributes to the happiness of all, a washerwoman for cleanliness; an affectionate wife for domestic happiness. 0 God cast aside a wicked person bent on teasing, murdering, and offering opposition."

"O God, create a man of iron determination, for the implementation of vow; a loud-voiced man for proclamation; a comprehensive speaker for establishing propriety of conduct; a mute for unending lawless discussion; a lute-player for festivals: a conch-blower for calling neighboring and distant people; a forest guard, for the forest protection; and drive a way a creator of uproarbent on uttering frightening sounds; a flute-blower intendingsing ingsongs of lamentation; a forest-burner contemplating the destruction of jungles."

Their calendar which continues to be used by all in India.

Yajur. Ch. 2.122

"May the mighty space unite with oblations and butter. May it unite with the 12 month of the year and 8 life-giving agencies and vital breaths. Let the sun be harnessed with all its rays. May pure water rain whenever duly consecrated oblations are offered."

Yajur Ch. 3/6

"The earth revolves in the space. It revolves with its mother water in its orbit.. it moves round its father, the Sun."

Yajur Ch. 3/9

"Just as God reveals for humanity all the four Vedas - the store-house of knowledge, so does fire in the shape of lightening exist in the space, and become the source of rain and knowledge. Justas God through the Vedas displays all sciences, fire and lightening so does the Sun develop our physical and spiritual forces. Sun illuminates all objects. God is resplendent. This is the manifestation of His Glory." On getting pure water from heating it read hymn 16 in Ch. 3 of the

Yajur "The learned knowing the eternity, luster, thousand-fold service and usefulness of Fire, get pure water from it."

Yajur Ch. XVIII 40

"Moon is pleasant, receives light from the sun and imbibes its rays. Its Asterisms, and its rays present in the atmosphere, are full of luster.

In the next hymn 41 is written

"Air is quick and pervades the whole universe, retains sound in the atmosphere."

A query is made "What is the support of the universe? What is the material cause of the world in the beginning? What was its nature? Whence God, doer of the myriad things, the Seer of all, producing the Earth and Heaven covers them with His mighty power?

Yajur Ch. XVII 18

In the next hymn the reply is given "God keeps an eye on the whole world." In the same chapter hymn 26 says "God is the Creator of the whole Universe, full of knowledge, Ubiquitous, Sustainer, Maker,. Seer, and Foremost of all. In Him the seven rishis live in enjoyment according to their desire. He fulfils their lofty ambitions."

The sequencing in the order in Creation comes in hymn 3 2 in the same chapter. "Firstly, was created air; secondly, was created the Sun which sustain the earth, thirdly, was created the cloud that fosters plants, waters and souls, and helps the retention of lives in material objects, is the guardian of many and be getter of rain."

"God has set the Sun in the midst of the Heaven. It attracts rain water and pours it down is red, protects us thoroughly possesses diverse colored rays, rotates, keeps clouds under the check the clouds and different worlds, and guards them, it pervades lightening, the efficient cause of light."

Yajur Ch. XVII. 60

In this chapter we find several Hymns on the Yoga, its power and uses. Read hymn 70 "O Yogi, thought has the knowledge of innumerable usages, immense power of meditation, hundreds of accomplishments of life, and thousands modes of activity. Thou art the Lord of thousand fold possessions. To thee full of knowledge may we offer our obeisance in truthful words."

The other hymns that follow continue to describe the power a Yogi has. For instance in hymn 79 of Yajur XVII. Read,

"O Sage, seven breaths are thy fuel, seven flames are thy flames of knowledge, and seven organs of perception are thy sources of wisdom. Thou hast seven beloved mansions. Seven priests in seven fold manner pay thee worship. With knowledge and fine speech fill full these seven sources of learning."

Here is appreciation of intellectual speeches. Yajur. XVII. 97

"As maidens deck them selves with gay adornments and exhibit their beauty to join their husbands, so, where prosperity reigns, where yagna is performed, there the intellectual speeches are sanctified on all sides, which I enjoy again and again."

They knew about **copper.** Yajur. Ch. XVI. 6

"O people, your king is most auspicious, with limbs strong like copper, brilliant like fire, slightly red and brown."

**On stones and gems.** Yajur. Ch. XVIII. 13

"May my stone and ruby, my refined and rough clay, my clouds and corns, my mountains and their products, my sand and pulverized, my banyan tree and mango trees, my riches and silver, my iron and weapons, my sapphire and brilliant gem; my gold and precious stone, my lead and wax, my zinc and brass, multiply through government arrangements.

The subsequent hymns also talk of their possessions and ownership. For example, read the hymn 21 in the same chapter talks of "May my ladles and their contents, my good substances in the air and its purifying acts" ....or read "my sun and the means of my livelihood, my air, my nation and national policy, my Earth and its trees, my uniform statesmanship, and control of senses, my undecaying possessions and ephemeral body, my light of religion and day and night, my fingers, powers, four directions and sub-directions, be glorified through the grace of God."

**About Seasons and the Names of the Months**

Chapters 14 & 15 of Yajurveda talk of seasons (Shishir and greeshm) and months (chaitra & baishakh) and use the same terms for seasons and months that we do today.

Yajur. Ch. XXII. 31

Perform yagya to make comfortable and pleasant the month Chaitra., the Baishakh, the Jaishtha, the Asharh, the Shravan, the Bhadra, the Ashwin, the Kartika, the Margshish, the Paush, the Magh, and the Phalgun.

Yajur. Ch. XVII. 59

"This sun, in the midst of heaven, like an aeroplane (viman) filling the earth, sky and air's mid region, with its light."

Yajur. Ch. XVIII. 41

"Moon is pleasant, receives light from the sun and imbibes its

rays."

Yajur. Ch. XVIII. 41

"Air is quick, pervades the whole universe, and retains sound in the atmosphere. Its parts are well-known as givers of vigor and movers in the atmospheric vapors."

Yajur, Ch.XXV. 8

"People should know the working of the lightening the best food grain for the earth; the union of the quarters; the continual filling of the space with light by the sun. Clouds are like the soul that sleeps in the heart. Pericardium is vast like the atmosphere. Entrails of the belly are like water. Both parts of the neck are like a lovely pair of male and female goose. Sky is like kidneys. Mountains are like belly's ducts, which receive the meals. Clouds are like the spleen. Paths are refreshing like water."

The arteries on the right side of the belly are like pain, pleasure and sorrow. Streams are known for inundation. Both flanks are like lakes. The Sea is like the belly. The gastric fluid is like the ashes."

Yajur, Ch. XXXIII. 7

"The skilled merchants should utilise fire in making automobiles travel for 3339 miles. Fire and water should be employed in making them cover the atmosphere."

Yajur. Ch. 1. 9

"O Yemen! Increase the store of goods acquired by honest and fair means to be used in the service of humanity, May your life be constantly devoted to this principle. May the spiritually minded people also, not give up this humanitarian work. May your life be constantly consecrated to the performances of five daily duties. The heat of the sun destroys dirt and odor, and draws substances consigned to fire, in their at omic form for the purification of air" ...Ch. 1. 10" "I follow the researches made by the learned in the application of water and fire."

Yajur Ch. XII. 68

"O people, use various implements for cultivating the earth. Employ ploughs and yokes. With the knowledge of science of agriculture and full of consideration, bequick to sustain and nourish yourself." & 76 "O Cook, the preparer of palatable meals, please with vegetarian preparations, thy friends, the learned, the guests, the officials, and the Pranas and Apanas, the protecting parents and the children."

Yajur Ch. XII. 76

"O Physicians imbued with mani fold wisdom and deeds; protect my body from disease, with medicines having hundred and thousand growths. Cure your bodies well."

**On Arithmetic**

Yajur Ch. 24

"May my One and my Three, and my Three and my Five, and my Five and Seven, and my Nine and my Nine and my Eleven, and my Eleven and Thirteen, and my Fifteen, and my Fifteen and Seventeen and my Seventeen and my Seventeen and my Nineteen, and my Nineteen and my Twenty one+and my Twenty nine and my Thirty One, and my Thirty One and my Thirty Three etc. increase or decrease by addition or subtraction. (N.B. The odd digits of arithmetic have been cited 1+2 =3; 3+2 = 5 and 33-2=31; 29-2=27 here etc. to show that the Vedic scholars knew both additions and subtraction.)

Yajur Ch. 25

"May my Four and my Eight, and my Eight and my Twelve and my Sixteen and my Twenty, my Twenty and my Twenty Four and my Twenty Four and my Twenty Eight, My Forty and Forty Four etc. increase or decrease by addition and subtraction."

Yajur Ch. XVII. 2

"O learned person, may the materials of my yagna, like the milch kin, be the giver of happiness to me"!

"They may be one, and ten, and ten tens, a hundred, and ten hundred, a thousand and ten thousand and a hundred thousand, a lac and hundred lacs, a million, and ten millions, a crore, ten crores, hundred crores, thousand crores, its ten times Maha Padma, its ten times Shankh, its ten times Samudra, its ten times Madhya, its ten times Prardh. May these bricks of my altar be a source of happiness to me, like the milch cow in this world and the next world."

Yajur. Ch. XVII.

It contains mathematical equations running into billions of numbers.

(Remember these figures are given in connection with the altar for the yagnas which later gave birth to Vaastu sastra. This quote also contradicts the statement of Bertr and Russell that Indians learnt their Zeros from the Arabs ignoring the fact that the Arabs themselves call these numerals Hindsa i.e. from Hindustan.)

**Medical science (Diseases and Cures)**

Yajur Ch. XII. 76

"O Physicians! Imbued with manifold wisdom and deeds; protect my body from disease, with medicines having hundred and thousand growths. Cure your bodies as well. Know the innumerable vital parts of your body. O mother thou should to also do like this." 84, "Just as a thief steals into the cattle-fold, by breaking into the wall, so do all well-known plants come out of the earth tearing it asunder, and drive out from the body whatever malady there is."

Yajur XII. 86

"O medicines! When ye creep in a patient part by part, joint by joint, ye destroy his pulmonary disease, as a strong man destroys the delicate bodily parts of the foe." 87 "O Physician! Try to extirpate tuberculosis through well-nourished diet through control of breath (pranayam) and through medicines that which fully relieve the patient of its pain."

**Dress**

Wearing of turban by villagers (Yajurveda, Ch. XVI. 22) 'Homage to the turban-wearing.')

**On cooked food and digestion**

Yajur Ch. 2/11

I have prayed to the Effulgent, all sustaining God. May the Lord Father accept my prayer. Our digestive faculty digests the food in the stomach. In this universe created by the All-Blissful God, I take that food through the qualities of attraction and retention, of inhalation and exhalation; and the forces of purification and permeation of the invigorating air, throughout the body. Cooking my food in the burnt tire I eat it with my mouth.

**Variety of food-grains known to them**

Yajur. Ch. XIX. 21-23

They talk of barley, wheat, rice, jujube, corns etc. and the uses of milk and curd, honey etc.

Yajur. Ch. XVIII. 12

"May my rice and my barley, my pulses, my sesarnum and grams, my kidney beans and their cooking, my millet and its cooking, my excellent rice of wild growth and their cooking, my wheat and its cooking my lentils and other food grains prosper through the Grace of God."

**Names of birds and animals**

Yajur. Ch. XXIV.

Contains the names of birds/animals and sea creatures like fish, crocodiles etc. About their temperament Yajur, Ch. XXIV. 3 "The bright aired; the wholly bright haired beasts possess the qualities of the sun and moon. The white, the white-eyed, the reddish beast, possess the qualities of fire, the protector of cattle. Beasts of burden possess the qualities of air. Beasts with heavy limbs posses the qualities of vital breaths. Sky-colored beasts belong to the cloud."

**On built houses and the Vaastu sastra**

Yajur. Ch. XXVI. 16

"O learned person. I admire the house, high in the altitude, full of foodstuffs; well ventilated and airy, grand in sight and extremely commendable. May it be durable like the Earth."

Yajur Ch. 1

"I resort to agriculture and craft for removing the poverty and ministering happiness to all. May I feel joy in my domestic life. May our houses be sufficiently commodius, airy fully comfortable and built in the middle of an open space. May our life be in conformity with the Vedic teachings. O lord! We pray unto thee to preserve and protect whatever gives us happiness."

In the same chapter verse 14 says

"May your home be comfortable. It should afford no shelter to the wicked. May your house serve as the skin of the skin of the earth. May all persons acquire houses like yours by the grace of God. Clouds receive moisture from the forests, reside in the vast space and receive water from air. May God impart this knowledge of clouds and building houses, which serve as skin of the earth."

In Ch. 2 of the Yajurveda hymn 20 it is desired,

"Let me live in a comfortable house; praying to Thee and doing noble deeds."

**On the doctors, their fees and behavior**

Yajur. Ch. XXVIII. 7

"O Physician, regular in thy meals and recreation just as two physicians, givers of happiness, expert in the diagnosis of physical ills, excellent amongst the learned, dispellers of the disease, friendly to each other, wise, full of the knowledge of medical science, experienced in the art of medicine, adept in medical treatment, treat the ills of the soul, amass wealth for worldly progress, attain to longevity, so should thou do!"

Yajur. Ch. XIX. 12

"Just as a lady doctor well-versed in the science of medicine, with healthy organs of the body; physicians and surgeons, having mastery over the Ayurveda, learned persons stretch out the healing sacrifice, for prosperity with their speech, so shouds to thou."

**On the variety of poetry meters and the importance of Yagnas**

Yajur Ch. IV. 37

"O God! Just as learned persons, utilise Thy created objects by oblations, so should we utilise them. The Yagna is the advancer of our progeny, wealth and houses; dispeller of diseases, best ower of heroes, remover of the idles and cowards from amongst us, and giver of happiness in manifold ways, may that conduce to our benefit. O learned persons may be perform this yagna, and live happily in your houses".

"O Lord, dauntless art Thou; Let us avoid in a Yagna the use of fire that burns corpses, and the use of fire that ripens the raw commodities, and endows us with nobler qualities. Through thy teachings remove our miseries and confer bliss on us."

In the hymn 19 Ch. 1 in the Yajurveda is written,

"The Yagna is the 'giver'of happiness, puts an end to the selfish and miserly habits and protects the mid-regions as the skin protects the body. May the performer of the yagna realise its importance. The proper recitation of the Vedic hymns is yagna itself. The yagna performed on special occasions also protects the body. The yagna is the sustainer of the illustrious sun, the embodiment of the Vedic lore. May we realise the yagna as the bringer of rain and the giver of spiritual knowledge."

Hymn 21 Ch. 1

"I fully harness the yagna for the attainment of happiness and material prosperity".

Hymn 24 Ch. 1 The rishi says

"By the impulse of God, Giver of bliss, I perform the yagna free from violence (hinsa); for the attainment of noble qualities and association of the learned; through the life-giving breath, vitalising air and through the rejuvenating rays of the sun and the moon. Ayagna is the recipient of the rays of the sun that ripens a large variety of object sand is full of inunense luster and innumerable rays. Ayagna is illuminating the sources of rain. With the aid of yagna we could remove our miseries."

Yajur Ch. 1 Hymn 26

"O omnipotent God, the giver of happiness, may we subjugate wicked on this earth where the sages perform the yagnas. May we associate with the learned and thus spread freely the system of education as propounded in the Vedic hymns. Just as my light of knowledge is valued by all, so should yours. The ignorant moving in the dark who are opposed to the learned, and whom the learned disapprove for their antagonism to knowledge, should be brought round to the path of virtue by hundreds of means available and let the restriction on them be not removed until their enlightenment. May the wicked be not blessed with prosperity and the pleasure of knowledge. O ye dutiful may ye persistently follow the path of virtue!"

Yajur Ch.1 27

"I perform the yagna with the recitation of Vedic verse in Gayatri, Trishtup, and Jagati meters. O Earth thou art beautiful, a source of happiness, a fit place to dwell comfortably, full of corn, milk, honey, sweet juices and fruits."

**The value of a mantra**

Yajur Ch. 4. 24

"O learned person this is Thy share of the sacrifices allied with Gayatri verses so may he say unto me a student of science. This is Thy share of the sacrifice allied with Trishtup verses so he may say unto me, the seeker of the essence of the things." "This is Thy share of the sacrifice allied with verses in Jagati meter, so may he say, unto me a student of science..." May thou attain to sovereignty detailed in Vedic verses. May he thus preach me the art of kingship unto me, full of affluence. "O learned persons just as ye are my purifying preachers, so am I your worthy disciple, endowed with virtues and wealth. May ye develop this sacrifice (Yagna) as well."

**On the supremacy of Knowledge**

"May ye thriving, justice-loving, wise-learned persons, preachers of knowledge of the Vedas become supreme through knowledge. Let all seekers of Truth, devotees of learning and action, attain to happiness. Preach my noble word that brings all kinds of joys."

Yajur Ch. XI. 22

"O Learned Geologist! wealth giver just as a strong horse jumps up so should'st thou attain to greatness in this world; acquire absolute, beautiful happiness free from pain, desirable from a saintly life. May we in the enjoyment of happiness, explore the pervading electricity full of brilliance."

Yajur Ch. XI. 23

"O seeker after Knowledge! Just as I with learning Ghee, clearly manifest the properties of air, that pervades all substances, that moves transversely, is vast vitality, highly powerful with the oblations of corn, vastin velocity, and visible, so I make thee also understand the properties of air."

Yajur. Ch. XXVIII. 27-46.

"Meters Brihati 36 syllables; Pankti 40 syllables; Trishtup 44; Jagati 48; Virat 33; Gayatri, Atichhandas, Ushnik; Anushtap; Dwipada; Kakup, Ati Jagati.

Yajur. Ch. XXIX. 8. May Bharati, the speech of the Adityas, illuminates our yajna. May Saraswati the speech of the Rudras, be our helper. May Ida, the speech invoked in accord by the Vasus give us happiness. (Bharati is speech; Saraswati is learning, and Ida is intellect-rationality) see also, hymn 33.

**Qualities of a ruler**

Yajur. Ch. XXXIII. 26.

"He alone is fit to be elected the head of the state, who possesses power, knows how to arrange his army in different military arrays, is majestic the sun, challenges for battle his impious foes, chastises the wily and deceitful persons, kills the dacoits hidden in the forests, and makes apparent the words who diffuse happiness."

Yajur Ch. IV. 22

"O King famous for eloquence, brilliance, enmity to fraud, antagonism to the thoughtless, pleasing manners, dexterity, defeating the designs of the ill-minded, friendship and the art of befriending others, with longing for delight—come unto us."

# Chapter - 7

# The Upanishads or Quest for the Unknown

The Vedas are the most ancient extant literature of India. The traditional view is that the original Veda was revealed to the rsis. It consisted of one hundred thousand verses in four divisions. With time these divisions got mixed up. In the beginning of the Dvapara Age, Krishna Dvaipayana resuscitated the Vedic study and classified it according to the four ancient divisions. the Rk, Yajus, Sama, and Atharvan. Each of these is divided into two parts—Work and Knowledge. The first is mainly made up of hymns or mantras, instructions regarding rites and ceremonies; the second is concerned with the Divine or the spiritual knowledge. Each of these main divisions has three sub-divisions-samhitas or mantras, the Brahmanas and the Arayankas. The Brahmanas are mostly in prose containing detailed descriptions of the sacrificial rites and the modes of their performance. According to Sayanacharya (a fourteenth century Vedic scholar) eight classes of topics, viz. itihasa, purana, Vidya, Upanishad, sloka, sutra, vyakhyana, and anuvyakhyana i.e. history, old stories, esoteric knowledge about meditation, supreme knowledge, verse, aphorisms, explanations and elaborations are contained in the Vedas. The Upanishads are the appendices of the Vedas. Therefore, they are also called the Vedanta.

The term 'Upanishad' means "sitting near devotedly". Since they deal with esoteric knowledge one has to be very attentive to their content. While the Vedas deal mainly with the formless Divine - the One without beginning or end, the primal cause, the Upanishads deal with 'Self or soul and thereby for the first time ever establish a relation of an individual with the Unknowable. The Self or Soul resides in the heart of an individual but being imperishable it does not constitute part of the body. We should not forget that in the Vedas the nature of the Divine Being is unknown and in their invocations to the Supreme Power they are uncertain of its name and nature; therefore they continuously keep asking to which God we should offer our oblations (kasmai deva havisha vidhemam). While they desire to understand the reason as to why the Divine Being created this universe, they also wish to know the purpose underlying this creation. For the first time in the Upanishads they attempt to go into this question and come up with answers. None of these answers is however complete as none could possibly be. No one will ever know either the First Cause or the purpose of this creation. Still the seers and thinkers have kept on trying to discover the background to both these queries. What have they found out? We are not as yet sure. The Upanishads constitute answers to that kind of curiosity but in the end they too meet with limited success.

The number of Upanishad runs into more than 108; but only 18 are venerated because they have been considered both authentic and authoritative. In his commentary on the Brahma Sutras Shakaracharya included citations from only six of them and on the other ten he wrote lengthy commentaries. These he considered as the principal Upanishads. The 13 Upanishads are named as Katha, Isha, Ken, Prashna, Mundaka, Mandukya, Taittiriya, Aitareya, Chhandogya and Brihadarankya,; Svetasvatara, Maitri, and Kausitaki Brahman.

The Upanishads have some common features. For instance, although they deal with apparently differing conceptions, thematically they display similar concerns. Secondly, they deal with the insights of the saints and seers, and since these people were not builders of any systems they were content with recording their experiences. The other feature of the Upanishads lies in their form. Now here do they bother about the logic of presentation. They could be brie for lengthy; present their experiences in prose or poetry or in both. They could also start as abruptly as they could end. The worry is not about parts but about wholes-upon brief, comprehensive, unanalysed statements that deal with momentary experiences. The homogeneity in their content is striking. They contain apparently differing concepts but such is the content of all. These concepts are not evenly distributed or a single concept monopolises one Upanishad and the other some other. Swami Prabhavan and says, "it is true that one Upanishad may emphasise certain ideas, or certain view, more than the rest, or may even specialise as it were in a topic but these distinctions seem purely accidental and are not important." The partitions in all the 108 Upanishads (this number is given in Mukti kopanishad) may be done a way with and all of them could easily be reduced to one. This then is the principal characteristic of the Upanishads.

Another characteristic of the Upanishads worth mentioning is that they all are works of the seers or rishis. Their authors were interested in reporting insights which came to them in thought or vision, and not in making these insights superficially coherent. They were not builders of systems but recorders of experience. We should therefore be prepared for apparent inconsistencies; for obliviousness to one conception through temporary absorption in another. Nowhere must we expect to find the whole truth gathered together once for all in easy, conscious, triumphant formulations.

Still another characteristic of the Upanishads, commonly talked has to do with their form. Never were the ideas set down as an expositor might suspect- with less regard for his convenience. Nowhere is there a logical beginning and nowhere is there a logical end. Furthermore attention at all points is not upon parts, clearly recognised as parts, but upon wholes- upon brief, comprehensive, unanalysed statement, it may be, or upon such particular elements as round out, when taken together, a momentary conception.

These Upanishads are an excellent example of describing an 'Ideal' teacher. Not only must a teacher know his subject but also lead the life of a 'model' performer of all his functions. In our world today we rarely come across both such seekers of knowledge and such venerable teachers. "Approach a teacher," we read the command of the Rgveda "with humility and a desire to serve", and in the Upanishads it is said: "To many it is not given to hear of the Self. Many though they hear of it, do not understand it. Wonderful is he who learns of it. Intelligent is he, taught by a good teacher, and is able to understand it". Teaching being the highest point in learning (knowledge) it was imparted at private sittings only to qualified disciples. The traditional view is that the Upanishads being revealed texts they teach the same doctrine but the fact is that due to a variety of their interpretations by scholars and the problems discussed in them being ever so different it is not possible to regard them as homogeneous. All their teachings are not prominent. Some are mere flashes of thought; some are only hinted at; some are slightly developed, while some are often repeated, emphasised and often thoroughly dealt with. However, there is an essential unity of purpose in them. They usually describe the same fundamental doctrine which may be called monistic idealism or idealistic monism. It is not only the style that varies but these poetic-philosophic works differ in their presentation as well. While some of them are full of grand imagery, have charming and lucid expressions 'abounding in crystal clarity or in (prasad guna)'. others offer to mind philosophical doctrines and to the heart peace and freedom.

The Upanishads develop monistic ideas scattered in the Samhitas. During the Brahmana period the philosophical ideas were overlooked and instead emphasis was laid on rituals and sacrifices. It is the Aranyakas that brought them back to the realm of philosophy, which incidentally was the basic purpose of the Upanishads. That is how the Karmakandis were removed from the first rank and placed next to the thinkers and philosophers. Thus, we find Narada telling in the Chhandogya, Sanatkumara: "I know the Rg-Veda Sir, the yajur, the Sama and with all these I know the Mantras and the sacred books besides much Gandharva knowledge too. But I do not know the Self..." "It is interesting to note that Sanatkumara calls this knowledge mere 'Words' or Lower Knowledge. In the Mundaka Knowledge is described both as lower and higher knowledge. The Knowledge that is available in the form the Vedas and such disciplines as Grammar and ceremonies constitutes lower knowledge or Apara vidya but what forms part of Para vidya or higher Knowledge constitutes the Knowledge of the Self. In the Chhandogya Upanishad (1, 12.4) occurs a satirical piece on the sacrificial nature of the yagnas emphasised by the Brahmins in which a procession of dogs marches along saying"Aum, Let us eat.Aum, Let us drink May the God Varuna, Prajapati and Savitr bring food here, yea bring it here. (Aum).

Chhandogya belongs to Samveda and is revealed in 10 Chapters. The first two chapters discuss the problems of liturgy and the other 8 chapters constitute the Upanishad itself. The most significant part of this Upanishad is that it offers a hierarchy of important values until it brings one face to face with the Reality itself. The Upanishad tells us the importance of the word Aum (which as we know is the sound that reverberates across the Universe) and its main priest is Udgitha The rest of the chapters detail the philosophy it contains.

We have already mentioned the important role a teacher plays in teaching esoteric knowledge. Few teachers could venture entering this area. About a good teacher it is commonly understood according to ancient Indian literature that a teacher not merely teaches directly through words but also presents a model daily life for his students to follow. Swami Prabhavan and cites a few lines of a verse which speak of the functions of an ideal teacher:

"Pleasant indeed are the study and the teaching of the Vedas

He who engages in these things attains to concentrate

And is no longer a slave to his passions;

Devout, self-controlled, disciplined in spirit

He rises to fame and is a blessing to mankind."

Majority of the Hindus regard the Vedas as the highest written authority. Any subsequent scripture if one has to regard it as valid, must be in agreement with them; it may expand them, it may develop them and still be recognised, but in no case should it contradict them. For him they are the expression of Divine truth; because he regards its truth to be verifiable immediately, at any moment in his personal experience or he would reject it.

The word 'Atman' originally meant the *breath* and then gradually acquired the meaning of feeling, mind, soul and spirit. Shankaracharya cites an old verse giving the different connotations of the word 'Atman'. According to that verse, 'Atman' means that which pervades all, which is the subject and which knows , experiences and illuminates the objects; and which remains immortal and always the same. The true Self is the main topic of investigation in the Upanishads. For instance, in the Chhandogya Upanishad we find a development of the concept of the Self in three states of being - waking, or dreaming or the empirical Self. The gods and demons the twin opposites i.e. Indra and Virochana go to Prajapati to learn about the Self. The teacher asked them to fulfill the condition of being a student. After meeting the requirement they asked the teacher about the Self. The teacher Prajapati told them to either look into the water or into the mirror and learn about it. While Virochana was satisfied with this teaching, Indrahada doubt about its veracity. Therefore, he went again to Prajapati to clarify his doubt. Once again he had to fulfill the condition of being a student and having fulfilled the condition he asked about his doubt: "How could the body reflect the Self?" If the body is beautiful or well dressed then would the Self too look beautiful or well-dressed? Would the Self perish when the body perishes? Prajapati now tells him that he who is seen in dreams roaming freely is the Self. Indra again feels doubtful of the truth of this statement. How could one not feel fear or pleasure in the dream state? Prajapati teaches him the enjoyer of deep dreamless sleep is the Self. Indra once again thinks How could Self be totally unconscious of his whereabouts feeling nothing, knowing nothing and willing nothing? He goes again to his teacher and asks about his doubt. He once again fulfilled the condition of being a student i.e. living in the Ashram for thirty-two years. The teacher is now very happy with Indra and tells him: "The body is not the Self, though it exists for the Self. The dream experiences are not the Self though they have a deep sleep. The Self is not an abstract formal principle of deep sleep. The eye, the body, the mental states, the presentation continuum, the stream of consciousness are all mere instruments and objects of the Self. The Self is the ground of waking, dream and sleep states and yet it transcends all. The Self is universal, immanent as well as transcendent. The entire Universe lives and moves and breathes in it. It is immortal and luminous, self -proved and beyond doubt, as the very principle which makes doubts. It is the ultimate subject and it can never become object and which has to be necessarily presupposed by all knowledge."

Indian scholars have found this statement to be very significant and comparable to many a statement and utterances of famous European philosophers and thinkers. For example, it reminds one of empiricism of Locke and Berkeley and the skepticism of Hume. It sounds like the flux of Heraclites, William James and Bergson the Copernican revolution of Emanuel and the abiding contribution of Hegel, the positions of Green, Bradley and Mc Taggart– all of them have been anticipated in this dialogue long back.

This is not the first time that some student of Indian philosophy has written all this about the Vedic philosophy; others like S. Radhakrishnan too have given names of thinkers and philosophers both in the West and the East who came close to writing such truths. Recently a Chinese thinker also wrote that India conquered China without sending a single soldier. Buddhism which spread across China and Japan too has had its roots in the Upanishidic thinking. And the Upanishads as we all know are part of the Vedas. The Atman is the transcendental background of both Self and not Self and its reality is beyond any doubt. Professor R.D. Ranade in his well-known work 'A Constructive Survey of Upanishadic Philosophy' wrote about the origins of the doctrine of Maya in the Upanishads.

1. Ishopanishad tells us that the veil that covers the Truth is golden, so rich, gaudy and dazzling that it takes away the mind of the observer from the inner contents. (Isha 15.3)
2. Kathopanishad says how we live in ignorance and thinking ourselves wise, move about wandering, like blind men following the blind. (Katha l, 2, 4 and 5)
3. Mundakopanishad compares ignorance to a knot which a man has to untie before he gets possession of the self in the recess of his heart. (II. 1.10)
4. Chhandogya tells us that while Knowledge is power, ignorance is impotence. (1.1.10)
5 Brihadaranyaka compares Unreality to Non-being to darkness to Death. (I.3.28)
6 Prashna tells us that we cannot witness the realm of Brahma unless we have shaken off the crookedness in us, the falsehood and the illusion. (I. 16)
7. Brihadaranyaka tells that there is no duality. Maya is a semblance, an as-it-were, an appearance. (II. 4. 14)
8. Chhandogya tells us that Atman is the only Reality; everything else is a mere word, a mode, a name. (VI. 1. 4)
9. Shvetasvatara describes God as a Mayin who creates the world by His power. (IV. 9)

The Upanishads are correctly regarded as the fountain head of all Indian philosophy. Bloomfield in his book The Religion of the Vedas remarks: “There is no important form of Hindu thought; heterodox Buddhism included which is not rooted in the Upanishads.” Even the heterodox Jainism has taken its idealism and its doctrine of Karma from the Upanishads even as Buddhism derives its idealism, monism, absolutism, the theory of momentariness of all worldly things, the theory of Karma, the distinction between the distinction between the empirical and standpoints, and the theory that Ignorance is the root cause of this cycle of birth-and-death and Nirvana can be attained by right knowledge alone from the Upanishads. Sankhya derives its theory Prakriti (from Shvetashvatara) and of the three Gunas from Chhandogya, the doctrine of Purusha, the relation of mind intellect, and the soul from Kathopanishad and the doctrine of Linga-sharir from Prashna. Isha preaches the combination of Karma and Gyana; Mimansa takes up Karma; Vedanta takes up Gyana; and some take up the combination it self.

The most significant characteristics of the Upanishads are described by Ramamurti Sharma in his book Bharatiya Darshan Ki Chintan Dhara (Manatees, Delhi, 2001). According to him all six Indian philosophies have their roots in the Upanishads including all the schools of idealism and materialism. The Vedas contain the seeds of all Indian philosophies including Jainism and Buddhism. The interesting point is that instead of opposing or contradicting each other they present an integrated view both developmental and progressively evolutionary viewpoint .They provide the philosophy of the Vedas. This philosophy is essentially spiritualistic. What appears seemingly to contradict the Vedic view is holistic and highly supportive.

Dr S. Radhakrishnan in his translation of thirteen important Upanishads brought out by George Allen and Unwin Ltd. London 1951 under Muirhead Library of Philosophy series (1951) accepted thirteen Upanishads as important. He followed the line pointed out by Shankaracharya as many others have done both before and after him. All Upanishads describe a kind of hierarchy in knowledge and finally decide that what begins in Brahma also ends in Him. He is the great May in and all that what we see is only a result of our ignorance. Once one knows the truth one is relieved of the cycle of birth and death. The entire spectrum the real and the unreal is more like Yajurveda's two birds that sit on a tree while one merely looks on without tasting the fruits on the tree and the other indulges in eating the same. While the one who only looks on is the Unmanifest and therefore remains unseen and free from any blemish, the other one tastes and faces problems. It is the manifest which is linked with the world and happens to remain involved. This is lshvara or the one whom we could reach out in times of distress.

The major Upanishads are the Brihadaranyaka, Chhandogya and Svetavsatara, besides Tattiriya. The story of Satyakama is mentioned in the Chhandogya Upanishad. All students of philosophy are familiar with it. It relates the request of Satyakama to his mother to tell him about his father as he wanted to become a student where it was customary to inform the teacher about his Kul and gotra. His mother replied that she-did not know the name of his father as she served many a master in her youthful days. If he liked he could add her name to his. That is how he became Satyakama Jaabala. When asked by his teacher he related truthfully the inquiry he had made in this context and the reply he got. The teacher immediately accepted him as his pupil saying that only a Brahmin could speak the truth. The teacher without teaching him anything asked him to take 400 cows and come back when they became one thousand. He accepted the teacher's word and took charge of the 400 cows and a couple of bulls. Having gone to a pasture he acquired the ability to look after the animals and also to sustain him self during the absence of cooked meal. Slowly and gradually he learnt how to converse with animals. A bull became his mentor during this period. It is this Bull who informed him once that now the number had reached a thousand of cows as commanded by his teacher therefore it was time that he moved toward the Ashram. On his way back the Bull taught him about Brahman, "The East, West, South and the North are the four quarters of Brahman". The Bull said then: "This verily is the four quartered foot of Brahman named the Shinning. Fire (Agni) will tell you the other quarter". Agni told him, "The earth is one quarter, the atmosphere is the other quarter; the sky is one quarter and the ocean is the fourth quarter. This is Brahman's four-footed quarter- the Endless."

"He who meditates on this four-quartered Foot of Brahma as Endless wins endless worlds and becomes endless in the world".

Aswan came now to teach Satyakama the third quarter. "Fire is one quarter, the Sun is the other quarter; the moon is the other quarter and lightening is one quarter. This is the Brahma's four-quartered foot- the Luminous He who knowing this worships Brahma's luminous four-quartered foot himself becomes luminous. A diver-bird will tell you another quarter." The diver bird told him about the other quarter "Breath is the one quarter, the ear is one quarter, the eye is the other quarter, and the mind is the other quarter. This then is the four quartered foot of Brahma named possessing a support. One who worships on this four quartered foot called 'possessing a support' comes to acquire the support in the world."

When Satyakama returned to his teacher, the teacher was impressed by the glow on his face. He inquired about the reason for this glow and asked Who taught you Satyakama?' "Other than men," was the reply accompanied by a wish to be taught by the teacher himself. One who is taught by the teacher attains the best result."

The story of Satyakama does not end here. As a teacher he did not prove to be ideal. He kept Upkosala-his student, tending fires for 12 years without giving instruction in sacred wisdom and also did not allow him to go back home although all others were allowed to go as was the custom. He refused to listen to his wife either despite her repeated requests not to neglect his obligation. We have here a case in which a student went on hunger strike until he was taught by his teacher. Even when teacher's wife asked him to eat he refused. The fires that had been tended all this while said to themselves that this neglect was not desirable therefore they decided to teach him. They said, "Life is Brahman. Joy is Brahman. Ether is Brahman." Upkosala said, "I know that Life is Brahman but Joy and Ether I do not understand." They said to him, "Joy, verily, is the same as Ether and also vice versa." Then Garhapatya tire explained to him, "Earth, Fire, Food and Sun are all forms of me, the person seen in the Sun, I am he, I am He." "He who meditates on the Fire destroys sinful actions, becomes possessor of this world, reaches full life and lives brightly. His descendents also do not perish. Both in this world and the other world we serve him who knowing this meditates."

Then, the anvaharyapacana instructed him. "Water, the quarters, the stars, the moon are all forms of me. The person seen in the Moon is me, I am He." He who knowing this meditates on the fire destroys all sinful acts. His descendents also do not perish. Both in this world and the other world we serve him who knowing this meditates.

The ahavaniya fire instructed him. "Breath, space, sky and lightening are forms of me. The person seen in the lightening, I am he." "While the anvaharya fire is that on the altar on the southern side; the ahavaniya fire is on the eastern side.

He who knowing this meditates on the fire destroys sinful acts, becomes possessor of the world and lives his full life and lives brightly. His descendents also do not perish. Both in this world and the other world we serve him who knowing this meditates on the fire."

Then the fires told Upakosala, "Upakosala dear, you have this knowledge of ourselves and knowledge of the Self. But the teacher will tell you the way." When the teacher returned he asked Upakosala "Your face shines like one who knows Brahman. Who instructed you?" He answered indirectly about his instructors. The teacher asked him, "What did they teach you?" On receiving his reply, the teacher told him "They, my dear, have indeed told you this; But I will tell you this that as water does not cling to the lotus leaf, so evil deed does not cling to him who knows it."

This is what the teacher taught Upakosala, "The person that you see in the eyes is the self. This is immortal, the fearless, this is Brahman.

If one drops melted butter or water into this (eye) it goes away by the side. He is also Vamani for he brings all desirable things. He is like Vamani who shines in all the worlds."

"Now for such a person whether they perform the cremation or not, he goes on to light from light into the day, from the day in to the half month of the waxing moon, from half month of the waxing moon into the six months when the sun moves northwards, from the months into the year, from the year to the sun, from the sun into the moon, from the moon to the lightening. Then there is a person, not human. He leads them to Brahman. This is the way to the gods, the way to

Brahman. Those that proceed by it do not return to the human condition, yes they do not return,"

In the Chhandogya Upanishad there is also a story of Svetketu Aruneya and Pravahan Jaivali in which the latter asks the former whether his father has instructed him. When Aruneya responds in the affirmative, Jaivali asked, "Young man, do you know to what place men go from here?"

"No, Sir"

"Do you know how they return again".

"No Sir." "Do you know where the paths leading to the gods and leading to the fathers separate?"

"No, Sir"

"Do you know why that yonder world never becomes full?"

"No, Sir"

" Do you know how in the fifth libation water comes to be called person?"

"No, Sir"

"Then why did you say that you were instructed?

*Then he went back to his father and asked "Why did you say that you istructed me without actually instructing me?"*

The father, Gautama replied, "The questions you told me I too do not know how to reply even one of them".

*The story goes on to conclude that the father had to go to the King and ask him the answers to the questions he had put. It is the reply of the King that should interest us. The king responded. "Stay for some time and I shall tell you. Thus, far this knowledge has not reached any Brahmin before you. In all the works this knowledge has remained with the Kshtriyas only." Thereafter he teaches Gautama this secret knowledge. It is to be noted that whether it is Videha or Pravahan. Jaivali or Ashvapati Kaikeya etc. they are all Kshatriyas who possess esoteric knowledge and not the Brahmins. While the Brahmins performed rituals, it was the prerogative of the Kshtrivas to perfect this secret knowledge. The characteristic of Knower is that he rises above want and loses fun in acquiring. The detachment brings them close to Moksha or the cycle of birth and death.*

This true knowledge results in total detachment from world wealth, glory or power and also helps one learn the art of meditation and the value of Silence. For Jaivali Space, Earth, Ether, Fire and Water etc. are the various organs or Forms of the Universal Self.

There are *two more* noteworthy references in this story. One refers to the need for Knowledge of the Universal Self, which according to the King should be shared with all including the Chandalas since this Self dwells in them too there by saying that sacred knowledge is not to remain the exclusive right of any particular caste or community and the second refers to a woman's sexual organs, which are like fuel, which invites smoke, the vulva is the flame, what is done inside is the coals, and the pleasures the sparks.

The third characteristic of the Upanishads is that they use a language which is both symbolic and real. Therefore, it is difficult to be sure where and when they are employing symbolism and when the real. Most of the explanations given in them are beyond the ordinary knowledge of the human beings.

We know for sure that they did not have access to any technology and yet they surprise us by their subtle scientific knowledge and calculations far be yond the abilities of machines.

The Upanishads contain discussions about the inquiry of the Ultimate Truth/Universal Self–its nature and the manner in which one could realise the Truth. They are the first records of the curiosity of the Man about the nature of the Reality. Being the appendices of the Vedas they are also called the Vedanta. Not that all answers to human queries can be discovered in them, nevertheless the heights they reach is worth all the labor involved. The insights are as significant as the themes under discussion. One is struck by diction and the hierarchy involved in the thought processes. It is in the Chhndogya Upanishad the divine nature of the soul is described as *'tat tvam asi.' It is not to be confused with accidents* with which it is generally confused. The idea is to identify the antah purush.

From the objective side the ultimate Reality is Brahman. Brih means to grow or to evolve. In the beginning it meant sacrifice, prayer and thereafter it acquired its present meaning the Ultimate Reality. In the Chhandogya it is said to be Tajjalan i.e. Tat or from which it arises, Ja into which it will return la by which it is sustained and lives an. The evolution of the elements of Brahman is given in the Taittiriya Upanishad. From Brahman arises ether, from ether air, from air fire, from fire water and from water earth. This is pure science. We read today the Universe is made up of these five elements. But the real evolution theory is described in the Kosha theory. For life to take birth we need the basic element Anna i.e. matter. Once matter is available we can have life in various forms. This is one stage when Prana or life is possible. The third stage is that of movement or consciousness i.e. mana or the Desire is born. The next stage of evolution is when we start discriminating between one object and the other or we start making choices as we know for sure what is good for us and what is not good for us. This stage is called Vigyanmaya i.e. the exact or distinct knowledge. And once we know what is necessary to know us we reach the stage of happiness or Bliss i.e. Anand. The highest stage has now been reached. The matter now becomes Mind and therefore the condition we reached is Turiya. The highly evolved individual will reach the ultimate and now nothing remains either to disturb or achieve. This five stage evolution is the best scientific description of the Marxian theory of evolution, "Matter becomes Mind when it reaches a nodal point." In a way we could easily say that the original Vedantists anticipated not only materialism or Sankhya but Marxism too.

The hierarchy of elements is offered thus: After knowing that Word is lower than Speech and Mind is assuredly greater and higher than Speech. Will is higher than mind and mind is next only to Thought. Contemplation is higher than thought. Understanding is higher than Contemplation. Then on in the hierarchy come Strength and Food. Thereafter in the ascending order come Water, Heat (Agni), Ether, Memory, Hope, Life, Truth then thought and understanding., The precondition for understanding to develop one should have faith, steadfastness, activity and happiness. When one sees nothing, understands nothing that is the infinite. But when one sees something understands something else that is finite or small. The infinite is the same as the immortal, and the finite is mortal. The infinite cannot be established in anything other than himself. This is Brahman. Here we are close to describing the Infinite as the First Cause.

The researches in the area of psychology come very close to describing the importance of thought and the power of the Intellect. It is when we meditate, reflect or think that we come face to face with the powers of the mind and see beyond the reaches of the physical eye. Last Frontiers of the Mind by Mohan das Moses. (Prentice Hall of India, New Delhi, 2005). This book on Psychology tells us that the function of the Mind is to cognise. Thinking therefore is the logical end of cognisance. The researches on Brain-Mind have brought us to a point where we are not decided whether or not Mind and Brain are two separate entities or just one. It is however clear that Brain is the mechanical part without which Mind cannot function. The product of the Mind is Thought via Intellect. We are able to cognise because of the Mind. The ultimate goal of cognisance is to know and be able to distinguish between the True and False. Knowing Truth brings happiness and failure to do so Unhappiness. This is what compares well with the Kosha theory. Now read what Moses has to say: "Aristotle called Hippocrates 'The Great Physician'. In the modern time the great neurosurgeon Wilder Penfield was so fascinated by Hippocrates that he called him a great man who helped him to discover the electric discharge in the brain and learn that once these discharges fail to occur the Brain goes dead and cognisance fails. The brain enables Mind to cognise. In 1987 Colin Blakemore compared brain research and philosophy to two mountaineers who were trying to climb the same mountain from two sides "virtually unaware of the effort of each other without the knowledge of the benefits of joining hand." Descartes firmly set consciousness at the centre of the Brain-Mind theory. To the question what separates an animal from Man he answered Cogito Ergo Sum I think therefore I am. Cartesian dualism has evoked strong feelings. Will Durant said, "It began the great game of epistemology, which in Leibniz, Locke, Hume and Kant waxed into a Three Hundred Year War that at once stimulated and devastated modern philosophy." Descartes however continued to influence philosophy of Mind and the neuroscientists. Descartes pinpointed the pineal gland, a cone-shaped piece of tissue as the base of brain to interface the body. Later on it was found that human beings alone do not possess the pineal gland and that this gland does not play the same grand role as was thought earlier."

In 1870 two Prussian Military medical officers discovered that Brain needed electrical charges to function. The philosopher William James called the relationship between Brain and Mind as "the ultimate of the ultimate problems." The neuroscientists reduced the two hypotheses, one, that the action of the brain explains the mind and two; there are two elements - the brain and the mind. The greatest neurosurgeon of the time Sir Wilder Penfield (1975) declared in his lecture at Oxford that "Mind exists independent of Brain." Penfield wrote a book titled Mystery of the Mind in which he explained the theory that Brain and Mind are two distinct elements and that they exist independent of each other. Sir John Eccles and Sir Karl Popper also came to the same conclusion, that these two are independent of each other. Sir John Eccles and Wilder Penfield cited case studies to reinforce the duality theory in their discovery. They had discovered in their researches that disembodied minds were vividly aware of the ongoing surgery.

It is important to remember that contemplation or thought/intellect has been considered by the Upanishads as the highest element. It matters little how they reached this conclusion but it anticipates later day achievements of the studies in the area of psychology.

Scholars like Max Mueller felt surprised at the content of the Vedas and the advance type of knowledge they contained and the style they adopted. I have no quarrel with scholars like him but their definition of the 'primitive' must be highly personalised. It is the arrogance of western knowledge on the ascendance looking down upon a subject people in a non-machine society.

It may be remembered that with the arrival of the British (i.e. East India Company) in India and of other trader- colonisers (french. Norwegians. Portuguese, etc.) we had a spate of missionaries whose express purpose was to convert Indians to their variety of Christianity. They were surprised both by the quality of Indian craftsmanship and also by the richness of their literature. They found it difficult to excel Indians in their craftsmanship and therefore gradually they found ways to destroy the local craft and thus they were able to sell their goods here. It is a long and tragic story of the way the indigenous crafts and their makers were destroyed. They also wanted to destroy Indian beliefs and their literature that sustained them. They were happy to imagine and also brought out scholarly treatises to prove that Indians were 'primitive' people and their sacred and literary books were products of inferior quality as compared with their own. It is not the place to go onto the whole history of how and why they devoted their time and attention to study what India had already got. Not only were they surprised to discover that the ancient Indians had a language which was far richer than the language of the Greeks and their thinkers and the Epics too were far superior and older than their fourth or fifth century B.C. literary works. Although Indians had been trading with Rome during Roman Empire but it was not generally known that Indian learning too had travelled to Europe via Persia. This error of judgment has been committed even by Bertr and Russell who wrote once that both numerals and the decimal came to Europe from Persia. He overlooked the fact that Vedic mathematics was far advanced and older than that of the Persians. Even now the Arabs and other Middle Eastern countries call their numerals 'hindsa' or from India. Read, for instance, Yajurveda Ch. IX. 20 to get an idea of what these Indian ancients knew, "For the attainment of full knowledge, noble deeds; for the attainment of happiness, religious life; for the attainment of definite object, activity, for the advancement of wisdom the habit of reading and writing , for retention of knowledge, truthful speech; the arithmetical measurement of the day; the science of arithmetic; the checking the waste of time in infatuation, a word of wisdom for the fool who revels in vice, a word of caution; for the degraded, wicked soul, advice to ward off evil deeds; for the strong person amongst the low and despicable, speech revealing the true nature of things; for the attainment of God the Lord of the Universe, the knowledge of Yoga, for the king knowledge of all affairs are essential." Although enough material has been cited from the Vedas to counter the argument that ancient Indians were Primitive people this small citation if understood is sufficient for the purpose.

While ancient India was an important country for trade and conquests but our formal scholarly contact came via the conquering armies of Alexander the Great and his teacher Aristotle. *It is one date that no one can contest.* We know for sure when Aristotle came he saw a fully developed Buddhism whose centre was modern day Afghanistan. A Buddhist university was located in Taxila with a student population of ten thousand and its Vice-chancellor a well known scholar and an Emperor by the name of Chandragupta Maurya a ruler of Pataliputra who was willing to contest Alexander in the warfare. To call Indians 'primitive' is therefore indefensible. Even so the missionaries had their Bible and the text of the Bible saying that world was created only some six thousand years back. Be that as it may it is these people who brought Indian languages and their literature to Europe. This contact yielded rich dividends both for us in India and the Europeans. This is how Indians learnt English and through that medium modern sciences and they (the English/Europeans) the Indian languages and her literature. Max Muller studied the Vedas and the Upanishads and declared them to be the products of a 'primitive' people but there were others too like Schopenhauer who found the Upanishads solace of his life and the solace of his death. Also there were several other English scholars who produced dictionaries of Sanskrit and even formed An Asiatic Society of Bengal and which later on became simply the Asiatic Society with headquarters at Calcutta. What surprised Max Mueller was the way this vast literature was preserved over numerous centuries in the absence of writing material and a script. I find Max Mueller highly illogical. How can "primitive" people produce. philosophical and scientific works like the Vedas? Also, how could they develop a system of preserving such a voluminous literature orally? Later day studies have proved beyond any reasonable doubt that the Vedas contain knowledge which is far beyond the physics and mathematics of modern times.

It would be interesting if some one were to 'cite' a single example of a primitive people trying to describe poetry in terms of syllables and their numbers. Read for instance, Yajurveda Ch. XXVlll, 27 to 45 and decide for yourself. Here is the mantra number 27 "O charitably disposed, just as virtuous person becomes united with the immortal, vast like space, immersed in the contemplation of the Beautiful God, deathless in its purity, full of strength, enjoyer of space and pure water, extending over all, and attains happiness, preserving celibacy for 36 years like 36 syllables of Brihat meter, full of knowledge physical organs, Vedic lore...having action, worship and knowledge as its sons, and enjoys nice pleasure, so shouldst thou do!" Or read 45: "O learned person! Just as Omniscient God, Fulfiller of our desires and aims, strengthens the long lived, virtuous soul, as a teacher strengthens the pupil, so shouldst thou with the pleasant Ati Jagati verses perform Yagnas."

Also I doubt if any primitive people would have jewelry of gold with studded diamonds in it. The Vedas continuously refer to both. In my opinion gold jewelry cannot be prepared unless one knows how and where to find gold and a way to convert that to some degree of purity. Their knowledge of geology is both amazing and also modern. Read the following excerpt from the Rgveda: """I describe the special features of Fire (Agni). It takes every type of matter forward. It softens iron ore etc. it burns everything. *It emits light. It beautifies. It is set up before everything else. It performs many functions and is used during many activities. It is an instrument for attracting attention, give and take and for food preparation. Fire creates inside earth all varieties of gems and ores like gold, silver, iron, and diamonds.*" Rgveda 1/1

I have no desire to digress from the main topic but a careful study of the Rgveda would take one's breath away when one came across the type of society and the life they lived. Not only they knew how to build boats that could ferry both goods and passengers across the turbulent seas but they knew how to keep their boats lighted for the night journey. I think it is time some one collected all the names of metals they knew and grains they sowed and then compared how much had India progressed during those times.

I have in the following pages a reference to a place where contemplation is best done: "In the solitude of the mountains and confluence of streams a sage develops his spiritual force, contemplating on God through yoga." O learned person! I admire thy house, high in the altitude, full of food stuffs, well-ventilated and airy, grand in sight and extremely commendable. May it be durable like the Earth!

Also ask the 'primitive' people to produce something to match this kind of numbers, and calculations:- "O learned person! May the materials of my yagna, like the milch kine be the giver of happiness to me! They may be one, and ten, and ten tens, and ten thousand and a hundred thousand, a lac and ten lacs, a million, and a crore, ten crores, a hundred crores and thousand crores, its ten times MahaPadma, its ten times Shankh, its ten times Samudra, its ten times Madhya, its ten times Paradh. May these bricks of my altar be a source of happiness to me, like milch-kine in this world and the next world!"

It is interesting to remember that the vedis of the Yagna needed millions of bricks or ishtikas and in the process they also developed both geometry and Vaastushashtra. Different types of Yagnas required different type of Vedis. I need hardly point out such numbers and the geometry would be hardly common in Primitive societies.

For those who are not familiar either with the style, content or the rituals followed in a typical ancient society I cite a Upanishad or two for its content. I leave it to the judgment of the reader hows/he takes it. I cite brief ones both from the list of Shankaracharya and out side his ambit. The ones selected are Ishopanishad and Maitreyi because they are small and are sufficient to give a reader an idea of what these Upanishads contain. While one is translated by Dr S.Radhakrishnan, ex-President; and the other is rendered into English by some unknown translator. The style of presenting their content is very attractive and the content ennobling and edifying. Brihadaranyaka would have suited us the most for giving the reader not only an idea of the caste distinctions and their functions but also the type of questions that bothered the ancient minds. Its (Brihadaranyka Upanishads) content is both rich and varied, the stories told are detailed, and also because it touches upon those aspects of life which are even today relevant for a Hindu. I find the Brihadaranyka interesting because it contains three generations of famous teachers, reference to woman's genitals and their uses vis-a-vis men's needs besides the status a woman enjoyed in that society, at the same time the stories it contains are very edifying and highly esoteric. But as it is the ones cited below are in no way inferior either in terms of sacred knowledge or style or content of the narration.

Hence, Ishavasyopanishad first:–The *Isha,* also called the Ishavasya Upanishad derives its name from the opening word of the text Ishavasya or Isha. It belongs to the Vajasneyi school of Yajurveda, The Vajasneyi Samhita consists of 40 chapters of the Upanishad is the last. Its main purpose is to teach the essential unity of God and the world, being and becoming. It is not interested so much in the Absolute in itself: Parambrahmaas in the Absolute in relation to the world Parmeshwara. lt teaches that life in this world and life in the Divine Spirit are not incompatible.

**Invocation**

"Purnamadah purnamidam purnatpurnamudacyate.
Purnasya purnamadaya purnamevavasisyate."

That is full, this is full. The full comes out of the full. Taking full from the full, the full still remain full.

This invocation for peace is 'Santi Mantra' from Shukla Yajurveda. Brahman is both transcendent and immanent.

The birth or the creation of the universe does not in any manner affect the integrity of Brahman.

From the Isavasya Upanishad are the following 18 mantras which explain the relation between God and the world, work and wisdom.

**God and the World**

1. Isavasyamidam sarvam yatkimca jagtyam jagat.
   Tena tyktena bhunjitha ma gradhah kasyasvidhdhanam.

Know that all this whatever moves in this universe is enveloped in God. Therefore find your enjoyment in renunciation; therefore do not covet what belongs to others.

**Work and Wisdom**

2. Kurvanneveha karmani jijivisetsatam samah.
   Evam tvayi nanyathetoasti na karma lipyate nare.

Always performing works here one should wish to live one hundred years. If you live thus as a man, there is no other way than this by which karma or deed does not adhere to you.

**The Denying Spirits**

3. Asurya nama te loka andhena tamasavrita.
   Tamste pretyabhigacchanti ye ke catmahano janah.

Demonic, verily are those worlds enveloped in blinding darkness, and to them go after death, those people who are slayers of the Self.

**The Supreme is Immanent and Transcendent**

4. Anejadekam manaso javiyo nainaddeva apanuvan purvamarsat.
   Taddhavatonyanatyeti tisthat tasminnapo matarishva dadhati.

The spirit is unmoving one, swifter than the mind. The senses do not reach it as It is ever ahead of them Though Itself standing still It outstrips those that run. In It the all pervading air supports the activities of beings.

5 Tadejati tannaijati taddure tadvantike.
  Tadantarasya sarvasya tadu sarvasysasya bahyatah.

It moves and lt moves not. It is far and It is near. It is within all this. It is also outside all this.

6. Yastu sarvani bhutani atmanyevanupasyati.
Sarvabhuteshu catmanam tato na vijugupsate.

He who sees all beings in his own self and his own self in all beings; he does not feel any revulsion by reason of such a view.

7. Yasmin sarvani bhutani atmaivabhudvijanatah.
Tatra ko mohah kah shokah ekatvamanupashyatah.

When, to one who knows, all beings have verily become one with his own self, then what delusion and what sorrow can be to him who has seen the oneness?

8. Sa paryagacchukramakayamavranamasnaviram suddhama-papaviddham.
Kavirmanisi paribhuh swayambhuryathathathyato'rthan, vyadadhacchasvatibhyah samabhyah.

He who has filled all. He is radiant, bodiless, invulnerable, devoid of sinews, pure, untouched by evil. He the seer thinker, all pervading, self-existent had duly distributed through endless years objects according to their nature ignorance and Knowledge.

9. Andhantamah pravisanti yeavidyamupasate.
Tato bhuya iva te tamo ya u vidyayam ratah.

Into blinding darkness enter those who worship ignorance and those who delight in knowledge enter into still greater darkness, as it were.

10. Anyadevahurvidyaya anyadahuravidyaya.
Iti sushruma dhiranam ye nastadvicacakshire.

Distinct is the result, they say, of knowledge and distinct they say, is the result of ignorance, thus have we heard from those wise who have explained to us these.

11. Vidyam cavidyam ca yastadvedobhyam saha.
Avidyaya mrityum tirtva vidyayamritamasnute.

Knowledge and ignorance, he who knows the two together crosses death through ignorance and attains life eternal through knowledge.

### The Manifest and the Unmanifest

12. Andham tamah pravisanti yeasambhutimupasate.
Tato bhuya iva te tamo ye u sambhutyam ratah.

Into blinding darkness enter those who worship the unmanifest and into still greater darkness, as it were, those who delight in the manifest.

13. Anyadevahuh sambhavadanyadahurasambhavat.
Iti sushruma dhiranam ye nastadvicacakshire.

Distinct, indeed they say, is what results from the manifest and distinct, they say, is what results from the unmanifest. Thus, have we heard from those wise from those who have explained to us these.

14. Sambhutim ca vinasam ca yastadvedobhayam saha.
Vinasena mrityum tirtva sambhutyamritamasnute.

He who understands the manifest and the unmanifest both together, crosses death through the unmanifest and attains life eternal through the manifest.

### Prayer for the Vision of God

15. "Hiranmayen patrena satyasyapihitam mukham.
Tattvam pusannapavrnu satyadharmaya drstaye."

The face of Truth is covered with a golden disc. Unveil it. O Pusan! so that I who love the truth may see it.

16. "Pusanekarse yama surya prajapatya vyuha rasminsamuha.
Tejo yette rupam kalyanatamam tatte pasyami yoasavasau, purusah so'hamasmi."

O Pusan! The sole seer, O Controller! O Sun! Off-spring of Prajapati, spread forth your rays and gather up your radiant light that I may behold you of the loveliest form Whatever is that person (yonder) that am I.

17. "Vayuranilamamritamathedam bhasmantam sariram.
Aum krito smara kritam smara krito smara kritam smara."

May this life enter into the immortal breath; then may this body end in ashes. O Mind! Remember, remember what has been done. Remember! O Mind, remember.

18. "Agne naya supatha raye asman visvani deva vayunani vidvan. Yuyodhyasmajjuhuranameno bhuyistam te namauktim vidhema."

    O Agni! Lead us, along the auspicious path to prosperity. O God! Who knows all our deeds, take away from us deceitful sins. We shall offer many prayers unto thee.

    Maitrayana- Brahmana

    (800=400 BCE)

Maitrayana- Brahman Upanishad, named after its narrator, the teacher-Sage Maitri, is one of the shortest Upanishads and perhaps written toward the end of the Vedanta period. The present excerpt is part of a dialogue between king Brihadratha, who has renounced the world and a guru - Sakayana. The king is unwilling to do anything at all for himself because he believes when he dies everything else around him will also come to an end and he would he reborn as a new being. As a reward for his holiness the Guru teaches him about the 'soul'/Self, which resides in all human beings but is not part of the cycle of death and birth. No matter what shape a human being adopts in the next birth it remains with it- akin to Plato's ideal and the real. This concept is common to Judea-Christian and Muslim theology wherein body and soul are conceived as distinct entities of which one is perishable and the other not.

Both the Vedas and the Upanishads are concerned with the Ultimate Reality. Therefore they keep repeating the mantra - "Who is to be worshipped? To which god do I pay obeisance/? Who ought to be the object of my worship?" This Upanishad too like all others is also devoted to the same subject. Here is the text of this Upanishad.

### Chapter 1

Once upon a time a mighty king - named Brihadratha, after bequeathing his throne to his son renounced the world and all its pleasures. Thereafter performing the highest penances, he stood facing the sun with uplifted arms and prayed for the appearance of some saint to guide him toward his future course of action. After a lapse of thousand days his prayers were answered and there appeared a saint named

Sakayanya. He addressed the king and asked him to rise, "Rise, rise! Choose a boon."

Bowing before the saint the king asked. "O Saint! I know not the *Self.* Thou knowest the essence of the Self. This I have heard. Teach the same to me."

Sakayanya replied, "This was discovered long back. What you ask me to tell is difficult to achieve. Ask for some other boon; O the scion of your illustrious dynasty!"

Touching the feet of the Saint with his forehead the King said, "What is the use of enjoying pleasures with this gross body which are as transientas the worldly pleasures themselves? This offensive body is no more than a mass of bones, skin, sinews, marrow, flesh, seed, blood, mucus, tears, phlegm, ordure, water, bile and slime. What is the use of enjoying pleasures in this body which is afflicted by lust, hatred, greed, delusion, fear, anguish, Jealousy, fear of separation with the loved ones, union with what is not loved, hunger, thirst, old age, death, illness, grief, and other evils?

We also know that this body is as perishable as these flies, gnats and other insects are; and like herbs and trees it grows and decays. This is not all. The mightiest of the rulers, the wielders of the powerful bows and maces one day lie dead before the eyes of their family and the lay alike. We might as well ignore these ordinary mortals. Look at the death and destruction of the Gandharvas, Asuras, Yakshas, Rakshashas, Bhutas, Ganas, Pishachas, snakes and vampires. We are witness to the drying up of the great oceans, the falling of the mountains, the moving of the polar star, and even the gods must depart from their seats. Since all this happens all around all the time I feel like a frog in the well. O Saint! Thou are the only hope for me. Take me away from this world and guide me to get lasting peace."

## Chapter 2

"The Saint was well pleased. He said to the king," O King Brihadrath! You are the standard bearer of the great Iskshavaku dynasty and you have proved it too. Having learnt about the Self, you have immediately renounced the world. You are renowned by the name of Maruti (the god of wind), and you are also happy. This is the Self "Which is that? O Saint!" asked the King.

Then explained the Saint, "He who without stopping to exhale the breath proceeds upwards i.e. who moves away from the gross to the abstract, and who gets modified, and yet remains the unmodified and succeeds in driving away the darkness of ignorance, that is the Self. This is what said the Saint Maitri. Sakayanya then added further," He who rests in peace, having risen beyond this gross body attains a miniscule form, and after reaching the brightest light attains his original form, that 0 king, is the Self. This is the immortal Brahma.

Now then, this is the science of Brahman and the essence of all Upanishads. O King this was told by the Saint Maitri Nowl shall tell thee We learn from the past that there were once the Valakhilyas who hadmoved away from all forms of evils and were vigorous and passion less. They said to Prajapati Kratu "O Saint! This body is without intelligence, like a cart. Tell us which supernatural power has made it intelligent. Who is the driver, whatever thou knowest O Saint, tell us."

Prajapati responded, "He who in Shruti (the Vedas) is called 'Standing above' like passionless ascetic amidst the objects of the world. He indeed is the pure, clean, undeveloped, tranquil, breathless, bodiless, endless, imperishable, firm, everlasting, unborn, the independent one, stands in his own greatness, and by him has this body been made intelligent. It is he who is the driver."

Then they asked, "O Saint! How come has this body been made intelligent by the one who has no desire, how can he be the driver?"

He replied, "That Self which is miniscule in size, invisible, incomprehensible, called Purusha, dwells of his own 'Will' here in part, even as a man who is fast asleep wakes up of his own will. And this part of the Self, which is entirely intelligent, reflects in innumerable individuals like the sun gets reflected in different vessels of water at the same time; knowing the body.... attested by his conceiving, willing and believing, is Prajapati (the creator of all) called vishva;. By him, the intelligent is the body made intelligent. It is he who also is its driver."

Then they said to the Saint, "O Saint! If this body has been made intelligent by such a being the one that is above desire then how come he elects to become the source of such a creation?"

In the beginning Prajapati stood alone. He had no happiness in being alone. Meditating on himself he created many creatures. He looked at them and discovered that they were all like stones-bereft of understanding-more like lifeless posts. He had no happiness. He thought.

I shall enter these and may be they spring into life. Making himself like air he entered into them. Being one he could not become many. Then he divided himself into five - and thus assumed five forms each with well defined functions viz. Prana (Soul) which moves above, Apana (which moves downward); Vyan (that which upholds them both); Udana (that which carries the grosser material of food to the Apana); and that which brings the subtler material to each limb is called Samana.

After Prana, Apana and Samana comes the job of Vyan, and in between them comes the rising of the Udana.

(These five names of the divided air or wind which had constituted the lonely Prajapati are basically symbolic in nature because in reality this Upanishad is trying to tell us that the Reality is no more than air or Breath or Prana, So long as one breathes and is able either to belch or break wind etc one is alive. Therefore, Life is Breath or air or Prana-invisible, yet it is possible to ascertain its existence or non-existence).

Thus, having divided himself in five forms he lies hidden in a secret place in the body assuming the nature of the Mind and Prana (Soul) as his body, having true concepts and free like ether. Feeling even thus that he has not attained his object he thinks within his heart 'Let me enjoy the objects.' Thereafter he breaks open the five apertures (or through five senses) enjoys objects. The five senses — ear, skin, eye, tongue and nose activate five organs in the body-speech, hands, feet, anus, and the sex organs. These act like the horses to the body or chariot, mind becoming the charioteer, while the temper becomes the whip-thus starts the cycle of existence going round and round endlessly without achieving anything substantial. This is how the body becomes intelligent in which the invisible Prana lives on detached.

This indeed is the Self, which seemingly fulfils the desires and is also seemingly overcome by the fruits of his efforts. That is how he keeps wandering from one body to the other while remaining free.

Being invisible and bodiless he is beyond pleasure and pain. He is totally detached without any feelings whatsoever. He is like one of the two birds on the tree of life of which one is merely an onlooker while remaining in the company of the other which does taste the fruit of its efforts and therefore is subject to both the pleasures as well as the pain. The former is pure, firm, subtle, undefiled unborn, unmoved-free from desire, a mere spectator, who rests in himself. Having concealed himself in the cloak of these attributes he appears as the sole enjoyer. The infinite is happiness. There is no happiness in anything small (finite).

Now comes the point where Knowledge becomes Bliss. The fact is that Real knowledge is Bliss and ignorance is tantamount to unhappiness. When it knows the Reality one is happy because he reaches a state wherein attachments become transitory, everything else seems hollow.

Knowledge and ignorance, he who knows these two together crosses death through ignorance and attains life eternal through knowledge.

Ishopanishad 14.

# Chapter - 8

# Corruption, Debauchery and Misuse of Power

### The Great Indian Tradition

In the past few months, especially in the light of misuse of power and amassing of wealth by a handful of men and women in the Commonwealth Games; IPL, ICC or the major road construction works connecting the four metros in India has attracted the media attention. No one is spared criticism as if we have suddenly evolved into a class of people with missionary zeal who are out to reform and cleanse Indian society in a single go. The media seems so zealous of its own noble role that it seems to have forgotten that it by itself has not been free from these blemishes in the past; if not in the present. We have and perhaps justifiably so a very high opinion of our Judiciary but unfortunately the reality is only partially correct. In this branch of public service at least money making is relatively speaking unknown and the mighty and powerful are non-existent. We find it difficult to believe that the Vedas could talk of debauchery and illicit relations, besides drinking, betting and gambling etc. What is not available on these subjects in the Vedas or the Upanishads it is available in our Smritis. After all the Vedas are holy books and it is impossible for us even to think that our seers and rishis living a secluded life in sylvan surroundings would even know of such mundane blemished and moral compromises. The truth is however very different.

My purpose in writing this small paper is merely to point out that the Vedas and Upanishads do make a mention of all these vices-if, they can be called so. My purpose is not to justify any of these failings or moral compromises. My role is to remind ourselves that it is a rare individual who realises the truth that in a transitory world amassing of weal this ridiculous because instead of giving us any satisfaction, it only enhances the desire to have more and more until such time when it. becomes a cause for pain and not pleasure.

Few of us have an idea that the record of these moral deviations are traceable to the most ancient of India's revered books like the Rgveda and the Upanishads. The details given in them amaze us because it is difficult to believe that such a society would even know about these moral failings that afflict us today. Human beings will always remain human, easy to succumb to temptations instead of rising above these levels. Therefore, I would like to stress upon the point that these failings are common to the entire humanity and have been so down the history of human race. History records that persons like Socrates are rare. Perhaps he might even be a lone example who refused his friends drinking the deadly potion especially when they had bribed successfully the system itself. For him death was preferable to any sort of moral duplicity. I think it is instructive to read what our ancestors did in the past and derive some benefit for our solace.

*Now read one little moral deviation and moral compromise after another.*

The story of Satyakama is mentioned in the Chhandogya Upanishad. All students of philosophy are familiar with it. The story relates the request of Satyakama to his mother-to tell him about his father as he wanted to become a student where it was customary to inform the teacher about his Kul and gotra i.e. about the family details His mother replied that she did not know the name of his father as she served many a master in her youthful days. If he liked he could add her name to his. That is how he became Satyakama Jaabala. This is one story which throws light on the moral standards of both servants and their masters.

Everyone knows in India that *eight types of marriages* were sanctioned by the ancient Aryans. If the Vedas mention

(Rgveda, 2/32/4) on the one hand the marriage by choice of the two - i.e. the girl and her spouse; the Brihadaranynak Upanishad has no hesitation in approving forcible and violent marriage. Read (VIA. 12) Brihadaranyaka "If a man's wife has a lover and he hates him, let him put fire in an unbaked earthen ware spread out a layer of reed arrows in an inverse order soaked in clarified 'butter'. You have sacrificed in my fire, I take away in breath and out-breath, You so and so..." It does not require much intelligence to interpret this part of the message. On birth control read this passage in the same Upanishad (VIA, 10) "Now the woman whom one desires (with the thought that she may not conceive) after inserting the member in her, joining mouth to mouth, he should first inhale and then exhale and say, "with power, with semen I reclaim the semen from you". Thus, she comes to be without semen.

You could read also the disobedience of a son who accuses his father for not teaching him well enough. The name of the son is Svetketu Aruneya who accuses his father Gautum and the king in question is Pravahan Jaivali of Panchala who had failed in his test of esoteric knowledge. The chapter in this Upanishad is titled Life after Death. (Second Brahman) Like Vidheha he too is a King who is knowledgeable in the art and science of sacred and spiritual knowledge. Indeed this kind of knowledge was the prerogative of the Kshatriyas alone.

The *types of marriages* allowed in the ancient times are mentioned in the History of the Dharmasastra. Indeed the Hindus practiced eight types of marriages. These marriages had social sanction. Modern law declares some of them rape; abduction etc. and regards them as punishable crimes but not so in the past. The ancient Indians however had thought otherwise. The ancients accepted pishach and rakshash marriages too. How popular these marriages were is however beside the point. Ravana in the Ramayana abducted Sita to make her his principal wife down grading his existing Queen, Mandodary.

Now let us read the History of Dharmasashtra by P.V. Kane Vol. I. Chapters 11 to 16.The chapter 11 talks of multiple marriages in which man has the right to have several wives, even concubines while a woman had no such rights. Rgveda (10/ 145) and Atharvaveda (3/18) mention the feeling of less or more love for one against the other and a sense of jealousy is mentioned in both. Multiple marriages were common among teachers and Yagyavalkya - a great spiritual teacher, is one such example. Mahabharata presents a typology of teachers. Two types of teachers are mentioned prominently. Kripacharya and Dronacharya are shown as courtiers. They can witness what their masters do but are not supposed to do plain speaking. There were others who lived a peaceful life in solitary huts and did their job honestly. The courtiers are witness but do not oppose their masters. These twin teachers of repute are witness to Draupadi's humiliation but they keep their calm.

If it is immoral to share a woman like a piece of property then it is outright reprehensible to use her as a stake in gamble. Even seers were not averse to this practice. Tattiraiya Brahmana *(3/8/4)*declares women as property. Shatpath Brahman (13/411*19/)* talks of having four wives: - (1) the senior queen. Mahishi (2) the most preferred or vavta. (3) parityakta or the rejected one; and the (4) palagali or from some lower caste. Vajasneyi Samhita (23.24; 26,28) contains a few mantras wherein Brahma, Udgata and Hota i.e. the Vedic priests have descnbed all the four classes of women in their rank order. I suppose this is enough to prove a point that women had a very low position in that society. They could be asked to share their bed with more than one person but they had no right to a choice of their lovers. In the Mahabharata Draupadi was shared by all the five brothers and she was made a pawn by Yudhishthira-the senior husband, in gambling while all the other four other brothers who too shared her bed merely looked on. One can read a gambler's lament in the Rgveda (10/34). In gambling stakes matter and where pawn plays an important role. Yudhishthira lost everything in gambling because Shakuni knew the art of cheating and knew how to manipulate stakes. Yudhshithira declares that he could not run away from raising stakes when challenged. There is also a mention of prostitution in that society. See Rgveda (1.167, 4) (2, 29,1). Rgveda ( 1,66,4; *1.117,18; 1.34/3* etc.) relates such practices as women having secret lovers, putting illegitimate children by the wayside etc some thing which is a daily news item today..

We remain strangely enough a highly caste-based society. The Rgveda (X.90); Yajurveda (Ch. XXXI. IV) and Atharvaveda (XIX, VI. VI) endorse this societal division on caste lines.. Over the past number of centuries while the world has changed several times over we remain in this regard what we were in the past. The latest debate in our Parliament over caste census 2010 is a case in point. The first caste-based war in a law court is mentioned by King Sudrak in his drama The Little Clay Cart (Mrichchakatikam) in which a respectable Brahmin is brought to court on framed charges by the Kayasthas. It is here for the first time not only Kayasthas are mentioned as a caste they are shown as intellectual crooks. They showed their real colors during the Mughal times. Today if the Brahmins find Kayasthas as their principal intellectual adversaries in the job market then as a community, they must be accepted as their equals, if not better, Caste based politics makes us unique in modem world. The caste as we all know is not derived from the Purush Sukta. If Brahmins are born superior to other castes, then who gave birth to the Chanadals? If God is omnipresent and created all then who created this class of people? If it is He who created all then how does one can be counted as superior to another human being? The absurdity of this logic is therefore unacceptable. In the Rgveda itself we have support for this logic. The Vedas describe the qualities and characteristics of different castes and communities. For example, Vaishya or the business class is described in the Yajurveda (Ch. XXXV. 1). Businessmen who torment others, and are inimical to the learned should get away from here. May the Beautiful God grant this soul, the singer of Vedic hymns full opportunity with the luster of knowledge during all days and nights of life.

The Vedas knew of *adulterous women*. Therefore they desired to be protected from women who are given to adultery. Read for instance Yajurveda (Ch. XXXVII, 12). "Strong in conviction in the upper direction, in the over lordship of a learned master of the Vedas, give me energy. Being filled with a reflective mind, protect me from women given to adultery."

Now read the *qualities of King* that are ideal for a society and compare our contemporary rulers with them. "He alone is fit to be elected the head of the State, who possesses power, knows how to arrange his army, in different military arrays, in majestic ways like the sun; challenges for battle his impious foes, chastises the wily and deceitful persons, kills the dacoits hidden in forests, and makes the words of preachers who diffuse happiness."

Interestingly, look at the *desires of the people* of that society and try to compare our desires with theirs. Their desires are as mundane as are ours "Oh God! Thou art our well wisher the eternal knower of everything. Thy kindness may we see for a hundred years; may we live for a hundred years, may we listen for a hundred years the Vedic lore; may we preach the Vedas for a hundred years; may we live content Independently for a hundred years yes even beyond a hundred years, see, live, hear, preach and be not dependent. (Yajurveda XXXVI, 24)

In the next chapter i.e. Yajurveda Ch. XXXVII. 7) they desire to be associated with the Lord of Wealth. Our ancestors did not live in sylvan surroundings and had the same desires as we have today and neither was that society any different from ours. They had identical problems and similar desires as we have even as they too had their quota of thieves, burglars, prostitutes and gamblers, bad rulers and dishonest and immoral teachers.

Not unlike us our ancestors too did not live in sylvan surroundings. They naturally had similar life and shared most of our weaknesses and strengths. They had many of our problems and had similar desires as we have these days. They too had their quota of thieves, burglars, prostitutes and gamblers, good rulers and bad ones even as they had sincere and good teachers alongside bad ones. They had both Kripacharyas and Yagyavalkyas. In brief, human nature has hardly changed ever since. We have not evolved into superhuman beings and until this happens we must learn to live with our venial sins.

# Chapter - 9

# Modern Equations: Traditional Solutions

(Traditional Knowledge in a Knowledge Society)

*This essay examines the usefulness of reading the Vedas in the modern times.*

"A technologist first builds a transport to travel on earth, second in the water and the third capable to fly in the sky. 0 person! Such technologists impart happiness, triumph and make us powerful. It connects or regulates such movements in the ocean with thoroughness. Likewise, they should train more people to multiply the number of more technologists." Rigveda, 2. 18.2

**Meaning of 'Traditional Knowledge'**

Before we define *Knowledge* let us try to understand the use and meaning of the term 'traditional' first. Tradition lexically means "the handing down of opinions or practices to posterity unwritten", i.e., something society remembers to be useful and even after repeated trials finds the results consistently uniform. This is the scientificity of a tradition. All traditions have two components-the uncritical ritualistic, and the other one 'open' for a dialogue before a change. All societies have to deal with both. The uncritical and the ritualistic form of a tradition, if followed make a society 'closed'. Invariably such societies get dominated by priesthood and become inimical to progress. It is the 'open' societies that welcome criticism, dialogue, dissent and eventually progress. The best indicators of 'openness' are the multiplicity of educational managements and a variety in the school curricula. Such societies alone welcome criticism or questioning of a tradition and ignore the classes who oppose change or variations in social practices.

**Defining Knowledge**

How does one define a 'Knowledge Society'? Firstly let us try to understand the meaning of the term Knowledge. Knowledge is nothing more than rational, cumulative, classified graded bits of information, which can be openly questioned. Information is a single point illumination of a query, which most of the time is an uncritical reply and whose source is invariably difficult to identify, A Knowledge Society is characterised by 'openness' and acceptance of new ideas and innovations. Being progress-oriented it is forever ready for a dialogue, experimentation and rationality. It is possible that some of us may hold the view that knowledge societies are a modern acknowledgement of a reality and that such societies have appeared only recently. This is not true. Such societies have existed in the past also and their quantum and the level of knowledge continue to surprise us. In fact, in a number of areas such as philosophy, ethics, science, literature, architecture etc the Greeks, the Egyptians, the Chinese and the Indians reached pinnacles of glory.

There are areas in which the ancients have yet to find their modem-day match. For instance, in Philosophy, Bertrand Russell acknowledges that the entire development in this field could easily be summed up in a single footnote to Plato's *Republic.* The Pyramids continue to amaze us for the way they built vaults to preserve their dead and the material used to keep their remains unblemished. We have yet to find a match to Confucius or Lord Buddha and for the Aristotle's theory of the 'golden mean.' We have not succeeded to add a new plot (story) to the seven identified by Aristotle or excel the use of Divine intervention in resolving a complex situation in dramatic plot.

Knowledge by itself is both multi-dimensional and unique. It has a typology of its own. Besides being eternal and contextually identifiable, knowledge has a variety and its set goals. For instance, human knowledge is different from that of the animals. Each Discipline as a Knowledge area has its own stock mostly different from that of the others and, even when the new stock is merely a derivative it seeks to explain the differences from remaining independent and un-submerged. Knowledge is distinguishable both by its age or the geography. When exported it changes its allegiance too and acquires a new identity such as Indian/American or Australian English. Knowledge could be static and/or developmental. The only thing that characterises knowledge is that it changes its hue, control, definition and the state of development in terms of politics whether religious or otherwise. Therefore, while knowledge in a democracy is always on the rise/development in an autocracy or dictatorship can never be similar.

This means Knowledge exists in varying stages of development - some nascent, other developing or some fully developed. All traditional knowledge need not be developed afresh. In a way knowledge remains forever amenable to critical examination. Each sage of advancement has a context to consider. For instance, in the Indian context our society lives in varying stages of material and social development. A few of us have grown materially and intellectually so advanced that a comparison with European society appears legitimate. But the majority lives in conditions of extreme destitution and intellectual poverty. Generalisations therefore become irrelevant.

One must therefore remember that societies are not homogenous. Just as it is impossible to find everybody to be identically healthy or sick, humans continue to offer a variety in existence. Similarly, there is no question offirding everyone equally accomplished or well-read. Therefore, all societies are identified in terms of groups of people who differ from each other either racially or culturally and who have characteristics that help keep their identities distinctly definable.

**The suitability of the Vedas as a source of perennial knowledge**

The Vedas are correctly regarded as repositories of all kinds of ancient knowledge and the acme of ancient Indian wisdom. In them lie the seeds (at times the finished products) of our modern knowledge. For instance, there is hardly any branch of knowledge viz. music, astronomy, physics, modern mathematics, yoga, alternate medicine, philosophical systems, literature, grammar and prosody, etc. whose foundations cannot be traced back to them. A few know that the binary system, which gave birth to computer sciences, has its origins in the

Vedas. The yoga and the alternate medicine, which are the current rage in the West can also be traced back to the Vedas. True, we have outgrown many of the Vedic discoveries and findings. But there are numerous areas of knowledge where we are still groping in the dark alongside the ancients. In some ways the contemporary astrophysics has brought us back to the *Nasdiya Sukta* to compare notes. Be that as it may, we share with them the desire to learn and discover.

We find the Vedas contain two types of knowledge–one that is eternal, this knowledge is given to us as a finished product; and, the other that changes with time and people. The knowledge they give us about the nature of humans-like health, moral or religious code, philosophy etc is liable to change either through deliberate efforts or time. The reason is simple. Each, age and Time defines its health, morality, and material requirements. But the constants like the need to work for a living, do business, undertake travel, evolve methods and modes of governance etc. remain constant with plenty of scope for redefinition in their form an el content. The Vedas offer us a variety of knowledge most of it being eternal! or constant. They also lay the foundation for a possible variety and scope for advancement.

Traditional knowledge has it own uses. The Vedas informed us way back in time that, "O people! You should discover the attributes and 'myths of wind and sun', they create water and juices of all types by penetrating through the clouds and make prosperity. The rain water does not stay with the sun. The origins of the water give knowledge about the sun and let us know that." Rig-Veda 2.30.2 It is perhaps the Vedic times that the Indian farmers know the meaning of wind direction, the movement of the seven stars (Saptarshi), the usefulness of the sun, and the moon, relationship of months with seasons and the interpretation of the color of the sky with prospective disturbances, etc. They have been told over a period of time when certain birds appear, sing or squeak that portend a change in weather or when the black ants move from one place to another along with their household wares it signifies climate shift. For our purpose it is enough to understand that all these simple tit bits of knowledge passed on from generation to generation come in handy since they help supplement the predictability of scientific time-tested human awareness and information.

If we wish to define the uses of traditional knowledge we shall have to conclude by saying that the entire stock of human knowledge is built up on the information handed down from one generation to another and eventually this amounts to measuring the level or extent of a society's progress. The ones who lag behind get classed as backward or 'developing' and are those who neither create new knowledge nor store the knowledge that is readily available in the form of traditions. Besides they do not possess in adequate measure the necessary wherewithal of transferring it either.

What we call scientific or objective reality is something that has a lineage of tradition. Repeated experiments or testing the reliability or validity of an information/hunch/*or*/ hypotheses makes the information thus gathered scientific - because it could be demonstrated anywhere to show consistency in the results. In a manner of speaking therefore 'traditions' in most cases are nothing but scientifically valid truths whose origins/sources have been forgotten or are just not readily available for comparison. This does not qualify for a sneering act on the part of those who generalise knowledge as a derivative of some available source other than mere oral tradition.

In the case of this country our traditional knowledge has withstood the test of time. The illiterate farmer is nearly as good a weather forecaster as a weather reporter who has the benefit of scientific gadgets. This comparison may not hold good always, but the predictability of both sources of information is seldom questionable.

## Traditional Knowledge as conceived by the National Knowledge Commission

The National Knowledge Commission (NKC) too has assigned a certain role to this traditional knowledge in their scheme of things. Although one may not agree with the definition of the traditional knowledge given by the NKC (p. 22) it is true that the 'appropriate application of this knowledge can enrich people's lives and livelihoods, provide alternative means of sustenance and generate substantial employment.'

NKC has written that it is examining the following aspects of traditional knowledge:–

1. The principles that should govern the documentation and use of plant based drug formulations; traditional knowledge;
2. Traditional agricultural practices;
3. Culinary traditions;
4. Traditional water-harvesting techniques; and
5. Traditional products, services and art forms not included above.

As it is, the NKC has already received "a report on the traditional health sciences for their globalisation". I suppose the reason why a Report on this area of traditional knowledge was the first to be submitted is because this branch of health sciences is more well-known and its practitioners have always been available ever since the times when *Atharvaveda* was compiled. But then there are other areas too that are equally well-known and nearly as much traditional - a few that have a direct bearing on our daily life and are linked with our food habits, naturopathy, environment our rationality and mental health.

Though it is not possible to include all these areas in this paper or go into details of the benefits that may accrue if we were to learn the truths that were recorded in the Vedas but for the benefit of those who wish to learn about them, only two or three aspects of that knowledge are presented. We must remember that in this country a section of our population reveres the Vedas although they shall never read them or learn anything from them. Faced with the energy crisis the modemm an should know that the Vedas had exhorted in their time the scholars to "know the nature and properties of energy and should take the optimum use of that knowledge." Rg-Veda 2;9.1

What is most intriguing about the Vedas is that they come all of a sudden not unlike a bolt from the blue without any precedence/ continuity or knowledge of the state of society that produced them. We know practically nothing about the pre-Vedic people, the state of their material /literary development, their social organisations/customs or preferences, etc. The usual support for any historical statement that one derives from subject areas such as archeology, written word, etc.

provide no help to an individual trying to piece together a picture of the time that preceded the Vedic age. In fact, a Marxist like S.A.Dange, for instance, has with the help of Engels tried to superimpose our contemporary logical analytical system on the times to which he doesn't appear to have had any clue.

**Connotation of certain terms in the context of the Vedas**

It is important to define a few terms used in the context of the Vedas. It may interest some to know that *Sukta* means what is pleasant to hear or something nice that has been said. In all, the Vedic *Samhitas* (as distinguished from the literature based on the Vedas such as the *Brahmanas, Upanishads, Aranakyas* etc.) consist 01, 20,500 mantras. The other thing worth noting is that a number *ofRgvedic verses* appear in the other Vedas too. The Vedic prose is rhythmic. The Vedas contain the earliest recorded poetry and prose literature of the human race. The Vedas are no *sastras* i.e. they are not systematised knowledge with a set of any scientific terminology. In most cases they summarise the insights gained over a period of time.

Samhitas means compilations. The Suktas and the mantras that are compiled under Rik are called Rik Samhita or the Rgveda. Similarly, the mantras compiled under Sam or Yajus are called Samveda or Yajurveda. The Atharvaveda is so called because Rishi Atharvan wrote a substantial part of it. For a long time the Atharvaveda was not regarded as part of the trayi tradition. Generallyit is believed to be the last Veda because its content reflects a society very different from the society in the earlier Vedas. It seems by then the Aryans had come in contact with the local tribes and aborigines who believed in sorcery, magic and other satanic powers and all these impacts got reflected in the mantras of this particular Veda. In her book A Short History of the Vedic Literature, Eastern Book Linkers, 1994, Delhi, (p. 9, Hindi), Dr Pushpa Gupta advances reasons for accepting the Atharvaveda as the last Veda. According to her (a) religion had peaked by then, (b) it deals essentially with the material world that deal with mundane occurrences of human existence, and (c) thereafter no new prayers were written.

The meaning of a few terms generally used while talking about the Vedic literature is explained earlier. For instance, the *Sukta* means good poetry, or *Mantra* means speculation or summary of thought presented in quintessential form. The term *Samhita means* compilation. On the basis of the meaning and the nature of the content the *Vedas* are called *Veda-trayi.* This use does not denote that the reference here is restricted to three Vedas only and the fourth Veda i.e. the *Atharvaveda* has been excluded. At the same time it is generally taken to mean that only the first three Vedas count and the fourth does not get similar weightage.

Though technically the word Veda means knowledge/gyan, the Indian tradition holds that the Vedas contain both the contents and purpose of the karmakaand i.e. the sacrificial rituals as well as the jnankaand i.e. the spiritual knowledge. On the basis of these twin purposes of the Vedas the sacrificial aspect of them is contained in the Brahmanas and the jnan/or the spiritual aspect of the knowledge is dealt with in the Upanishads, In fact, Apastamba titles both the mantras and the Brahmanas as the Vedas.

It is believed that internal evidence available in the sruti/or what was revealed or heard is indicative of the gradual complexity of language development that took place then. The ancients preserved the Vedas through oral tradition. It is common knowledge that to keep any language unchanged for a long time is simply impossible. A living language will invariably change both because of its natural tendency to absorb new words and idioms in its repertoire and to keep modifying pronunciations with each successive generation. This linguistic reason forced the ancients to devise a system that prevented such a change to occur. They, therefore, evolved a regular disciplinary system known as the vedangas i.e. the limbs of the Vedas. It was felt necessary to lay down general rules for pronunciation of words properly. Change in pronunciation leads to change in the interpretation and meaning of the words. This necessitated the formulation of *shiksha* and *chhandas.* The *vedangas* are six in number. They are: (1) *Shiksha* (orthography), (2) *Chhanda* (prosody), (3) *Nighantu* (lexicon), (4) *Jyotis* (astronomy), (5) *Vyakarana* (grammar) and (6) The *Kalpa* (rituals).

The ancients also divided knowledge into several areas of specialisations. These knowledge areas are called the up (mini)-Vedas or the minor Vedas. These are: (1) *the Ayurveda* (the science of medicine and cure), (2) the *Gandharva-veda* (the system of aesthetics),

(3) the *Dhanurveda* stands for the system of defence sciences, and (4) The Arthaveda means economics or the science of wealth i.e. the production, distribution and utilisation of wealth for the development and growth of this kind of knowledge it is more than obvious that the ancients must have taken a very long time. In fact, the form in which the Vedas themselves have been made available to us makes an interesting reading.

I have taken up for discussion first that area which is currently of the greatest concern to the Mankind, *namely—Environment.* Let us see what the Vedas have to say about it.

Long before others came to realise the value of environment the ancient Indians had perhaps intuitively learnt that trouble comes from unknown sources and therefore, it is better to take care of the immediate neighborhood first. This neighborhood is environment. By definition environment means "The aggregate of circumstances surrounding organisms or group of organisms including the social and cultural conditions affecting the nature of individuals or community." Hence, the following prayer:

"May the five types of men, born to offer (the butter of) affection, and eager to perform the sacrifice, be pleased with my discharge of the function as an invoker; may *the earth preserve us from the troubles that come from heaven."*

"May you, spinning the thread of divine knowledge, follow the splendid light of the illuminator, and protect the pathways well..."

"The great river of life-conflicts flows alone, be alert; rise up, cross over, my friends; here let us leave those who are wretched and hence unhappy; may we cross over (this river) to secure auspicious boons." Rg-Veda X.54.5-7

The present write-up is addressed to those who have a very vague idea of how knowledgeable the ancient Vedic society was. In whatever form the Vedas have survived, they tell us enough about the Nature, Life and the concerns of the ancient Indian. Since I have for my write-up selected the Vedas as the principal area for exploration I have gone by the text that is available; therefore I have not bothered to include any analysis of the archaeological findings of Indus Valley Civilisation to show how the urban populace of those times had evolved amazingly the most sophisticated and scientific urban water supply system and also the sewage systems that have been excavated.

The Vedic society is no less advanced and knowledgeable about the world around them. The Vedic Seers appear to have foreseen the catastrophe Man was likely to invite for his own destruction, therefore they had forewarned against indulging in such acts.

The appreciation for '*enlightened person*' is remarkable for the ancients. Read what they have to say, "O men! I praise an enlightened person who shines and purifies like the fire kindled well with fuel, which is steadfast in non-violent sacrifices, pure, purifier, and liberal donor, respected by many scholars, void of malice, wise with knowledge and humility and highly learned." Rg-Veda 6.15.7

Experience informs us that mere knowledge is rarely enough to prevent trouble, and it is also true that we rarely listen to reason until the catastrophe takes over and we are left with nothing else but regret. In the modem high-tech world people have little time and even less patience to go deeper into any text even when it might have enormous value for one's guidance. Indeed, it is no longer considered necessary to read scriptures or may be it is even considered un-intellectual, if not infradig, to try discovering any particular sense in reading them. Perhaps it is the job of a priest who is put paid for his services to read the same out in bits and pieces on ceremonial occasions.

**Contemporary Environmental Concerns and the Vedas**

Indian historians took considerable time to discover the meaning and the message that the Vedas carry and that too only when the Western scholars had started using the Vedas and their text for purposes other than those of mere scholarship. One must admit that it is the West that initially led the path back to our glorious past and furnished insight to find for us gems that had been lying hidden in the obscure homes of the neglected but venerable scholars.

I propose to cite here relevant hymns on each of the manifested contemporary environmental concerns from the text of the Vedas and show that the ancient Indians had the knowledge of the environmental problems but their future progenies, alas! They did not have the 'Will' to act. The message is clear. If we failed once there is still time to mend our ways. This is the sole purpose of learning History. Historians as interpreters of facts are capable of delivering subtle messages to the posterity.

Although all the four Vedas were supposed to have appeared simultaneously the common belief is that the Rg-Veda came first. It is in this Veda that we *see vayu* or air being regarded as the soul of human beings. They realised the value of the air and talked of its curative powers. "Lord *Vayu* is the soul and spirit *of Indra* and all other gods and living beings and is the seed of the world. Such a divine Lord flows according to its Will. We can only hear it but cannot see it. We bow before this lord *Vayu.*" Rg- Veda X.168.4. Additionally they came to realise that air had its own curative powers. Therefore, they prayed, "O *Vayu!* Bring your medicines and do away with all the ailments here because you are the only one who is full of curative powers." In the history of Indian philosophy there is discussion about the evolution of the concept of *Atma* or the source of life, which was at different points in time was variously identified with air, water, food etc. Even now we call soul *as prana vayu.* Since they rated all these 'elements' as divine and identified them with soul or life itself, it was unimaginable for them to have even thought of polluting any one of these.

Read, for instance, their feelings about *Mother Nature*:-

"I address this new laudatory hymn, with all sincerity of heart to the fire Divine, who loves it; and appreciates; may He hear our voice; may I be in the center of His heart like a loving well-attired wife meeting her husband."

"I address this new laudatory hymn, with all sincerity of heart to the fire Divine, the absorber of water, to whom the oblations of herbal juices (mixed with curds) are offered and in whom every living being like vigorous horses, bulls, milching cows and barren ones, sheep and goat are consigned to the cremating fire."

"The vast heaven, the spacious firmament, and the glorious unbounded earth; pay homage to the fire divine, Lord of the cosmic sacrifice; Nature's bounties such as lightening, the sun, the water, the wind and the cosmic intelligence, with potentialities purifies, recognise him with one accord."

"The rivers flow along with the dashing storms and sweep over the boundless earth, with them the circumambient lightening, spreading over a wide space thundering in the belly (of the firmament) bedews everything that lies within." Rg-Veda, X.92. 1-4.

In terms of Western history the concern for environment dates back to 1962 (which is very recent) when Rachel Carson wrote *Silent Spring.* This book focused on the enormity of ecological damage brought about by industrial waste being dumped into the rivers. Then came the papers by Barbara Ward and Rene Dubois in 1972 "Only One Earth." Their project had been funded by llNDP. It brought to the fore the confict between biosphere of Man's inheritance and the techno-sphere of His creation. Since then the voices of concern for the safe upkeep of this creation have not been silenced. The concern clearly is about keeping the environment livable. The express desire is for striking a balance between material prosperity and human sustenance. The 'Club of Rome'—funded by independent scientists, too has shown similar concerns and proposed almost identical schemes to sustain life on this planet.

The 'Limits to Growth,' brought out in 1972, reported research findings based on a data collected at global scale on a mathematical model. The model predicted Doom and stated that continued resource shortages, crowding, pollution, famines etc. will soon control current trends in population growth, natural resource exploitation and capital investment in agriculture. As expected the model was heavily criticised. Since then the problem remains where it was seen for the first time. As of today the problem is whether or not based on non-renewable resources is it possible to maintain a certain rate of sustained growth forever? We unfortunately are no longer ideologically neutral.

The Indian concern for the environment is as old as our civilisation's origins. But did the ancients understand the meaning of the term 'environment'? Perhaps they did. But then what exactly do we mean by this term. "The environment (after all) is sum total of water, air and land inter-relationships among themselves and also with the human beings: other living organisms and property." This definition appears in the Environment (Protection) Act, 1986.

In modern terminology if one wanted to have a comprehensive knowledge of the subject the minimum requirement is to go through several stages of a variety of subject areas, such as Botany, Zoology, Microbiology, Genetics, Geology, Bio-chemistry Bio-technology, Oceanography, Atmospheric science, Statistics etc. It would appear as though we hold the view that if the ancients spoke on all these subjects with equal command like us then alone they would be considered knowledgeable enough for our good, failing which, let us keep them under covers for a few recluses and the lonely.

Let us examine the Vedas on all these counts all the same.

For instance, see in this quote a desire that we have in common with the ancients, i.e. work so that one could meet one's physical needs and an airy house to live in. "I resort to agriculture and craft for removing poverty and ministering happiness to all. May I feel joy in domestic life! May our houses be sufficiently commodious, airy, fully comfortable, and built in the middle of an open space." Yajurveda, Chapter 1.11

For an obvious reason an individual engaged in agriculture knows the value of timely and plentiful rain. In this sense we have not outgrown this basic requirement.

" Let us see with respect that earth, which loves the rains and is looked after by the clouds, in which is grown foodgrains like rice and barley, and where live all the four castes, and the other five types of people. Atharvaveda/12/1/42

As one reads the Vedas one is made to realise that the ancients suffered from the same weaknesses as we do, but they prayed to get rid of them through sustained efforts called the *yagnas*. For them," the yagna keeps away the thieves, refines and sweetens the speech, is productive of food stuffs and is the best ower of knowledge and vigor. *Yajurveda.* Ch. 1. 16

We see in the following few pages the *type of knowledge* they had of the Nature and its capacities. They desired that we do not transgress boundaries and remain within acceptable limits to avoid catastrophe. See here their knowledge about fire /heat.

"I describe the special features of Fire. It takes every type of matter forward. It softens iron ore etc. it burns everything. *It emits light. It beautifies It is set up before everything else. It performs many functions and is used during many activities. It is an instrument for attracting attention, give and take and for food preparation. Fire creates inside earth all varieties of gems and ores like gold, silver, iron, and diamonds.*" Rg-veda l/1

In the following quote the reader could see that they had knowledge of Vaastu and were fully acquainted with the powers of the Nature's Elements.

"O husband and wife! We want to construct a house for you; that is fully lighted by the strong rays of the Sun. For Sun is strong and capable of giving happiness yielding light". Rg-veda 1/155/6

About the *Solar energy* they say :

"Learn carefully about the presence of *Vaishwanar* Fire in us all. The same Agni/Fire is located in all worlds and the same is working through *Vaishwanar* Sun doing all kinds of work such as producing light, growth of plants etc. Rg-Veda *1/98/1*

Here is a hymn from *Yajurveda* (XXXIII. 92), which talks of the functions of Sun: "Just as the Sun, set in Heaven, the benefactor of humanity, increasing in power on Earth, ripens medicines and grows food, removes darkness of night with his lustier, shines forth, so should ye dispel ignorance".

"Just as lightning destroys insects that disturb sleep and spread disease, let us enjoy all the fruits and favors granted to us by the Sun and the wind and thereby let us feel safe against Nature gods." Rg-Veda! *10/36/4*

Or read their knowledge about the relationship of Sun with the formation of clouds and feeding rivers with plentiful water:

"O Gurudev! Just as strong, light -emitting Sun attracts the waters of these rivers toward itself and having done so distributes them through clouds all over again on the land, so do you attract students and instruct them with eclat". Rg 7/34/10

The Seers therefore enjoin us to learn to "Respect that special Guru who is powered by education, who is familiar with the work of

*Agni, Vaayu, Sun* and other deities and knows all about the names, places and the births. You should respect those Gurus too who understand the speed of air and the lightening and who can tell you the exceptional ways to Salvation." *Rg-veda* 7/58/1

They offer a lesson or two in human psychology for *compassion toward one and all.*

"May that intellect which is inside me let that be full of feelings of welfare for others. It is because of that the industrious, reflective and patient men work to gain both knowledge and the riches, and undertake to give charity, worship gods and work for mutual benefit, and that which is located in all living beings." *Yajurveda 34/2.*

"Even as all spokes in a wheel are joined together in the center may my intellect also carry feelings of welfare for others because of the coming in of knowledge from the *Rgveda,* the proper methods of actions from the *Yajurveda* and of worship from the *Samveda.*" *Yajurveda* 34/5

We could see their concern for the education of all, more particularly of girls. At least in this sense they were far ahead of us. While discussing methods of instruction, the Seers also talk of how to practice writing. Incidentally, the following lines throw light on a historically disputed domain. Few historians dispute the fact that the Vedic people had no script and therefore writing was unknown to them. I suppose it is possible to resolve that contentious issue whether or not the ancients knew how to write, what to write and the lack or otherwise of a script. The fact that they knew about the written word can be established even otherwise. For instance, on the demerits of gambling the *Rgveda* (10/34/2) says that the faces of the dice carried written symbols. At another place; viz. Rg-veda 10/62/7, there is a mention that the ears of the cows have the number 8 written on them.

Additionally, these lines also show that *education of girls* was common and prevalent. In their opinion female teachers are better teachers than their male counterparts.

"O girl students! Just as intelligent teachers introduce writing and reading of letters with the help of fingers, you should know lady teachers who know innumerable subjects and possess immeasurable learning.

For your balanced development such an intelligent teacher will herself make all arrangements." Rg-veda/7/15/9

In case this is not enough to establish their knowledge about *language*/linguistics then see elsewhere they mention that mere reading is never enough because people learn at a pace which differs from individual to individual:

"A few do not understand the secret of the language even after reading it, a few others do not realise the reality even after listening to it but *there are others for whom the language presents her true form as does a beautiful bedecked bride reveals herself before her husband.*" Rgveda 10/71/4

"Language through its own symbols explains the wide expanse of knowledge and is able to illumine all intelligence fully. Therefore, one should put language to good use." *Rg-veda 1/3/13*

We see here the functions of language per se and its symbolic nature. It perhaps holds a lesson or two for the modern day linguists.

What did the *Rgveda* say about the nature of the universe (cosmology)/astrophysics that we live in? We may have advanced in varied ways but about the origin of the galaxies, stars and planets we arc still nowhere being close to certainty. Even today we have not gone beyond the realm of conjectures in numerous academic areas such as astrophysics for instance; then how could we expect the ancients to be definitive about their knowledge, who definitely had no access to the present day scientific instruments, which make a Hawking so knowledgeable and relatively certain? According to the ancients the universe consisted of three regions-the earth (prithvi), heaven (dyauh), and the intermediate world or the antariksha. We are familiar with the term earth, but not with dyauh because this is one term which was employed to denote the vault of the sky, which is the place where the sun and the stars shine. They had an idea that there was an invisible world too where these stars and the sun retired after their daily ritual! duty was over.

The Rgvedic hymns sporadically mention the abodes of padam of Agni, (1.72.2), Indra Pusan (1.162,2), Vishnu (1,154,6) etc. In reality they appear to think that the universe consisted of four regions. The name of the fourth region is Satya Lok. Read Rgveda. (1.35.2), which says "Causing immortal and mortal to rest God Savitr returned (to his abode) by way of the Satya Lok (i.e. invisible) world; he comes on the golden chariot observing the worlds." The Satya Lok was considered the abode of Brahma, the Creator. The later day developments have only added certain more Loks to the list. Only as a passing reference I mention here the seven loks that the Puranas talk about. From Bhu-lok upwards are Bhuvar Lok, Svar-Lok, Mahar Lok, Jan Lok, Tapo-Lok and the Satya Lok. Similarly, by that time the idea of seven 'nether' worlds had also grown and developed. They were called atal, sutal, vital, and patal etc. according to the depths at which different unwanted creatures supposedly lived.

## Vedic Concept of the Origin of the Creation

Numerous references are made daily to the unusually wonderful understanding these Rishis had of the origin of the Creation, especially to the scienuficity of their observations. For instance, the subject of Creation interested these Rishis immensely. The Rgveda talks of it in the Hymn 10/ 129/7 and Yajurveda in 10/129/3 etc.. It does amaze one to imagine that even with out the benefit of any of the modem equipments and gadgets they could be, at times, so precise in their observations. For instance, the Vedas hold the view that in the beginning there was nothing but darkness. It was the state of Nature, which could drown all without a trace. That extensive Nature, which is hidden in the Cause form, the same with the shinning glory of the divine God appears in the physical form as its effect. Compare this piece with the findings of modern astrophysics and take your own decision.

Read the *Nasdiya Sukta* and feel surprised at the latent modernity of reasoning and logic:

"What was the state during the Pralaya or total annihilation? Who is the Creator? What was the principal cause of Creation and what its principal instrument? During Pralaya there was no evil or good nor did the atoms fill the horizons? What was shrouded and by what? Who was the Protector? Did only the deep seas exist?

There was no death nor was there any life. Even the day and night had not taken birth. The lone Creator breathed without any life breath by his own will. Nothing superior existed beyond him.

In that dark existed, the un-manifested Nature like seamless water. Everything looked small before him. Nature gradually manifested itself because of the austerities of the Supreme Being." Rg-veda 10. 129 i-v.

A Desire was superimposed on what existed in the form of inner self during Pralaya The seers could thus realise that the Good was latent in the Evil even as the light is in the dark. The creation could arise out of the un-manifested Nature. Slanted bright rays spread out of these three-God, Soul and the Nature. What was below was as amazing as the one who could serve as receptacles for that amazing semen above. If one went deep into the description of the origins of the Creation itself we start dealing with the eternal questions of Philosophy whose definitive answers continue to elude us. Our understanding of the Reality is as remote today as it was when the ancients were trying to grapple with it.

In a hymn the seer says, "One thing that is beyond this world is matter, the material cause of this world another thing even beyond this is the soul which is remote in rareness and not within reach of ordinary man." (Atharvaveda, Book V, XI. VI)

**The Art and the Science of Architecture**

Interestingly, the Atharvaveda carries a section on the Vaastu sastra-the art and science of architecture. Here a number of hymns talk of God being present in a three-room school or the eight-room school. One cannot imagine of a three rooms or eight rooms building without proper measurements and even building materials.

"Like the animal heat in the body and foetus in the womb I, the master of the house live in the houses, which are built with two wings, four wings, six wings, eight wings, and are constructed in appropriate measurement." Atharvaveda/9/3/21

In fact, so great is the insistence on the proper measurement of the size of the rooms and the accurate mixture of mortar that one could seriously start thinking about the presence of the ubiquitous modem day contractor in that society too. One would be amazed to read about their express desire to make lighting arrangements that are necessary for a large room. The mention is of electricity and also of teaching aids. I must say I have failed to be specific because I do not know whether this light is not lightning and teaching aids something very elementary and highly primitive in character. These hymns in question are: Atharvaveda 9/3/1 and 9/3/11 and many more. The fact that God is present in all these classes of the school does suggest that schooling was carried on in built enclosures and not under the shade of the trees or in the hermitages only.

**The Idea of the Vedic Guru**

It is not quite correct that all gurus had equal competence. But in terms of their insistence on respect there is near unanimify. The impression that we have is that the Guru did not charge fees. May be he did not do so in the beginning. But no student could leave the residence of the teacher without paying the appropriate amount in terms of tuition fees/guru-dakshina.

On pupil's return home the following hymn specifically desires that the teacher should make some relaxation in the strict rules that one followed.

"O the best Guru! The restrictions that you had imposed on us regarding food, sensuality and travel, please relax them now. O luminous with *knowledge,* Gurudev! *We shall* continue to observe all the *pure vratas,* and shall continue studying with unbroken regimen, the Vedas." Yajur. 12/12

In fact, there is a mention that at the time of leaving the Ashram the student does say that he would like to know about the time one could leave the school and when does he invite the teacher home. Atharvaveda (11/5/26) describes how glorious the student looks on the completion of his education.

But here is one mantra wherein the teacher refuses to be admired by a student whom he regards to be a fool.

"O you, my pupil ! Who shuns practice in learning, even if you are ready for employment immediately, I do not like your praise because you cannot repeat properly even those lessons that have already been taught. You, who are famous amongst fools, I do not like any praise from you. I would much prefer you becoming properly educated and earn reputation than what you are Right now. That would enhance my reputation." Rg-Veda/7/22/5

"The teachers who teach at the lower levels and offer expertise may they improve and grow. Those that teach at the middle and higher stages let them too progress and develop. The teachers of Som-knowledge let them too progress. Let all these teachers teach us the techniques and methods of prayer and the yagnas. Besides these teachers, those who know the techniques of the yagnas and are aware of *the way the Universe was created and are free from crookedness and have long lives may they too impart us instruction"* Rg-Veda 10/15/1.

Let us now take an example of their concern for *keeping rivers free from pollution*:

"O God! Cast aside the vile man who pollutes rivers..." says the Yajurveda XXX, 8 and the hymn goes on to command, "Nishad's son, hankering after libidinous women; a degraded arrogant, friend of person harmful like a tiger; an uneducated person attached to low dancing and singing women; the demented, given to the application of magical rites; an untrustworthy person *who* befriends *the serpents* and *fools, a non*-gambler, who creates unnecessary excitement; a woman who creates split among the Pishachas, the thorny woman who favors the free booters."

Look at the way they *desire the trees to be protected,* "He, who rears trees by erecting barriers round them...conduces to our happiness." Yajurveda XX.45

Read Yajurveda and see how in chapter XXII hymns after hymns are talking of protecting oneself against the physical ailments and blesses those that help preserve environment. Hymn 5 in the chapter admires one who "protects beautiful objects like the Earth"; The next hymn is even more explicit "Make the best use of fire. Take medicines. Derive joy for drinking water. Enjoy well the warmth and light of the Sun. Have knowledge of air and vital breaths. Perform yagna in fire."

They knew that "The Sun moves singly and alone. The moon is brought to life again. Fire is the remedy of cold. Earth is the vast field for production." *Yajurveda* Ch. XXIII. 46

To the questions: "What lustre is like the Sun's light? What lake is equal to the sea? What is more spacious than the Earth? What thing is beyond measure?" The reply is given in the next hymn. *Yajurveda* Ch. XXIII. 48 / "God is lustre like the sun. Heaven is a flood to match the sea. Sun is vaster than the Earth. Beyond all measure is speech." It is difficult to find an answer better than this one from a Seer.

**Of Birds and Animals**

I now cite from *Yajurveda* Chapter XXIV wherein the Seers talk of birds and animals and their attributes and characteristics and where to locate them. The loving manner in which they talk of these birds and animals underlines the fact that they knew their beans about environment and wished to protect it. These hymns begin from number 11 and continue up to 40. There is not a single animal known to a veterinarian practitioner that is not described along with its typical characteristics. Read for instance, hymn 18 "The animals of peace-loving parents are smoke–colored and of brownish hue. The animals of parents who sit in assembly for propitiating yagnas are brown and smoky-looking." The next hymn commands "O men, bring into use the pre-mentioned agricultural animals." Then comes the knowledge of the experts. "An expert in the knowledge of animals finds Kapinjalas in spring, sparrows in summer; partridges in the Rains; quails in autumn, kakras in winter and Vikaras in the Dewy season." The rishis describe also the uses of each animal according to the class of people for whom they are intended. It is not possible to reproduce all the hymns to show the knowledge of the Seers or their desire to preserve all these species but it is perhaps enough if we appreciate their knowledge and perception from the following hymn (40): "Rhinoceros serves all warriors in preparing their shield; the black dog, the long-eared ass. The hyenas are used for protection against the demons; the boar is for the king who wants to tear asunder his enemies; the lion is swift like air; the chameleon, the Pippaka, the vultures are used for making arrows; the spotted antelope is used for preparing mrigshalas for the learned people."

The next chapter (XXV) opens with a hymn for *protecting all objects worthy of desire*. Read this hymn in totality, "Learn for the teeth the act of biting; from the gums the method of protection; from tooth-sockets the way of pounding; sharpness from the fangs. Use the tongue tip for a learned utterance; learn the act of uprooting from the tongue; the use of palate by crying slowly; chew with both the jaws;

drink water with the mouth. Acquire the knowledge of oozing semen from testicles. Recognise the Aadityas from the beard; know the path from the eyebrows; know the sun and earth from their motion; lightening from the pupils of the eyes. Observe celibacy for the protection of the semen; acquire knowledge through high character. *Objects worth acceptance are worthy of preservation.* Objects after one's desire should not be resisted. Don't show disrespect to your own men. Friends and relation should be fostered."

Whatever else may have been the motive of these Seers in commanding Man to worship God and perform yagnas, one thing is certain. They knew well their *environment* and wished to protect it.

What better could one offer in terms their understanding of the Nature's cycle around them than the following quote:

"When the clouds cultivate the earth with its waters; then winds are blown (for the rain to fall). lightening is struck, vegetation comes to life and grows, sky pours the raindrops and the earth then gets ready for the welfare of the world." Rg-Veda 5/83/4

We should remember that the ancients wrote an entire Veda on the *science of medicine* called the Atharva-veda. They went into details how a herb has to be identified and then they describe its properties for different ailments. They achieved and left behind knowledge of an almost fully developed medical science, which is currently proving to be helpful to the entire Mankind. Therefore they had prayed, "O God, create a man of iron determination for the implementation of a vow a forest guard for the protection of a forest., and drive away a forest burner contemplating the destruction of jungles." Yajurveda, Ch. XXX. 19 one might as well put a question: "What else does a forest officer do other than protecting a forest and preserving wild animals and their habitat under his charge?" In the same chapter of the Yajur-Veda in hymn 10 the seer prays "O God create a physician for purifying our body with the eradication of disease; astronomer for the advancement of knowledge; an inquisitive man full of cravings for knowledge; an extra-inquisitive man for desire of extra-knowledge; and a question-solver for establishing moral law." If read closely one can see the hymn telling us that all knowledge is located in curiosity and for extra knowledge one has to put in extra effort.

"O Spiritual juice (of wisdom and devotion) thou hast been prepared carefully for the soul. Let diseases stay afar together with the fiends of lust, anger, greed, pride and jealousy." (Samaveda Hymn. 561) This hymn clearly states that "those who are double-tongued or crooked cannot take delight of drinking thee." It would be clear to the reader that disease or physical ailment is as good as being crooked or a doublespeak. It is much better to avoid them both. It is only then that "those who are of calm nature like the rays of the moon, (will) be full of strength and wealth of wisdom."

I cite here a hymn (Samaveda, 1837) that has been interpreted differently by two scholars of eminence viz. Satvalekar and Griffiths, whose two versions are given below. Meanwhile the reader should also realise that it is quite common for the hymns being interpreted differently by different scholars. This is precisely what I wrote in the beginning about the difficulty of agreeing on the common meaning of a hymn or even of a single word. The Vedas can be read for different purposes, as they are capable of giving more messages than one can imagine. In fact, it is impossible to understand everything they say and why do they say what they actually say. Majority of the Indians regard them as revealed books because no human being could have been so wise as to cover all themes and subjects, besides all aspects of human life as they do. Probably for this reason alone that F. Max Muller wrote the following:

"What can be more tedious than the Veda and yet, what can be more interesting, if once we know that it is the first word spoken by the Aryan man?

The Vedas have a two-fold interest for us. They belong to the history of world and also to the history of India, As long as man continues to take interest in the history of his race, and as long as we collect in libraries and museums the relics of the former ages, the first place in that long row of books which contain the records of the Aryan branch of mankind, will belong forever to the Rgveda."

So much for the glory of the Vedas! This praise comes from a man who learned Sanskrit and translated the Vedas only to make Hindus Christians.

Be that as it may, the first interpretation is of Satvalekar :

1. "O Omnipresent Divine Mother! Thou art source of happiness. So endow us with strength and pleasure of great vision (realisation) of truth."
2. Griffith's translation: "Yea waters, ye bring health and bliss; so help ye bring health and bliss ye us to energy that we may look on great delight."

It is interesting to note that this hymn has something to do with water. In the next hymn the reason why water is mentioned here is made clear. Because water is known to be the source of life as it is one of the five elements or tatva that constitute life and at the same time water is also a cure for numerous diseases even if used singly.

The hymn number 1638 from Samaveda has two meanings. One is an external meaning and the other internal. The external meaning is as follows: "O water! Let your most prosperous juice be ministered to us in this world with the readiness that affectionate mothers apply to their infants."

The other interpretation is spiritual in character. "O Divine Mother! May thy most auspicious juice of bliss be ministered to us in this world with the readiness that affectionate mothers supply to their infants."

The next hymn talks of *water being used for removing diseases*. It is significant that the use of water as a medicine was known to them and therefore, it becomes even more meaningful that this water has to be clean or pollution free. Look at it from an ordinary person's point of view. By the time the Seers came to writing the Atharva veda they had learnt through experimentations as well as through empirical evidence the curative value of the usages of both herbs and lotions including water. This Vedas are a living testimony to the fact that science grows only empirically. And the seeds of modern laboratories were first grown in the Vedas. This is one History lesson that one should learn from reading the Vedas.

Now I cite the Rg-Veda X. 1/ 46

"Lady of the Forest! Lady of the Forest!

Who seems to vanish from sight in the distance?

Why do you never come to the Village?
Surely you are not afraid of us.
When the grass hopper replies
To the lowing of the cattle,
As though to the sound of tinkling bells,
The lady of the Forest makes merry.
Some time you catch a glimpse of her, and think it is cattle grazing
Or a house, far away
And at the evening you hear the Lady of the Forest
Like the distant sound of moving wagons.
Her voice is as the sound of man calling his cattle.
Or as the crash of a felled tree,
If you stay in the forest in the evening
You will hear her like a far voice of crying.
But the Lady of the Forest will not slay
Unless an enemy draws near
She eats the sweet wild fruits
And then she rests wherever she will
Now I have praiser' the Lady of the Forest
Who is perfumed with balm and fragrant?
Who is well-fed although she tills not?
The mother of all things of the wild!

And what greater respect could Man show towards all the elements of Mother Nature than the prayer from Yajurveda, 36/17 for peace or recite the Shanti mantra, which desires that 'let there be peace in the heaven, horizons-where the Earth and sky meet, peace in the vegetation, peace on earth, peace in everything' etc., and this prayer is always sung at the end of any holy anushthan or ceremony and this Shanti mantra may be accepted as the ultimate for any environmentalist.

Here is a quote from the Chhandogya Upanishad (VI, 11, 1) :

Of this mighty tree, my dear, if someone should strike at the root it would bleed but still live. If someone should strike at the middle, it would bleed but still live. If someone struck at the top, it would bleed but still live. Being pervaded by the living self: it stands firm, drinking in the moisture (which nourishes it) and rejoicing."

**The Tree and the Human body (Brihadaranyka 3. IX, 28)**

Yagyavalkya says, "Venerable Brahmanas, whosoever among you wishes to do so, question me or I will question you." When no one speaks he goes on to compare a man with tree.

1. 'As is a mighty tree, so indeed is a man; his hairs are leaves and his skin is like the outer bark
2. From his skin blood flows forth and sap from the skin of the tree. Therefore when a man is wounded blood flows forth as sap from the tree.
3. His flesh is its inner bark, his nerves tough like inner fibers. His bones are the wood within and the marrow is made resembling the pith.
4. A tree when felled springs up from its root in a newer form; what does man spring forth when he is dead.
5. Do not say from the semen for that is produced from the live man. A tree springs from the seed when it is felled.
6. If a tree is pulled up again it will not spring again. From what does a mortal spring again when he is dead?'
7. 'When born, he is not born again for who should create him again? Brahman who is Knowledge bliss is the final goal of his who offers gifts as well as of him who stands firm and knows (Brahman).'

This comparison is a rare treat from Upanishad.

I have already referred to the twin state of knowledge being both developed and developing. We have seen how the ancients were concerned about preserving the Nature as God's gift and now I cite a case of knowledge which has continued to grow ever since it was given birth. The current rage for adoption of the Yogic exercises, make us think that this knowledge is very recent origin. This is far from being true.

This knowledge was readily available in the Vedas. However, what has been added to that knowledge is something quite unique. For instance, there are today numerous schools of the Yoga (the hath yoga, raj yoga, karma yoga etc.) and a few asanas may also have been evolved and even got patented during the course of development, but read what the Rg-Veda has to say on the subject. It is the seed knowledge which has thus prospered over a period of time.

"God who is realised through the practice of seven parts of Yoga consisting of *Yamas, Niyamas, Asanas (proper postures), pranayama (control of breath), pratyahara* (withholding from external effect) *Dharana* (concentration) and *Dhyana* (meditation) commands us in our own interest and is the constant giver of prosperity, riches and plenty." *Samveda* Book 2, Chapter 2. 101

Until this day the Vedas have not been studied in terms of knowledge they impart and their secular content has also not been classified in terms of knowledge areas/discipline. But if read carefully, the Vedas touch upon all areas of human interest; be it astrophysics, chemistry, mathematics, music, yoga, or philosophy, rules of governance, Parliamentary system, moral law, raising of army and its management etc. The Vedas have been preserved as collection of liturgies but the fact is that there are other ways to make their content examined and presented. Time has come when the secular content of the Vedas has to be classified, indexed and presented. In this chapter I have tried to discuss this very role the Vedic knowledge can play. This should serve as an example for future prospective researchers. The basic role of traditional knowledge is to offer ideas and suggest areas for further research. We must accept the fact that growth in knowledge is limitless comparable to the cosmos whose dimensions remain hidden from human ken.

I shall not go into details about the real and unreal knowledge. Our problems arise because of our basic ignorance. One who knows the Truth behind this prapanch attains Moksh or freedom from the cycle of birth and death.

# Appendix

## शान्तिमंत्रः

ॐ पूर्णमदः पूर्णमिदं पूर्णात्पूर्णमुदच्यते।
पूर्णस्य पूर्णमादाय पूर्णमेवावशिष्यते।।
।। ॐ शान्तिः शान्तिः शान्तिः ।।

–शुक्ल यजुर्वेद

## ईशावास्योपनिषद्

ॐ ईशावास्यमिदँ सर्वं यत्किंच जगत्यां जगत्।
तेन त्यक्तेन भुञ्जीथा मा गृधः कस्यस्विद्धनम्।। 1 ।।

कुर्वन्नेवेह कर्माणि जिजीविषेच्छतँ समाः।
एवं त्वयि नान्यथेतोऽस्ति न कर्म लिप्यते नरे।। 2 ।।

असूर्या नाम ते लोका अन्धेन तमसाऽऽवृताः।
ताँ स्ते प्रेत्याभिगच्छन्ति ये के चात्महनो जनाः।। 3 ।।

अनेजदेकं मनसो जवीयो नैनद्देवा आप्नुवन्पूर्वमर्षत्।
तद्धावतोऽन्यानत्येति तिष्ठत् तस्मिन्नपो मातरिश्वा दधाति।। 4 ।।

तदेजति तन्नेजति तद्दूरे तद्वन्तिके।
तदन्तरस्य सर्वस्य तदु सर्वस्यास्य बाह्यतः।। 5 ।।

यस्तु सर्वाणि भूतानि आत्मन्येवानुपश्यति।
सर्वभूतेषु चात्मानं ततो न विजुगुप्सते।। 6 ।।

यस्मिन्सर्वाणि भूतानि आत्मैवाभूद्विजानतः।
तत्र को मोहः कः शोक एकत्वमनुपश्यतः।। 7 ।।

स पर्यगाच्छुक्रमकायमव्रणअस्नाविरँ शुद्धमपापविद्धम्।
कविर्मनीषी परिभूः स्वयंभू-र्याथातथ्योऽर्थान् व्यदधाच्छाश्वतीभ्यः समाभ्यः।। 8 ।।

अन्धन्तमः प्रविशन्ति येऽविधामुपासते।
ततो भूय इव ते तमो य उ विधायाँ रताः।। 9 ।।

अन्यदेवाहुर्विद्यया अन्यदाहुरविद्यया।
इति शुश्रुम धीराणां ये नस्तद्विचचक्षिरे।। 10 ।।

विद्यां चाविद्यां च यस्तद्वेदोभयँ सह।
अविद्यया मृत्युं तीर्त्वा विद्ययामृतमश्नुते।। 11 ।।

अन्धं तमः प्रविशन्ति येऽसम्भूतिमुपासते।
ततो भूय इव ते तमो ये उ सम्भूत्याँ रताः।। 12 ।।

न्यदेवाहुः सम्भवादन्यदाहुरसम्भवात्।
इति शुश्रुम धीराणां ये नस्तद्विचचक्षिरे।। 13 ।।

सम्भूतिं च विनाशं च यस्तद्वेदोभयँ सह।
विनाशेन मृत्युं तीर्त्वा सम्भूत्यामृतमश्नुते।। 14 ।।

हिरण्मयेन पात्रेण सत्यस्यापिहितं मुखम्।
तत्वं पूषन्नपावृणु सत्यधर्माय दृष्टये।। 15 ।।

पूषन्नेकर्षे यम सूर्य प्राजापत्य व्यूह रश्मीन्समूह।
तेजो यत्ते रूपं कल्याणतमं तत्ते पश्यामि योऽसावसौ पुरुषः सोऽहमस्मि।। 16 ।।

वायुरनिलमृतमथेदं भस्मान्तँ शरीरम्।
ॐ क्रतो स्मर कृतँ स्मर क्रतो स्मर कृतँ स्मर।। 17 ।।

अग्ने नय सुपथा राये अस्मान् विश्वानि देव वयुनानि विद्वान्।
युयोध्यस्मज्जुहुराणमेनो भूयिष्ठां ते नमउक्तिं विधेम।। 18 ।।

**—Swami Chinmayananda**
Discourses on Isavasya Upanishad
Central Chinmaya Mission Trust
Bombay–400 072